THE
GREAT
FEUD

THE GREAT FEUD

THE CAMPBELLS & THE MACDONALDS

OLIVER THOMSON

SUTTON PUBLISHING

First published in 2000 by
Sutton Publishing Limited · Phoenix Mill
Thrupp · Stroud · Gloucestershire · GL5 2BU

British Library Cataloguing in Publication Data
A catalogue record for this book is available from the British Library

ISBN 0 7509 2374 1

Typeset in 11/13pt Photina.
Typesetting and origination by
Sutton Publishing Limited.
Printed in Great Britain by
Biddles Limited, Guildford, Surrey.

CONTENTS

PART 3: THE DIASPORA

Where did you come from, baby dear?
Out of everywhere into here.

George Macdonald (1824–1905)

Or like a poet woo the moon
Riding an armchair for my steed
And with a flashing pen harpoon
Terrific metaphors of speed.

Roy Campbell (1901–57)

PREFACE AND ACKNOWLEDGEMENTS

Most history books follow the narratives of countries, empires, great heroes or socio-economic trends. This one traces two genetic finger-prints that just happen to have intertwined in an interesting and often dramatic way all over the world. The selection of events may at times seem otherwise quite random and it is most unlikely that the topic will ever appear on any school or university exam syllabus. But I hope it will provide entertainment, give cause for thought and at least cast some new light on many events in world history. This multiple biography is full of excitement, waste, cruelty, sadness, talent, triumph and disaster – just like life.

My thanks go to Alastair Campbell of Lorne, Unicorn Pursuivant, who is writing the definitive history of the Campbells, for his advice, to Dan Byrne of New South Wales, to Dr David Caldwell for his photograph of Finlaggan, to Sarah Moore of Sutton Publishing for her skill and patience as an editor and to my wife Jean for her unfailing support and for sharing many journeys of exploration.

NOTE ON SPELLING

Most of the names in this book can be spelt several different ways and particularly in the early stages there is no such thing as a definitive spelling. Gillespic is interchangeable with Archibald and Celestin, the Latin version, as is Alastair or Alasdair with Alexander, Ian with Ewan and John, Angus and Aeneas. MacDonald with or without an 'a' is like Macdonnell or Macdonell simply an anglicised version of MacDomhnuil. The MacDonalds of Glencoe and Ardnamurchan are also referred to as MacIains. St Bride can be St Bridget. Place names have different versions like Cawdor and Calder, or Tioram and Tirrim, or Dunyveg and Dunnymhaig. I have not made any purist rules on name spelling, just tried to prevent spelling authenticity from impeding the narrative. If anyone is offended by any of my choices of spelling, I apologise.

CHRONOLOGY

1513	James IV and Earl of Argyll and several other Campbells killed at Flodden
1519	Campbells persecute MacGregors
1543	Second escape of Donald Dhu
1568	Mary, Queen of Scots' forces under Earl of Argyll defeated at Langside
1577	Campbell attacks on MacDonald territory
1583	Glenlyon Campbells attacked by Glencoe MacDonalds
1588	Sorley Boy acquires Spanish Armada guns
1603	James VI becomes King of Great Britain
1614	MacDonalds recapture Dunyveg, then lose it again to Campbells
1620	Black Duncan attacks MacGregors
1644	Irish MacDonalds join Montrose
1645	Huge defeat of Campbells at Inverlochy
1646	MacDonalds massacred at Dunaverty
1647	Death of Alastair MacColla
1650	MacDonald and Campbell prisoners transported to America and West Indies
1661	Execution of Marquess of Argyll
1685	Campbell settlements in New Jersey and Carolina
1688	Battle of Killiecrankie
1692	Massacre of Glencoe
1700	Battle of Toubacanti
1707	Union of Parliaments
1715	Battle of Sheriffmuir
1739	Major emigrations of both clans to America
1746	Battle of Culloden. Flora Macdonald helps escape of Prince Charles
1758	Battle of Ticonderoga
1776	Campbells and MacDonalds on both sides in American War of Independence. Glengarry MacDonells move to Canada
1784	John Campbell captures Annanpore
1786	Duncan Campbell sends first convicts to Australia
1796	General Jacques Macdonald captures Rome for Napoleon
1815	James MacDonell is hero of Waterloo
1827	Robert Campbell explores Pelly River
1838	Angus MacDonald explores Colorado River
1855	Colin Campbell leads 'thin red line' at Balaclava
1867	John Macdonald becomes first Prime Minister of Canada
1873	Mike MacDonald is boss of Chicago underworld

1905   Henry Campbell-Bannerman becomes Prime Minister of Great Britain
1924   Ramsay MacDonald becomes Prime Minister of Great Britain for the first time
1963   Judith Campbell meets John F. Kennedy
1983   Admiral McDonald invades Grenada for Ronald Reagan

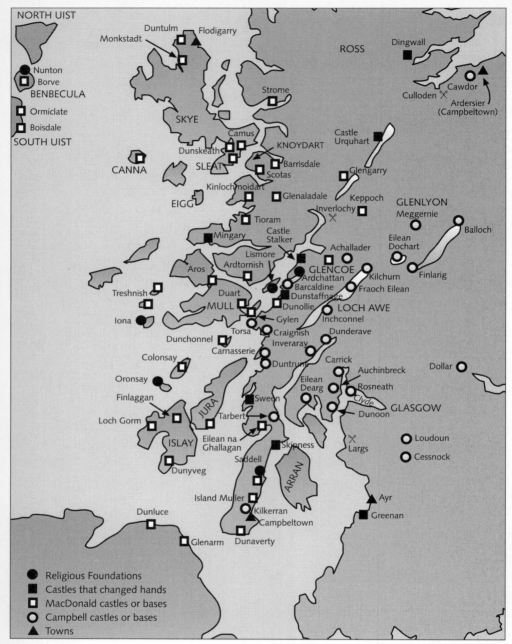

The main sites of the Great Feud.

Note: Locations – nearly all the locations mentioned in the narrative are also briefly described in the Tour section beginning on p. 165.

INTRODUCTION

This book examines the remarkable rivalry, sometimes bloody conflict, between two great families which originated on the west coast of Scotland, the Campbells and the MacDonalds. Starting with the violent death of a Campbell chief in 1296, the feud then went on for about 450 years. There were numerous clashes and cullings inflicted by both sides, among which the incident in Glencoe in 1692 just happens to have been the best publicised.

This all took place amid some of the most spectacular scenery in Europe, against a backdrop of gaunt island fortresses and remote medieval chapels. Yet despite, or perhaps because of, the bouts of mutual antipathy, both families continued to grow, to scatter over the world and to produce an amazing number of talented, energetic descendants including two British prime ministers, the first Canadian prime minister, a French duke, an Italian general, poets, actors, explorers, Indian fighters, soldiers, entrepreneurs, terrorists and criminals.

For convenience this book is divided into three parts, the first two set mainly in Scotland. The difference between parts one and two is that for the first, covering 300 years or so of the feud, the MacDonalds were opposed to the Bruce/Stewart dynasty in Edinburgh and the Campbells were supporters of it, whereas in the second period of around 100 years the roles were reversed: the MacDonalds became supporters of the failing Stuart (the spelling had changed in the early sixteenth century) dynasty and the Campbells became its implacable opponents. The third part of the book deals with the aftermath of the feud when the two families were splattered right across the globe. It takes in the trials and achievements of both clans in Ireland, France, North America, India, Australia, the West Indies and many other parts of the world.

Most histories of Scotland tend to focus on the concept of nation and wade into emotional quicksands as it ebbs and flows. This book shows two families who, though quintessentially Scottish, for the most part regarded the idea of Scotland as an irrelevance.

PART 1
THE FEUDAL FEUD

Unnatural, deadlie feudis quhilkis hes bene fosterit
amangis us this lait aig.

Statutes of Inchcolmkil, 1510

1
DEATH AT THE RED FORD

It all began in 1296 with an ambush. The place where it occurred was a lonely stretch of track called the String of Lorne, which leads to this day from the shores of Loch Awe to the area now called Oban. The victim of the attack was Sir Colin Campbell, Big Colin or Chailein Mor as he was known, and the spot where he died is still marked by a rough cairn of stones near the Alt an ath'Dheirig or Red Burn Ford, called red because this was not the first time that blood had been shed there. The perpetrator of the killing was almost certainly Lame John MacDougall, Lord of Lorne, eldest son of Ewan MacDougall, head of what was at that time the most powerful family in the west of Scotland.

So why did the attack take place? The facts are by no means clear. We certainly know that Colin Campbell was on his way to conduct a royal mission, to make contact and hopefully peace with the MacDonalds of Islay. Ten years earlier the last of the old dynasty of Scottish kings, Alexander III (1249–86), had died in a riding accident on the cliffs at Kinghorn, racing back to see his new young wife. Four years after Alexander's death his heiress granddaughter, the Maid of Norway, died in Orkney leaving no other obvious heir. The failure of the eligible candidates to agree on one of their own number left Edward I of England with the leverage to play kingmaker. He selected the pliable John Balliol from a number of competitors and at the time of the Campbell killing Balliol was vainly trying to bring his kingdom under control. The west coast was the most awkward area for him, because the only sensible method of transport was by sea and to use the water effectively it was necessary to have a bigger navy than anyone else. But two great interlinked families, the MacDougalls and the MacDonalds, between them controlled virtually every war galley available.

So was Colin Campbell on a fool's errand, hopelessly out of his depth in hostile territory? Lame John MacDougall as the ambitious heir of the leading family in the area owned huge tracts of Argyll and controlled it with a ring of powerful stone-built castles: Dunollie perched on the high rock above Oban Bay (where Fingal had tethered his dogs on the Clach a Choin), Dunstaffnage a few miles away on its commanding peninsula jutting into the sea, Aros on Mull and even more remote Cairnaborg and Isleborg Castles, built like pirate hideaways on the Treshnish Islands. The MacDougalls also controlled the cathedral island of Lismore, base of the Bishop of the Isles, which they had recently won by force from their MacDonald cousins. Both families had Norse blood in their veins, had sided with the Norwegian king against the Scots at the battle of Largs in 1263 and were shortly to ally with the English against Bruce, symptoms of their essential desire for independence from Edinburgh – anything was better than a powerful Scottish king. The nearest they came to supporting the native monarchy was when Lame John's relative, John Comyn, was still a potential candidate for the throne. Meanwhile, Edward I's puppet-king John Balliol was trying to establish a powerbase, the Bruce and Comyn had both lost out and were sulking in semi-retirement, the Stone of Destiny still lay at Scone Abbey and Edward himself was too busy conquering the Welsh to interfere.

This then was the complex web of diplomatic intrigue into which Colin Campbell was thrust. But where had he sprung from himself? His origin is shrouded in mystery. The name Campbell was unheard of until about thirty years before the attack on Big Colin. His father, Gillespic, was laird of Menstrie in the Ochil Hills, near Stirling, and it appears that he was knighted and given a new estate on Loch Awe with the island of Inchconnel as its centre. There he built a new stone castle as a royal bastion in this otherwise hostile territory controlled by the MacDougalls. But the Campbells also had an Ayrshire connection. Only two years before his death Colin bought Symington, an estate just a few miles from the Stewart stronghold at Dundonald, suggesting a neighbourhood link with the highly influential, shortly to become royal, family which had led the fightback against the Norse at Largs. Could that have been where Gillespic Campbell won his spurs? If so it ties in with the now rather discredited legend that Campobello was a sort of

Norman or bastard Latin name, that the family were Norman immigrants and had connections with a Campobello (conceivably a sort of Latin version of the Norman-French name Beauchamps) in Bedford. It also ties in with the fact that another Campbell called Arthur, clearly a relative, was governor of Doon Castle in Ayrshire until forced to surrender to the English; he later acquired Dunstaffnage Castle from the MacDougalls as his reward for supporting Robert Bruce. Perhaps even the rapid rise of another branch of the family, Colin's grandson Duncan who married the heiress of Loudoun, also in Ayrshire, helps corroborate the story.

But there is another totally different tradition, one publicised by the later Campbells to boost their credentials as genuine Argyll men. This version suggested that Gillespic Campbell of Menstrie had married Eva MacSporran, the heiress of an old Argyll family and daughter of Paul MacSporran, the hereditary pursebearer and last male heir of the O'Duins. This links with the other main theory about the origin of their name, that it meant 'twisted mouth' in Gaelic – a touch of the sinister even at that early period. The boar on the Campbell of Argyll coat of arms was held to commemorate their favourite ancestor, Diarmid the legendary boar-slayer, though another story attributed it to a much later Campbell chief who killed a boar in France (see p. 29).

This story does not tally with another which says that Gillespic married Margaret, one of the Sommervilles of Carnwath, a Norman baronial family in Lanarkshire. There is, however, also a reference to a Dugald Campbell who married Bridget the red-haired maiden of Craignish around 1220, daughter of the local toiseach or chief; they were said to have lived in the tiny island castle on Loch Avich known appropriately as the Castle of the Red-haired Maiden (Castael na Nighinn Ruaidhe), which is now no more than a pile of stones on a tree-covered islet.

Anyway, whatever his origin Big Colin was to be regarded as the effective founder of a new dynasty that after his death was destined to grow in size and power. His successors as head of this family were all known as Mac Chailein Mor.

But what of the third great family that formed the apex of this triangle in west Scotland? The MacDonalds were at this time junior to their cousins the MacDougalls, both families being descended four generations back from the great Somerled, King of the Isles. Somerled or Sorley had been a mixture of Scots, Irish and Norse. His way of life was inherently Viking, based on the use of swift war galleys or birlinns which he used to dominate the west coast of Scotland, Northern Ireland and the Isle of Man. He began the great tradition of divide and rule, playing off the king of Scotland against the king of Norway so that his own independence would be unchallenged. In later days the family reckoned their Irish pedigree was more politically correct than their Norse, so they chose as their ancestor Conn of the Hundred Battles, High King of Ireland, and Colla – hence Clan Cholla. And for many centuries there remained strong connections between MacDonalds in Ireland and Scotland. They were highly competitive and strongly motivated to succeed at all costs by legends such as the story of the red hand: in it one sibling racing against his brother cuts off his own hand and throws it far in front of him to win possession of a piece of land. This culture might help weed out weak successors but equally it could create disaffected also-rans.

After Somerled's somewhat undignified defeat and death at the battle of Renfrew (1164), where he rashly challenged the Scottish King Malcolm IV, his mini-empire was split into three between his surviving sons: Dougal, progenitor of the MacDougalls, took Lorne, Mull and Jura; Ronald and his son Donald, founders of the MacDonalds, took Islay and part of Kintyre; while Angus, whose line died out soon afterwards, took Ardnamurchan and the Northern Isles. During the Viking wars that dominated the next century all three branches often took the side of the Norwegian overlord rather than the Scottish king. In the face of the Norse invasion which climaxed at the battle of Largs the MacDonald chief surrendered Islay and Kintyre to Norway and helped the invaders, even though his eldest son Alexander had been named obsequiously after Alexander III, King of Scotland, and kept by him as a hostage in Edinburgh. It is therefore possible that the skirmish at Largs, where the large Norwegian fleet was forced by storms onto the hostile beach and took significant losses, was the first occasion when a Campbell and a MacDonald fought on opposite sides.

As well as regularly rebelling against the Scottish crown the descendants of Somerled also regularly fought each other. A particular sore point was control of the cathedral island of Lismore, one of several major religious foundations supported by these clans, and perhaps the one with the greatest patronage. Others included the lovely abbey in secluded Saddell, a nunnery and a new abbey on Iona, the priory at Ardchattan and numerous churches dedicated to the Irish saints Bride and Maelrubha.

So it was in the context of a continuing feud between the MacDougalls and the MacDonalds that the luckless Sir Colin Campbell set out along the String of Lorne through MacDougall territory to attempt peace talks with Angus, chief of the MacDonalds. But there was also yet another complication. After Largs the Norwegian kings clearly felt expeditions to Scotland were no longer worth the trouble. If independent-minded western clans like the MacDonalds wanted an ally against Edinburgh the obvious alternative was England. Equally for expansion-minded English kings like Edward I the clans of the west coast, with their excellent seamanship, well-maintained fleets and susceptibility to foreign luxuries, presented a very useful and cheap method of causing embarassment to the king of Scotland. So Colin Campbell was playing for high stakes.

One thing is certain. In the thirty years between the battle of Largs and the ambush at the String of Lorne, the Campbells had acquired a major estate on the dangerous Argyll frontier. There they had built themselves an impressive stone fortress on the island of Inchconnel where the ruined, ivy-covered keep with its fish-tailed arrow slits still looks down onto the black waters below. They had also demonstrated enough ability as royal servants to be entrusted by King John Balliol with a very delicate and important mission. Colin Campbell was killed before the mission could be properly started. Within a few months John Balliol had been thrust ruthlessly from the throne by Edward I and Scotland was plunged into twelve years of civil war. The cairn marking the spot where Colin Campbell was attacked is well worth a visit, as is his tomb in St Peter's churchyard, Kilchrenan, just across Loch Awe from his castle and no more than five miles from the spot where he died. The twenty years after his murder were to see great changes for the two main families in our saga, but first we will turn to the fate of the man who led the ambush and who, for the time being, was victor in the struggle, Lame John MacDougall.

2

THE RISE AND FALL OF
LAME JOHN

Sir John MacDougall, otherwise known as John Bacach, Lame John, was triumphant. He had destroyed the one man who might have been able to assert royal authority in Argyll. Colin Campbell's heir, Sir Neil, was a relative youngster and anyway the whole of Scotland was now in chaos with its king, John Balliol, humiliated by the all-powerful Edward I of England, while William Wallace was still an unknown squire. All this suited John Bacach admirably – a weak or almost non-existent monarchy in Edinburgh and a strong one in London far enough away not to interfere with him but rich enough to show appreciation of the nuisance that John could cause his own king. Though his father Euan, the nominal chief of the MacDougalls was still alive, John seems to have wielded unrestricted power from Dunstaffnage Castle and his word was now law. His sister was queen on the Isle of Man and John could sweep between his numerous castles in his extra-large galley, visiting powerful relatives like his uncle, the Red Comyn, at his superb castle of Inverlochy near the site of modern Fort William. From Dunstaffnage John controlled not only the rich lands of Lorne and the newly acquired Fincharn Castle on Loch Awe, but also Mull with its Aros Castle, Lismore Island with Coeffin Castle, Coll and the Treshnish Islands with their spectacularly remote Cairnaborg and Isleborg Castles. If his conscience troubled him at all he now had his cathedral on Lismore and the family priory at Ardchattan in which to pray, not to mention numerous fine chapels such as St Bride's at Dunstaffnage itself. And if his family had health problems they could resort to the healing well of Tobar na Slainte on Lismore.

Needless to say Lame John played no part in the rising of William Wallace in 1297, for Scotland was not an entity in which he had any real interest. He was the official Sheriff of Argyll and his kinsmen the Comyns who shared four earldoms between them tended to support London rather than Edinburgh in the power struggles of the early 1300s. For the time being so also did young Sir Neil Campbell, Robert Bruce and both the two MacDonald chiefs, Alexander Og and Angus Og. This alignment was, however, shattered in 1306 when, after a long period of frustration, young Robert Bruce lost his temper and killed John Comyn, his rival for the dormant Scottish kingship, and a blood relative of Lame John's. For Bruce, who had interests on both sides of the border and had already switched sides several times, there was now no turning back. Whatever other allies he might find in his bid to become an independent king of Scotland he could certainly expect no help from Comyns or MacDougalls.

Meanwhile, Sir Neil, the son of the dead Campbell ambassador, had also gone through a period of switching sides in the dangerous power struggle orchestrated by Edward of England. Doubtless his position in the few years after his father's death was extremely weak and he does not appear to have sought revenge against the MacDougalls. Though he was probably too remote or too busy to join up with William Wallace, one source claims he did, another that he and his brother Donald, who held Reid Castle in Forfar, were so frustrated that they planned to go on a crusade. But, like Robert Bruce, Neil found it convenient for the time being to support the English side. So he swore fealty to Edward I, was apprenticed to the famous Earl of Ulster (Robert Bruce's brother-in-law) for military training and promised a rich Cumberland widow as his second bride. Then, for reasons unknown, at this point Neil Campbell took the drastic decision which was to change his own fortunes and those of his family for ever: he gave up all the rewards of English patronage, including the rich widow, and changed sides to support the murderer and underdog claimant to the throne, Robert Bruce.

In every respect it must have seemed a most unfortunate move at the time. Bruce had very few allies, an extremely small military base, no real experience, no clear claim to the throne and was under sentence of excommunication for committing murder in a sanctuary. What is more, the Comyn family and their MacDougall allies were committed to his destruction. Campbell was present with Bruce at the first disastrous battle at Methven and the subsequent headlong flight westwards. There was then the humiliating further skirmish at Dalry, just east of modern Tyndrum, where they had stopped at the shrine of St Fillan for the still guilt-ridden Bruce to seek absolution from the local abbot for his crimes. The small Bruce party was severely mauled by Lame John at the head of his MacDougalls – this being the occasion on which one of them ripped off the new king's brooch. It was to be a treasured trophy of the family in years to come when they had lost virtually everything else.

Bruce was at this point reduced to a tiny band of supporters, including Neil Campbell, and they were all on the run. Bruce's own wife Elizabeth, his daughter Marjory and his sister Mary (who at some point, we do not know when, became Neil Campbell's wife), were shepherded away to Loch Dochart Castle, but all were later captured at Kildrummy Castle by a pro-English group. The reduced party fled down Glen Ogle to Balquhidder, across to Loch Lomond, down it by boat with Neil Campbell apparently organising a galley to take them down the Firth of Clyde. According to legend they had to evade the galleys of Lame John as they headed past Arran.

Just when or how Bruce or Campbell established a relationship with Angus Og MacDonald, younger brother of the clan chief, is a mystery, for his elder brother Alexander was certainly a pro-Comyn–MacDougall man, but Angus's help was absolutely crucial in first the survival and then the comeback of Robert Bruce. After a possible brief stop at Saddell Castle facing Arran, the group's immediate place of refuge was almost certainly Dunaverty Castle on the Mull of Kintyre. Sir Walter Scott's poem 'Lord of the Isles' gives a romanticised account of the whole episode with Angus's name changed for poetic reasons to Ranald and the castle to Ardtornish.

> Beneath the castle's sheltering lee
> They staid their course in quiet sea,
> Hewn in the rock a passage there
> Sought the dark fortress by a stair,
> So straight, so high, so steep
> With peasant staff on valiant hand
> Might well the dizzy path have manned
> 'Gainst hundred armed with spear and brand.

But Dunaverty was too exposed to the English or MacDougall navy and the Bruce party was ferried out of danger, probably first to the MacRuari stronghold of Garmoran, then back south to MacDonald property on Rathlin Island off the Irish coast. From there they plotted Bruce's next attempt to win Scotland.

The following year with MacDonald help Bruce sailed from Arran to make a landing at his own former castle of Turnberry and won a surprise night attack on the English force camped outside it. Thereafter, despite being harassed by superior forces which included Lame John and his men, Bruce scored minor victories over the English at Glentrool and Loudoun Hill (future Campbell territory), which were made more significant by the death soon afterwards of Edward I, described on his tomb as *Scotorum malleus* – Hammer of the Scots. Then Bruce made a show of threatening the MacDougalls with a large sea and land force: Lame John backed down and asked for a temporary truce in 1207.

A year later Bruce was ready to tackle Lame John in earnest and headed back to Argyll for the first time since his ignominious escape. The MacDougalls were waiting for him in what was then the much deeper (long before Hydro power) Pass of Brander by Loch Awe, a ravine in which no normal army of the time could avoid ambush. James Douglas is given the credit for leading an outflanking party up the steep sides of the ravine to surprise Lame John from the rear, making it hard for him even to escape to his galleys on Loch Etive. At last Bruce had won his revenge for Dalry and Neil Campbell his for the death of his father eleven years earlier on the String of Lorne.

The MacDougall empire was destroyed. Lame John and his father went into exile in England where the old man died at Carlisle in 1311. Lame John, still employed as an English admiral, had one further small military success when he captured the Isle of Man for the English in 1315, but he is last heard of as sick and poor, living in Dublin. He died in about 1318. It was not until 1330, in his grandson's day, that the family were at long last allowed to return to Dunstaffnage.

Meanwhile, it is worth emphasising that but for the help given by Angus Og MacDonald's fleet there would have been no comeback for Bruce, Scotland would almost certainly have remained an English conquest for the next few centuries, the Stewarts would never have become royal and the Campbells would probably have remained minor Highland lairds.

3

TWO MACDONALD BROTHERS

After Robert Bruce's destruction of the MacDougall authority in the west there remained only one significant power in the area left to conquer – Alexander MacDonald of the Isles, chief of the second largest branch of the great dynasty founded by Somerled. Just as that remarkable self-styled king had split his inheritance between three sons, so his descendant Angus MacDonald, who according to one account had married Colin Campbell or Mor's daughter, seems to have split it yet again between his two eldest sons, Alexander and Angus Og.

Just what the source of friction was between these two brothers – other than normal sibling rivalry enhanced by the ethos of the red hand – remains a mystery, but it is a reasonable assumption that Angus Og, being the younger, received a smaller portion and resented it. One of his castles, Dunaverty, on a steep rock near the Mull of Kintyre was, as we have seen, quite vulnerable to attack from the sea. Given the fact that his wife was an Irishwoman, Agnes O'Cathan, descended from Neil of the Nine Hostages, we can assume that some of his other estates were probably in Ulster or remote Rathlin Island, which he had used to shelter Bruce. To all this we may add the suggestion that there was a trace of bitterness in Alexander's character brought on by the fact that though christened after the king as a piece of belated flattery he was still sent far away from home at quite a young age to be a hostage for his father's good behaviour. This was after Angus Mor had unwisely backed Norway rather than Scotland in the campaign that ended in the Scottish victory at Largs. Younger brother Angus did do unexpectedly well from his marriage, for Agnes O'Cathan brought a very useful dowry of 140 Ulster warriors who settled in Scotland and provided him with an elite fighting force, later the Clan Chattan.

Angus Mor, the MacDonald chief, died soon after the killing of Colin Campbell at the String of Lorne. Just how long his eldest son Alexander Og survived him is not clear, but it can be assumed that dressed in the white robe of purity Alexander placed his foot in the foot-shaped hollow on the island rock of Finlaggan Castle on its loch on Islay and took the hereditary white rod of chieftainship. His younger brother Angus Og was perhaps already seething with jealousy. A possible extra cause of friction was Alexander's marriage to Lame John's sister Juliana and his close relationship with the MacDougalls. Whatever the cause, Angus Og had earlier, like most Scottish landowners, sworn fealty to Edward I and given him military assistance. Then, for no obvious reason, he switched sides to help rescue Bruce and Campbell after Dalry. Now he sided with the struggling Scottish king against both his own elder brother, Alexander, and the might of England.

Once King Robert was seriously back on the road to power he sent his brother Edward to attack Alexander Og MacDonald,* but despite a drubbing on the River Dee in Galloway the Lord of Islay managed to get away. Robert Bruce was perhaps at this time besieging the MacDougall castle of Dunstaffnage which he captured and handed over to Sir Arthur Campbell, the former commander at Doon Castle in Ayrshire. Now that he had the elder Bruce to contend with Alexander chose to shut himself up in Castle Sween in Knapdale. This great fortress, which he may have thought impregnable, is probably the earliest stone castle still standing on the Scottish mainland. Of all the western clans the MacSweens were the most definitely of direct Norse descent, for Sweyn was a common Viking name. The Sween responsible for this castle was supposedly an Orkney pirate who even, in about 1120, could afford to hire highly qualified masons, perhaps from Ulster, to build a sophisticated stone keep on the jagged rocks of this beautiful sea-loch. The MacSween descendants, Dugald, Lord of Glassary (d. 1260), and his son Eoin, lost out in the Scottish–Norway war, were deprived of their two great castles, Sween and Skipness, round about 1264, and retired

---

* This is one version; another source suggests that Alexander may have been killed in Ireland.

in exile to Ireland. Indeed, there is a surviving Irish poem about Eoin's expedition to try to recover his patrimony – 'Dal Chablaigh ar Chaisteal Suibhne' ('The Tryst of the Fleet at Castle Sween') by Arthur MacGurcagh.

There is no record of the details of the siege of Castle Sween by Bruce, though Alexander was said to have held out bravely for a few days. All that survives is a local legend that a headless horseman called the White Rider is to be seen charging through the castle gate on summer nights. When the siege was ended Alexander was captured without hope of escape and taken to Dundonald Castle, where he died in the dungeons. It is uncertain whether this castle was the Stewart keep of that name in Ayrshire or somewhere like Tarbert or Crinan where the name could be regarded as a generic one for any MacDonald stronghold. Alexander's six surviving sons escaped to Ireland where they founded the nucleus of the future MacDonald/MacDonnell clan of Ulster. His younger brother Angus Og was rewarded for his loyalty to Bruce by being allowed to take over all his brother's lands and a good proportion of MacDougall territory as well, the rest going to Campbells. Neil Campbell won back Inchconnel, Sir Arthur had Dunstaffnage and Duncan got the Castle of Dogs (Castael nan-Con) on a rocky outcrop of the small island of Torsa guarding the channel up to Loch Etive, with Reid Castle in Forfar as a bonus.

These events had two long-lasting consequences: the juxtaposition of two now hugely powerful families, each with the capacity to grow still more powerful and with a long-shared frontier between them, and a residue of dissatisfied and disinherited MacDonalds who could use their place of exile as a base for trying to restore their battered fortunes. It was thus the joint good fortune of Angus Og MacDonald and Neil Campbell in both backing the right horse in 1307 that set the stage for four and a half centuries of intermittent squabbling between the two families and a great deal of bloodshed on both sides. Significantly, it was a third brother of Alexander and Angus, young John or Ian, who founded the MacIain MacDonalds of Ardnamurchan, one of the poorest and most restless of the septs who were to maul and be mauled by the Campbells most fiercely 300 years later.

Meanwhile, Angus Og and Neil Campbell both lived out the rest of their lives on the same side, and both contributed to the victory over the English at Bannockburn in 1314, though one version of the story has Angus arriving with his troops at the very last minute. The poet John Barbour described Angus as: 'In battle stalward was and stout' and Sir Walter Scott put into the mouth of Robert Bruce the lines

> One effort more and Scotland's free
> Lord of the Isles my trust's in thee.

There is another obscure theory that some dispossessed Templar knights were among the contingents that came from Argyll to help Bruce, but there is no real evidence to back this up.

The king's sister Mary Bruce had been exchanged for an English prisoner and released back to Scotland after six years of captivity, four of them spent cooped up in a cage. Then, or possibly before, she became the second wife of Neil Campbell, who became known at the Ayr parliament as Nigello Cambel or Sir Nicholas de Chambelle, Lord of Ardskotnish. This was by no means to be the only time that the Campbells had an admixture of royal blood. Mary and Neil's son John was later made Earl of Atholl, but died in battle without heirs. (Some 330 years later the Earl of Argyll inaccurately claimed to be a descendant of Bruce through Mary and Neil Campbell when he was preparing his bid to replace the Stuart King Charles I.) Meanwhile, the family had to wait another century and a half before acquiring its own permanent earldom. But patience and determination were to be their hallmark.

Angus Og died at his home Finlaggan on Islay round about 1320. MacDomhuill de Ila, as what is possibly his tombstone (see p. 40) on Iona, described him, consolidated the sea-based mini-empire stretching from Kintyre to Ardnamurchan, which under his eldest son was to be formally recognised as the Lordship of the Isles. But it was one of his bastards, an Ian Fraoch (Heather) born to one of his mistresses called MacHenry of Glencoe, who was given an unpromising little estate in Glencoe and founded the MacIain MacDonalds of that glen who regrettably were to become the best known of all the family's branches nearly 400 years later.

4

HOW GOOD WAS GOOD JOHN?

There were in total four officially recognised Lords of the Isles and Good John, son of Angus Og, was the first. Even as far back as Somerled his ancestors had called themselves 'Rex' or 'Dominus Insularum', but their title had no governmental recognition. In retrospect the Lordship has been painted as the epitome of romantic Gaeldom, the flower of chivalry and the ethnically precious opponent of Sassenach centralisation. Indeed, there is something inherently attractive about a period when oared galleys with square sails raced across beautiful expanses of blue water, between purple-green islands with quaint castles astride sea-washed rocks, when ravens perched on the ships' masts to help navigation and Gaelic bards entertained the oarsmen with the heroic deeds of the past. It might seem natural enough for this Gaelic-speaking thanedom to resist the authority of Edinburgh dynasties and Anglo-Norman culture. The belligerent clansmen of that period have come to epitomise the struggles of an oppressed ethnic minority preserving worthily sustainable ways of life in antithesis to the poisons of capitalism. And, ironically, for all their long history of anti-Scottishness, they came to symbolise the apex of Scottishness.

All four of the official Lords of the Isles were extremely ambitious, and in this Good John set the fashion. Their basic policy was to expand the Lordship by seeking alliances with the English or any other groups who would help offset the centralising power of Edinburgh. This was made easier by the fact that of the seven Scottish kings who ruled during the Lordship period, four had long minorities and two of them were in English prisons for more than a decade each.

The other special feature of the four lords is that they tended to have large numbers of unruly sons, legitimate and otherwise. All were desperate for a slice of the action and all regarded force or an arranged marriage as perfectly normal methods of acquiring other men's cattle, money and land.

Good John found it all quite easy. The king he had to deal with for most of his period was David II (1329–71), who for much of that time was either a minor or a prisoner of the English. John neither contributed to David's royal war effort against the English nor much to the campaign to get him ransomed from captivity. In fact he backed the English-sponsored pretender Edward Balliol just to be provocative. The nearest he came to a pro-Scottish military contribution was when he went to France to fight for the Scots against the Black Prince at Crécy in 1369. It was a disaster; he was captured and ironically had himself ransomed at considerable expense. Perhaps the English thought that he was of more value to them sent back to make trouble in Scotland than kept in one of their dungeons. Certainly his captivity only lasted three months, much shorter than King David's.

John's greatest achievement was probably the handling of his marriage to his cousin Amy MacRuari. This lady was the niece of Christina, who had helped Robert Bruce in the dark days, so she and her brother were the sole surviving representatives of the MacRuari offshoot of Somerled's empire which held Garmoran, Moidart and the Uists. Soon after his marriage Good John had an extra unexpected piece of luck when his childless brother-in-law, Ranald, was murdered in a squabble at Elcho on his way to fight for King David against the English at Neville's Cross in 1346. Thus John's wife Amy inherited the entire MacRuari estates and dutifully handed them over to her husband.

No sooner had Amy done this than the grateful Good John renounced his marriage, an act perhaps made easier for him by the fact that he had become such a great benefactor of the church that the priests dare not refuse. Amy and their two sons, who were also disinherited from the main patrimony, were packed off to Garmoran where she built the superbly beautiful Tioram Castle by an exquisite sea-loch on the Moidart coast. From this castle there still leads a long drive of cairns to the pier from which the family could row over to the Eilean Fhionan where they restored the island chapel of St Finnan the

Infirm as their future resting place. There the ancient bell of St Finnan still rings its lament.

Amy seems to have been a woman of considerable piety whose only known sin was to have insisted on the murder of McInnes of Ardgour, the man she blamed for ending her marriage. She paid for new chapels on Isle Eorsay, at Kilmory Knapdale, Trinity on North Uist, St Columba's on Benbecula, a mini-monastery on Colonsay and an oratory on the island of Grimsay. At Tioram Amy's elder son Ranald founded a new sub-branch of the MacDonalds, Clanranald, which was to have a very active role right up to the Jacobite rising in 1745. Amy's other son Godfrey rejected his father's disinheritance plan out of hand and as a result was given nothing, though he eventually ended up with some estates on Uist and built Borve Castle on Benbecula as the family seat. The more obliging Ranald seems even to have acted as steward of Islay and regent for his stepbrother when Good John died. A beautiful carved cross on the island of Texa, near Dunyveg (Dun Naomhaig) Castle, has an inscription 'CRUX REGNALDI JOHANNIS DE YSLA' so it may be his monument.

Meanwhile, as the Black Death swept through central Scotland Good John took as his second wife Margaret, the daughter of Robert Stewart, now regent for the absent King David and, so long as David remained childless, heir to the throne of Scotland. A legend arose that John wore no hat at the wedding to avoid having to doff it to the king, but the king was a prisoner and could not have been there so this is perhaps just an illustration of the pride of the Lordship. Margaret brought as her dowry large tracts of Kintyre, which made a neat fit with John's Islay and Knapdale estates, giving him a consolidated spread of territory from the Firth of Clyde to Skye.

Thus by the time Good John died in 1386, having outlived David II by fifteen years, the MacDonald Lordship had expanded considerably and John's acts of rebellion had all been forgiven. In fact, he may have served briefly as Steward during the period when his father-in-law Robert was out of favour with King David and seems to have gone on an embassy to the Flanders wool merchants on the crown's behalf. But it was church not state that gave him his sobriquet 'Good' for his substantial expenditure on religious buildings. He rebuilt the chapel at Finlaggan, constructed the superb Augustinian priory on the beautiful island of Oronsay and built the tiny remote monastery of St Cormacthe-Sailor on the Eilean Mor at the mouth of Loch Sween. He refurbished Saddell and Iona abbeys and encouraged the building of numerous other churches throughout his domains as, according to MacMhurich, did his son Ranald who built the nunnery at Nunton on Benbecula and the two churches on Howmore. It is probable also that Good John was responsible for importing new sculptural skills to the area, perhaps through the Benedictine connection from Durham. His period saw the new fashion for elaborate carved tombstones with crosses, swords and intricate intertwining foliage that are found in large numbers on all the western islands, Kintyre and up the coast to Lochaline. Soon these stones also began to carry the effigies of mailed warriors in their bascinets and gambesons, with their galleys beside them, while the stones with shears or scissors, a sign of domesticity, were probably for their wives. These people may have lived often short and violent lives, but they had a high regard for elaborate memorials and their rich tradition of sculpture is one of the unique features of these tiny ruined chapels on offshore islands or remote parts of the mainland coast.

Good John outlived by a long way his opposite number on the Campbell side, Sir Colin Og. The expansion of the Campbell family was much less spectacular at this period, but Colin was a seasoned if impetuous soldier whose feudal obligation to the crown was a forty-oared galley. This was one of the single-masted *lymphads* (Gaelic, *longfhad* or longship), clinker built like a Viking galley but with a stern rudder. Ninety feet long with forty oars and a crew of over 100, it was about as large as they came on the Scottish coast. The average, as Denis Rixson has shown, was more like twenty-two oars. The smaller barges or birlinns used for inshore transport of men or supplies normally had from twelve to twenty oars. Two bits of oak preserved on the island of Eigg are all that have survived of these numerous craft, except for the stone images on thousands of tombstones.

Colin Og Campbell served with the two Bruce brothers in Ireland, as did a number of MacDonalds but probably the latter were hired mercenaries or gallowglasses, such as those who died with Edward Bruce at Dundalk in 1318. Colin earned a reprimand from King Robert for foolhardy chasing of enemies outside the battle zone, but he did later have one major military success: he stormed and captured Dunoon Castle from the English while David II was still a minor, then executed all the survivors – not an unusual occurrence at that time. As a reward he was given the custodianship of this important keep, which guarded the entrance to the Clyde. It also provided a foothold in Cowal where the Campbells began gradually to supplant the Lamonts as the leading family of the area, the clan's first but by no means last taste of encroachment into the territories of neighbouring families weaker than themselves. Theoretically the Campbells still pay a rent of one red rose a year to the crown for the now invisible remains of Dunoon Castle.

There was one other Campbell of note at this time, Sir Duncan of Loudoun, the sheriff of Ayr who fought with David II at Neville's Cross in 1346 and like him was captured by the English. His branch of the family was also destined to grow powerful, but not quite so rapidly.

5
BROTHER DONALD AND COLIN THE WONDERFUL

Donald MacDonald and yet another Colin Campbell were roughly contemporary as rival chiefs of the two great clans in the next generation. This was the period during which the mentally unstable King Robert III (1390–1406) was dominated by his brother the Duke of Albany. It also stretched on into the decades after King Robert's heir, young James I, had been kidnapped by the English with the possible connivance of Albany, in the best tradition of wicked uncles. Robert had tried to ship the young prince off to France for safety, Albany may have tipped off the English, Robert died of shock when he heard the news, and the boy King James I was destined to spend the next eighteen years in the Tower of London.

Donald, 2nd Lord of the Isles, led the MacDonalds for thirty-seven years (1386–1423) and was a nephew of the Regent Albany whose other nephew, young King James, neither of them really wanted to see back in Scotland. But if this was common ground it was limited, for Donald led a massive rebellion against Albany which very nearly succeeded.

By contrast Colin Iongantach (Wonderful) led the Campbells for a mere twenty-three years (c. 1394–1417) and presided over undramatic expansion rather than rash attempts at supreme power. He too, however, was well connected, having married Robert III's wife's sister. His son married Regent Albany's daughter, thus entwining the tentacles of the two leading clans. Unlike Donald he did assist in the effort to have King James released from the Tower and his son Duncan was one of those sent down to London as a hostage for the payment of the ransom money. In fact he was marked down as the wealthiest of all the young nobles who undertook this duty, a tribute to the way Colin Iongantach had built up the fortunes of the Campbell family – 'the sleekit Campbells combined claymore and parchment as never before'. Indeed, Colin was thought of as a bit of a miser who, according to one legend, buried some of his gold under the water round Inchconnel Castle to keep it out of the hands of his relations. Certainly as an old man he laid out money to build a smarter and more accessible new castle for himself on the new site of Inveraray. This tower house, now totally disappeared, stood on the banks of the River Aray, and was soon surrounded by a small town, but both were demolished in the 1740s to make way for the current ducal château and its garden.

It has been suggested that Donald MacDonald, 2nd Lord of the Isles, may have studied at Oxford (a theory based on his travel pass) and he spent some time as a hostage at court. Certainly he soon showed signs of very considerable ambition, perhaps partly goaded by the desperate desire of his two belligerent younger brothers to carve out independent baronies for themselves. The elder, Alastair Carrach, was described as 'a freebooter by nature', became one of the clan's best military leaders of the century and founded the new Keppoch branch of the family, which came to the fore in the Jacobite period. The younger, John Tanister, was even more of a rebel, so much so that he was exiled to Ulster with only one tiny foothold left in Scotland – the utterly remote castle of Dunyveg on Islay, with its safe anchorage for the MacDonalds in Lagavulin Bay, an area now better known for its excellent malt whisky. Fortuitously John married one of the Bissets of Antrim, and between them they founded the new branch of MacDonalds or MacDonnells of Dunyveg and the Glens, who years later became Earls of Antrim. John Tanister made up for his misbehaviour in Scotland by listening to his highly intelligent wife. She had spotted and adopted a red-haired amnesiac tramp who bore an uncanny physical resemblance to the recently murdered King Richard II of England, Ireland and Wales whom she had met when he visited Ulster. As Wyntoun the Chronicler put it:

> Quhen in the Islys schee saw this man
> Schee let that schee weel kend hym than
> That he was the King of Yngland
> That she before saw in Ireland.

This unwitting pretender, or mammet as he was known, was groomed, dressed up in appropriate finery by the Tanister's wife and handed over first to Donald, then to a very grateful Regent Albany to be used as an irritant against the new English King Henry IV. At the same time the Tanister started to make his mark in Ulster politics when he used a MacDonald naval force in Strangford Loch to help the MacQuillans, who later became the MacDonalds' main rivals in the area. In the end, according to the Sleat seannachies, John Tanister was murdered by a man called James or John Campbell at Ard Dubh on Islay. It appeared that a quarrel between him and his nephew had been engineered by Kinnon, the Green Abbot of Iona, and James I used this as an excuse to order Campbell to track down the Tanister. Once the deed had been done the king seems to have disowned the Campbell bounty-hunter and authorised his execution, an event of which no other details are known, but the line the Tanister founded was to have a truly remarkable future as we shall see.

Donald, Lord of the Isles' own wife was also destined to play a very important role in the history of the family. Margaret Leslie was sister of the Earl of Ross and potentially his heir. The earl's only child Euphemia had severe disabilities and Albany as both regent and her grandfather, was steering her towards a nunnery. He too had his eye on the Earldom of Ross, if for no other reason than to stop it becoming part of the MacDonald Lordship.

The aggravation between Donald and the royal Stewarts began as early as 1389 when the despised Robert III tried to complain about the way the Lord of the Isles' two restless brothers, Carrach and Tanister, were treating their mother, the king's own sister. This was perhaps when the Tanister was packed off to Ulster. The trouble resurfaced when the king's spoilt eldest son, the Duke of Rothesay, briefly displaced his ever-cunning uncle Albany as regent for the almost senile Robert III. The boy proved an extravagant, adulterous and unpopular regent and Albany, furious at being displaced, soon managed to have him locked up without food or water in a wing of Falkland Palace. Not long afterwards to consolidate his grip on the regency Albany had, as we have seen, contrived at least the temporary removal of the next heir, Prince James, by leaking advance news of his escape route to English pirates. Poor old Robert

III had dropped dead at his supper when he heard the news of the capture.

At about this time in 1402, with or without the connivance of Donald, Alastair Carrach cut a swathe through Inverness and burned half the cathedral city of Elgin. He apologised four months later and this was to become a familiar ploy of MacDonalds – commit a violent act of rebellion, then apologise humbly if there was a threat of retaliation and sit back knowing that it was more cost-effective for the government to accept the apology than to attempt to exact retribution by force. This was perhaps Donald's way of showing that he could exercise power in Ross. The prize of a mainland earldom was clearly becoming an obsession but the hunchback Sister Euphemia and the ever-watchful Regent Albany still stood in his way.

Donald was a regular visitor to London, for instance in 1388 to Richard II and twice to Henry IV in 1400. Five years later he was again being provocative by holding secret talks with Henry IV and the imprisoned James I (1406–37), not because he wanted James back, but because he wanted to destabilise Albany. The crafty regent had bullied poor Sister Euphemia into making his own son John, already the Earl of Buchan, heir also to the Earldom of Ross. Donald's negotiations included the idea of English military help if he tried to oust Regent Albany, perhaps to restore King James I, now aged about twelve, to his rightful throne.

In 1411 Donald, Lord of the Isles, tired of waiting, brought a large force over to the mainland. He captured Inverness and seemed to be heading to destroy Aberdeen but was met by an army of east coast barons – no Campbells that we know of – under the Earl of Mar. A battle followed at Harlaw on the slopes of Benachie, with broadswords, bows, axes and wooden shields. The Highlanders were perhaps rashly regarded as inferior. As Walter Scott put it in the mouths of their opponents:

> If they hae twenty thousand blades
> And we hae ten times ten
> Yet they hae but their tartan plaids
> and we are mail-clad men.

But they soon discovered that the two sides were well matched:

> Now haud your tongue both wife and carl
> And listen great and sma'
> And I will sing of Glenallan's Earl
> That fought on the Red Harlaw.

Scott's phrase 'Red Harlaw' summed up the one thing that is certain about this strange battle: that the casualties were high on both sides. In fact initially both sides seem to have thought they had lost. Nearly 1,000 MacDonalds were killed, but so too were large numbers of Lowland barons. Yet the MacDonald seannachies were soon composing poems about a great victory with Donald as the hero, while in contrast Donald himself was soon retreating rapidly back to his homelands with nothing concrete achieved. Yet as we have seen, invasion and withdrawal were becoming traditional isleman's tactics.

The MacDonald army had been egged on to battle with appeals to their roots by the hereditary MacMhurich bards:

> O children of Conn of a hundred battles
> Now is the time for you to win recognition.

Partly as a result of this the battle has been presented as one of languages and cultures, of Gaeldom versus Sassenach, Celt versus Teuton, Highland versus Lowland, Isles versus Edinburgh, clan loyalty versus fiendish Edinburgh centralisation or as John Major, the early Scots philosopher, put it 'Wild Scots' against 'civilised Scots'. It is seen as the turning point which determined whether Gaelic speakers would dominate Scotland or only its west coast, but the same argument could be made for Sheriffmuir or Culloden, and it is hard to envisage the Islesmen as desperately interested in controlling southern Scotland. Whatever the truth, the Regent Albany followed up Harlaw with a campaign that was unusually aggressive for him: Donald made no effort to withstand it. Instead, he attended peace talks at Lochgilphead where the Campbell chief Colin Iongantach was a local mediator; Donald submitted with no apparent effort to save face. Perhaps it was just the usual empty apology made on the basis that the government's troops would soon go away, but certainly Donald caused no further trouble for the rest of his life. He continued to live in a fantasy world of exchanging meaningless treaties as an equal with contemporaries like King

Sigismund of the Romans, Charles the Foolish of France and Henry IV of England, but he had no stomach for further invasions of Ross.

In his final years Donald perhaps lost faith in himself or began to be troubled by conscience. He is recorded as supplying a gold covering for the hand-bones of St Columba and silver goblets for the monks of Iona. There is even a story that he retired to the monastery as a monk himself, but an alternative suggests he died in Ardtornish Castle aged about fifty. Certainly he was buried on Iona in 1423, two years before James I at last returned from captivity and only three years after the death of his clever old uncle the Regent Albany.

Colin Iongantach Campbell had died six years earlier. He too had skeletons in his cupboard. He had quarrelled with his sons over money. He was reputed to have been forced to leap out of his burning castle wearing chain mail to cool off in the loch below. He had even deliberately burned down one of his own houses to avoid the shame of having to entertain some guests in poor surroundings. Of his wife we know little but he did have at least one bastard, Dugal Campbell, who was found a cosy niche as Dean of Argyll. There he proved a double example of clerical inchastity when he married the daughter of an Abbot MacAlaster. Compared with MacDonald flamboyance, Colin's career seems tame, but he had quietly become the wealthiest landowner in Scotland outside the royal house of Stewart, perhaps wealthier even than them.

6

HUMILIATION AND EXALTATION

The next generation of our two families coincided initially with a rule from Edinburgh that was for once extremely strict and effective. The returned prisoner James I flexed his muscles and used ideas he had learned from the long years of captivity in England watching Henry IV and his son Henry V. Our two protagonists are Alexander, 3rd Lord of the Isles, who took over from his father Donald MacDonald in 1423 and ruled for twenty-six years, and Sir Duncan na adh (Lucky) Campbell. He had taken over at Inveraray in 1414 and held the chiefship for very nearly forty years. Both Alexander and Duncan were to expand their respective territories considerably, but in Alexander's case it was at considerable cost.

Duncan Campbell has already been noted as the wealthiest hostage for the ransom payments on young King James (see pp. 21–2) and this enforced stay in the south had given him some experience of life in England. He had married Marjory Stewart, one of Regent Albany's many daughters, a contact which at the time was the right kind to have. Unlike other barons who suffered under James I for being too independent, Duncan continued discreetly building up the Campbell patrimony. In 1427 he gave up the old family seat at Menstrie beside Stirling in exchange for Glassary on Loch Awe, thus consolidating his grip on Argyllshire. Three years later he was ensuring that the Lochgoil area with its castle at Carrick went to another Campbell branch, that of Loudoun. Shortly afterwards he took over Loch Ranza Castle on Arran and at the same time began securing Glenorchy for his younger son Colin who was to be the founder of the second major branch of the family. This Colin Campbell (1400–78), according to his own descendants, had helped the Knights of St John during one of the many Turkish attacks on the Greek island of Rhodes, hence his soubriquet Black Knight of Rhodes (Colin Dubh na Roimh). The *Black Book of Taymouth* recorded that Colin: 'throch his valiant acts and manhead was made knecht in the isle of Rhodes . . . and was thrie sundrie times in Rome'.

When he returned from these adventures Colin had a succession of useful wives organised for him by his father, two of them Stewarts, so that his patrimony was built up quite rapidly. The final marriage was to Janet Stewart of Lorne, one of three Lorne heiresses all of whom had Campbell husbands, which increased the odds of Campbells taking over the bulk of this Stewart lordship. At the time it had no male heir and included not only Glenorchy and the upper end of Loch Awe but also the huge prize of Dunstaffnage Castle on the coast. In 1464, John the Leper, the last Stewart Lord of Lorne, was to make a final effort to acquire a new bride and produce a son, but he was murdered by an unknown Campbell at or close to the altar of his lovely chapel in Dunstaffnage. The lordship and its properties passed to various Campbells but mainly to Colin, the Black Knight of Rhodes. He and his third wife Janet then built the impressive pile of Kilchurn Castle on a peninsula jutting into Loch Awe. This inaugurated a long period of oppression against the MacGregors in this area, which was to see Campbell power spread steadily up to Loch Tay. The pretext for the attacks was the long-forgotten marriage of an Ian Campbell to a Mariota MacGregor.

Black Colin had one other mysterious claim to fame. After King James I had made numerous enemies for himself by the unaccustomed exercise of real royal discipline, he was murdered in the Blackfriars Priory, Perth, by a group including members of his own Stewart family. Afterwards Black Colin took some part – details unknown – in the tracking down of the murderers and was credited with arresting two of them, Colquhoun and Chambers. It could even be that he was the mysterious Knight of the Order of St John who took the murdered king's heart on a crusade to Rhodes and then brought it back to be buried with the rest of his body at the Carthusian priory in Perth. Such a theory is made plausible by the fact that between 1440 and 1443, when Kilchurn Castle was being built, his wife Janet had to supervise the masons because Colin was away on a crusade. Officially

Colin could not have been a member of the knightly Order of St John as he was far from celibate, but such rules could be overlooked and we know that there was a crusade organised in 1440 by Pope Eugenius IV. This was poorly supported by most of Europe but it did go to Rhodes and the Knights of St John did score a victory against the Mameluk Turks by sending a fleet to raise their siege of the Christian fort at Kastellovizo.

For some reason Black Colin was not rewarded for any of his services by the dead king's son but much later by his grandson James III (1460–88), who gave Colin the estate of Lawers. This extended the Campbells' grip on Loch Tay and created a new base for them that later provided some distinguished warriors and a male heir to enable the sonless Campbell barony of Loudoun to be kept in the family.

Meanwhile, Black Colin's father Duncan na adh had continued with his own royalty-pleasing career. In 1436 he accompanied Albany's son John, Earl of Buchan (and to the disgust of the MacDonalds also now Earl of Ross), on his fatal expedition to France. Buchan was killed fighting for the French against the English at Verneuil, but Duncan Campbell survived. It was from this period that there came the story of his slaying a wild boar, which became integrated in Campbell mythology with the boar of Diarmid as part of their coat of arms and their credentials as princes of Gaeldom (see p. 5).

Four years after this event came Duncan's one serious misfortune, the death of his eldest son Archibald, supposedly on a wintry trip back from Glasgow. This inspired Duncan to set up the new collegiate church on the Holy Loch, which was dedicated to the Irish hermit, St Mun, also as it happened the local saint of the MacDonalds of Glencoe who had their chapel on Eilean Munde in Loch Leven. Archibald was buried in the new church and so some years later was Duncan himself with a fine tombstone in the latest style showing his effigy in full armour. He left an estate on Loch Eck at Inverchapel to the custodian of his new church and also spent money on the island monastery of Inishail on Loch Awe, which was dedicated to Saint Findoca, one of the martyrs of the nine wells saga, and here too there is an ancient Campbell family burial ground.

By his death Duncan had been created 1st Lord Campbell and had served as Justiciar of the North leaving his title to his teenage grandson, Colin, whose tutor and guardian was the ubiquitous Black Colin.

Meanwhile, Alexander, 3rd Lord of the Isles and according to himself Earl of Ross, saw his powers both reach their greatest height and sink to their greatest depth. Unlike Duncan he had not been a hostage for the king's ransom, but when James came back he did sit at the trial of Albany's son Murdoch and joined in condemning him and his sons to death in 1425. In the period that followed, Alexander and the new king sized each other up and Alexander, foreseeing a reduction in his independence, seems quite soon to have started intriguing against James. The first tack was the usual one of divide and rule, appealing to the Danish king as a more distant alternative to a monarch resident in Edinburgh. But Eric VII was a highly unreliable ruler who shortly lost Sweden for his own dynasty and was then even deposed from Denmark. Meanwhile, the impetuously ruthless James I invited the Lord of the Isles and other suspect barons to a parliament in Inverness in 1428. Once they were in the town and defenceless he had about fifty of them arrested. Some were immediately executed, the rest including Alexander were shut up in various castles throughout Scotland and King James wrote a Latin poem to celebrate his triumph. The Lord of the Isles was offered inducements to become a pro-establishment courtier but clearly had no liking for the idea. Soon afterwards by some means he managed to escape from Perth Castle where he had been placed and set about seeking revenge for what he saw as the king's unchivalrous and outrageous behaviour. In addition, he was still irritated by the recent murder of his uncle, John the Tanister, by the king's Campbell hatchet man.

With 10,000 troops, including MacDonalds, Camerons and MacIntoshes, Alexander burned the town of Inverness and started to besiege the castle. Then, perhaps just in the MacDonald tradition of hit and run, he returned to the west at the end of June 1429. There in Lochaber near where Fort William now stands James I and the royal army caught up with him. At this point his Cameron and MacIntosh allies decided that they had had enough and deserted en masse. Without these additional troops Alexander must have been easily defeated, though no details of the battle are known. Realising that all his possessions could now be overrun by the king he decided to beg for mercy. Two months after Lochaber he arrived at Holyrood, and knelt in front of the high altar in his shirt and drawers, handing his sword hilt-forwards to the king. No doubt this was all part of a

pre-arranged spectacle in which Alexander's survival had already
been negotiated, but he went on with the charade, begging for his
life and Queen Joan the 'milk-white dove' went through the motions
of persuading her husband to spare the Lord of the Isles. He was sent
to Tantallon Castle at the mouth of the Forth and his mother, the
heiress of Ross, was put out of the way on the monastery island of
Inchcolm.

James I did now take some steps towards dismembering the lands of
the Lordship, with the territory of Alastair Carrach, Alexander's warlike
uncle, as the first target. The Stewart Earl of Mar was sent to enforce
this policy, but that experienced warrior Alastair Carrach took his
archers to the hills above Inverlochy Castle, near Ben Nevis, and began
an attack on Mar's army. This was turned into a notable success against
the royal army when a small fleet of galleys appeared in Loch Linnhe
under the command of Donald Balloch, Alastair's nephew, and son of
the redoubtable John Tanister of Dunyveg and the Glens. As Walter
Scott described it:

> Cast your plaids
> Draw your blades
> Forward each man set
> Pibroch of Donuil Dhu
> Knell for the onset.

Caught between two MacDonald forces Mar's royal army took a severe
mauling and had to retreat in disarray to the east.

James I must have been extremely annoyed and his first reaction was
to mount a new expedition immediately to go after Carrach and
Balloch. But doubtless his counsellors warned him of the huge expense
and probable futility of sending normal Lowland troops to try to catch
lightly armed islanders who could disappear into the mountains or out
to sea at the first hint of a pitched battle. So, perhaps also demoralised
by a new onset of the Black Death which was once more sweeping
through Scotland, he called off the expedition. Instead, another charade
was laid on in which the queen played her usual role of calming the
king down and Alexander was pulled out of the dungeons of Tantallon
to swear future good behaviour in return for the restoration of his lands
and titles.

Whatever promise Alexander made he seems to have kept for the remaining six years of James I's life. When John Stewart, the rival Earl of Ross, was killed at Verneuil in 1436 there was no longer any reason why Alexander should not rightfully claim the earldom inherited through his mother.

After the king was murdered at Perth the political situation changed: there was a six-year-old boy on the throne. Alexander was officially recognised as Earl of Ross by the regency group, most particularly by his ally Archibald, Earl of Douglas, also known because of his exploits in France as the Duke of Touraine. He was even appointed a justiciar in the north. He used his clan to harass his enemies in Lennox and to take revenge on the Camerons who had deserted him at Lochaber. Thereafter fewer official opportunities for disruption presented themselves. In 1443 the MacDonalds invaded Kintyre and two years later Alexander was once more in league with Archibald, Earl of Douglas, possibly in a scheme to dethrone the now teenage James II (1437–60). But before the plan came to a head Alexander died, leaving his own teenage son to succeed him. He did have other sons; it is unclear whether they were legitimate or otherwise but at that time the difference often meant little. His main wife was certainly Elizabeth Seton and his two other sons, Archibald of Lochalsh (born to a McPhee lady) and Hugh of Sleat (born to a Gillepatrick), were both to found major and violent new branches of the family. Sleat remarkably survived all the others, ultimately became the claimant for the by now meaningless Lordship of the Isles, and still carries a hereditary Irish peerage based on the Skye estates. Its early castles were at Duntulm in the north, and Dunskeath and Camus, or Knock, both on the fertile Sleat peninsula.

One of Alexander's final acts was to hand over the island of St Barr or Davaar Island, at the mouth of what is now Campbeltown Loch, to the monks of Saddell Abbey and he had already shown some favour to the church by yet another rebuilding of Iona Abbey in 1443 – there were some complaints about the monks' rough behaviour with their concubines, so their image needed some refurbishment.

Perhaps in this period there was little overt violence between MacDonalds and Campbells, but through most of this generation they had been on opposing sides. The borders between their estates remained long and vulnerable and the Campbell triple marriage of the three Lorne heiresses had removed the last major buffer zone between them.

As a means of identification in battle the MacDonalds had adopted a sprig of heather in their caps, whereas the Campbell equivalent was the gale or bog myrtle. Both are extremely common plants in the whole area, but one thrives better on high rocky ground, the other on the damp lower hillsides.

7

THE END OF THE LORDSHIP

The fourth and last official Lord of the Isles (excluding members of the British royal family who later adopted it as one of a quiverful of spare titles), John MacDonald, was in many respects an anticlimax. By a strange coincidence he was only about fifteen or sixteen when he succeeded Alexander in 1449 as both Lord of the Isles and Earl of Ross, a similar age to Colin Campbell when he succeeded his grandfather as Lord Argyll six years later. But in every other respect the careers of the two were very different: John did irremediable damage to the MacDonald family while Colin continued the steady progress of the Campbells.

Even his own seannachies described John as 'mean and moody, more fitted to be a priest or scholar than a military leader'. His irascible father had spent much time away from home in prison or fighting and perhaps was a poor role model; he died leaving John to inherit before he was old enough to cope. Though John was to be Lord of the Isles for forty-four years, longer than any other, surviving through the reigns of James II, James III and into that of James IV (1488–1513), he showed no sign of learning from his mistakes, was an uninspiring leader, an inveterate plotter and a fickle husband. The classic tactic of violent rebellion one minute and abject pleas for forgiveness the next was taken to extremes in his case.

John's Lordship started on an awkward note, for what had looked at the time like a most advantageous arranged marriage soon turned out to be a disaster both politically and conjugally. The bride was Elizabeth Livingston, daughter of what had been the most powerful family in

Scotland for several years. However, just as Elizabeth was romantically escaping from Dumbarton Castle to elope with John, the teenage James II seized power from his regents, purged the Livingstons and left the new Lord of the Isles with a wife who was no longer politically correct and not apparently even much to his taste.

With a new and headstrong young king flexing his muscles John wisely kept a low profile for the first four years of his Lordship, but in 1452 the balance of power was upset when the all-powerful Earl of Douglas goaded the king too far and was murdered by him and his friends in Stirling Castle. The earl's brother and successor James Douglas went into hiding but soon began to tempt the still immature Lord of the Isles to join him in rebellion against the murderous King James. Douglas, with backing from Henry VI of England, came to meet John at Eilean na Ghallagan Castle on West Loch Tarbert and dazzled him with gifts of fine wines, jewels and fashionable clothes brought from England. Still aged only twenty-one John led a force of some 10,000 MacDonalds onto the mainland and was defeated by the Earl of Sutherland amid considerable slaughter – in fact he seems never again to have taken personal command of his troops in a rebellion. Meanwhile, his more experienced uncle, Donald Balloch of Dunyveg and the Glens (John Tanister's son and the hero of Lochaber), had conducted another invasion on the Clyde coast with 100 galleys, destroying Brodick Castle and burning some Ayrshire villages, killing just a few local men, but stealing around 10,000 assorted livestock. Significantly no Campbells seem to have come out to oppose him. Donald Balloch also strengthened his family with an excellent marriage to one of the O'Neills of Connaught, which brought the family additional estates in Ulster, so that Islay gradually became less important for them – a development of great importance for the next generation.

Overall, with defeat in the north and some success in the south John might not have been totally disillusioned, but the last straw came when his ally the Earl of Douglas was drubbed by the king at Arkinholm a year later in 1455. John now submitted to the king and was pardoned for both his own and Donald Balloch's invasions. As a reward John had restored to him Castle Urquhart, a massive pile in the disputed territory of Ross and Lochaber, and Greenan Castle on the coast south of Ayr. Four years later John dutifully responded to the feudal call of his king and turned out with his 3,000 men for an attack on the English at Roxburgh and Berwick. In fact, so keen was he to impress that he volunteered to march at the front of the Scottish army to demonstrate his loyalty. He may have been gently amused at around this time to hear that Robert Campbell, Captain of Ordnance, a very early practitioner of what was then a highly suspect military technology, had been executed for helping the French against the English. Despite the fact that King James II was pretending to aid both sides in the English War of the Roses and hoping to drive a wedge for himself, the invasion came to nothing. James made a truce with the English and John headed back to either Ardtornish or Finlaggan Castle, his two chief residences.

All this time John had continued to hold treasonable correspondence with the rebel Earls of Douglas and Crawford. Meanwhile, his Campbell opposite number Lord Colin, still advised by his guardian the redoubtable Black Colin, Knight of Rhodes and Glenorchy, had helped the king so significantly in the battle against the Douglases that in 1457 he was rewarded with his own earldom – of Argyll. With Earl Colin at Inveraray now a major force in the west and Black Colin his close ally making steady inroads into MacGregor territory from his grim stronghold of Kilchurn, for the first time the Campbells were becoming a power almost as great as the MacDonalds. The murder of the penultimate Stewart Lord of Lorne in 1463 by a Campbell henchman of Alan McCowle meant that a final buffer zone between the Campbells and MacDonalds was removed and eight years later Earl Colin officially became Lord of Lorne.

Meanwhile, John's marriage, undertaken for political benefits that were never delivered, got into predictable difficulties. It had produced no children and judging by the age of John's most famous bastard – the curly-headed, hard-drinking Angus Og – he must have strayed from the marital couch at a very early stage. Equally, Elizabeth was a city girl and preferred the jollities of court life at Holyrood to the draughty loneliness of Finlaggan. To be trapped in a damp tower on a tiny island on a loch that was itself in the middle of another island must have seemed a severe penance and she spent as much time as she could in Edinburgh.

Three years after his previous attempt James II renewed his attacks on the English-held Roxburgh Castle. The Earl of Argyll was present, but as far as we know the Earl of Ross was not, when the king stood impetuously close to one of his own new cannon and was fatally injured as it exploded. As a result Scotland once more had a child king, James III: Earl John was likely to take unfair advantage of the regency and Earl Colin to be among its ardent supporters. Two years into the new reign John predictably announced that he was himself King of the Isles and as if to prove the point he lived in regal splendour. After he held a meeting at Ardtornish Castle with the two permanent rebels, Earls Douglas and Crawford, documents were produced signifying that in future the MacDonalds would be subjects of Edward IV of England, not James III of Scotland. Their agreement meant that the three Scottish earls would combine with English help to eject the Stewart dynasty and then divide Scotland between them under remote control from London. This secret treaty, later referred to as the infamous Ardtornish Pact, was ratified when John sent Ranald of Largie and Archdean Duncan of the Isles to London to sign it.

For the next few years things were quiet but in 1475 Earl Colin Campbell was one of the negotiators acting for James III in peace talks with the English. It was probably he who found out from the now friendly Edward IV about the treacherous pact made by Earl John MacDonald of Ross some ten years earlier. The English no longer saw any advantage in the Ardtornish agreement and felt free to spill the secrets of the three plotting earls, Ross, Douglas and Crawford, who had offered Scotland to them. James III was not an aggressive man in the mould of his father or grandfather, but even he felt constrained to demand that the treacherous Lord of the Isles be punished. John was summoned to Edinburgh from Islay but failed to appear. Colin, Earl of Argyll, was given the commission of fire and sword to bring John to justice – the first major confrontation that we know definitely happened between the chiefs of the two great clans. With no significant allies John made no fight of it but asked for a royal pardon in the customary way. It was much easier for the king to punish him mildly than to continue the difficult and costly attempt to take him by force. So the Lord of the Isles was deprived of the Earldom of Ross, which his father had made such huge efforts to acquire, and he lost control of Kintyre and Knapdale. However, he was still Lord of the Isles, still controlled the traditional MacDonald territories and still seems to have held the constableship of Urquhart Castle on Loch Ness. Furthermore, as his marriage was still childless he won the vital legitimisation of his bastard son Angus Og as heir to the Lordship and, amazingly, Earl Colin's daughter Isabella as his daughter-in-law. Ironically, the MacDonalds lost their earldom just a few years after the Campbells had won theirs, so this period, symbolically at least, marks the point where the clan on the way up passed the one on the way down.

Despite, or perhaps because of, his fairly mild punishment John showed a few years later that he had learned nothing from experience: he started to plot or condone plots against the government all over again. He was accused of illegally building up stocks of arms at Castle Sween ready for a new rebellion, and again he backed down.

At this point as MacDonald territory was being steadily eroded John seems finally to have lost the confidence of his more energetic relations. The most proactive of these, now that Donald Balloch was dead, was Donald Gorm MacDonald of Sleat, a violent, fairly desperate man based on the farthest edge of the clan territory in northern Skye. He is reputed to have locked up his own brother in Duntulm Castle, which was their base and is now a grim ruin with galley grooves scarring the rocks below. Nearby are a judgement mound and a hanging knoll. The family eventually abandoned the castle after someone dropped a MacDonald baby from one of the upper windows.

The other proactive MacDonald was Angus Og, John's hot-tempered heir, who deeply resented his father's lethargic performance. The ex-earl had indeed settled down to a life of idle self-indulgence, incapable of disciplining the assembly of knights that still met on the Council Island of Finlaggan. And still there were the expensive retinues of hereditary poets (the MacMhurichs), hereditary doctors (the Beatons) and hereditary lawyers (the Morrisons). He had also finally fallen out with his wife Elizabeth who at about this time wrote to the Pope complaining that he was trying to poison her. At some point Elizabeth and Angus Og seem to have become unlikely allies. They ejected the Lord of the Isles from his own island mansion at Finlaggan and he had to spend the night under an upturned boat. In revenge for this humiliation John signed over some MacDonald properties in Kintyre and Knapdale, which were not legally his anyway, to the Campbells. Most specifically, the key fortress of Castle Sween was taken from the MacMillan Constables, who had looked after it for many years and had put up the superb MacMillan Cross at Kilmory Knap Chapel. Now Castle Sween became a government/Campbell base for repression instead of a MacDonald one for rebellion. The rock at Point of Knap, which it was said would stay there as long as the MacMillans held Castle Sween, mysteriously fell into the sea where it can still be glimpsed at low tide.

The split in ranks between the MacDonald lordlings now erupted into open war. Attempted peace talks between the two halves of the Lordship were held at Tobermory but ended in deadlock. Half each of the MacLeans, MacLeods and MacNeills sided with John and the rest – together with the hard-core MacDonalds of Sleat and Moidart – supported Angus Og. In 1481 the two sides fought a naval battle in the Bloody Bay close to Tobermory and Angus Og easily defeated his father's armada. But now the government intervened. The Earl of Atholl was sent to sort things out and specifically to kidnap the child recently produced by Angus Og and his Campbell bride. This boy, the tragic Donald Dhu, was handed over to his grandfather Colin of Argyll and thrust into a cell at decrepit Inchconnel Castle, the Campbell's original home, where he was to spend the next miserable fifteen years.

Soon afterwards, around 1482, a MacDonald force under the almost psychotically violent Angus Og, and the old campaigner Donald Balloch, was sent to Inverness to frighten the populace. It had orders to induce them to pay all future taxes to John, not to James III, and to offer no further obedience to the Edinburgh monarchy. The rebel army met no opposition and headed south to Blair where it dragged the earl and countess out of the sanctuary of their chapel of St Bride and took them off into captivity.

The events that followed were even more bizarre. On their way back to Islay the galleys of Angus Og and Donald Balloch, laden with booty and prisoners, were hit by a storm and at least one treasure ship was sunk. Furthermore, it seems that the MacDonalds had picked up some plague germs from Perth or Inverness for 'they were suddenly stricken by the hand of God with frenzy and wodness'. So shocked were the two leaders by what occurred that they released their prisoners without ransom and returned as penitents to St Bride's Chapel to beg for the restoration of their health. Luckily for John his plot remained undiscovered at this point and the state of the country was so chaotic that his bastard's military venture went unpunished.

Meanwhile, the unsatisfactory reign of James III was drawing to a close. Like John of the Isles he was a rather indulgent father with a very aggressive young heir waiting impatiently to succeed. Edward IV of England likewise had an impatient, aggressive brother waiting in the wings to succeed him, Richard, Duke of Gloucester. It was Gloucester, in fact, who started the process that brought so many changes, for his invasion of Scotland forced James III to summon the army of his feudal barons at what was a very inconvenient time for him. He had created huge resentment among them all by his overt preference for upstart architects and other low-born favourites rather than military men. The barons, including Colin Campbell, Earl of Argyll, mutinied. Cochrane, the most hated of the favourites, was hung without ceremony from Lauder Bridge in the Borders. Earl Colin was sacked as Lord Chancellor and was probably one of those who became involved in treasonable talks with young Prince James about staging a coup against his bumbling father. But when the coup took place and culminated in the battle of Sauchieburn (1488), Earl Colin was conveniently away in London holding peace talks with the new English King Richard III. So he escaped the slight taint of regicide that lingered over those who took part at Sauchieburn – including the new King James IV himself. For not only had young James beaten his own father in the battle but he had then allowed him to be murdered by a man referred to simply as 'Grey'.

By a strange quirk of fate the Lord of the Isles, unlike James III, outlived his own rebellious son. Angus Og had exploited the civil unrest in the central belt of Scotland to launch yet another attack on the wretched town of Inverness. But he was murdered soon afterwards in a brawl in his rooms in the town by a wandering Irish harper called Dermid O'Cairbre, who was punished by being dragged behind a horse till he died.

Angus Og left the child Donald Dhu, half MacDonald, half Campbell, as theoretical heir to the Lordship. The unfortunate boy was already a prisoner in Inchconnel and was soon declared a bastard to undermine any claims he might later try to make. The tombstone on Iona that carries the name Angus Og (see p. 15) may well mark the grave of the one murdered in Inverness, rather than the illustrious predecessor of the same name.

Under the energetic new King James IV the fringe MacDonalds continued to strive suicidally to regain their former glories. Angus Og was replaced as leader by Alexander MacDonald of Lochalsh, the branch of the family based at Strome Castle on Loch Carron. A rebellion began as soon as King James decided that the luckless John of the Isles could no longer control his vassals and stepped in to strip him of all his remaining titles. Four generations after its inauguration the official Lordship of the Isles was no more.

John was sent packing from Islay to live out the rest of his life as a pensioner, possibly at Lindores Abbey or nearby Dundee or Paisley. By coincidence one of his last acts as lord had been to hand over the delightful church of Kilberry in Knapdale to the Bishop of the Isles, who was based at Lismore. By a strange chance this very same year, 1493, Colin Campbell, Earl of Argyll, died having doubled the territory of his earldom in his own lifetime. The latest addition was Rosneath, given as a reward by James IV for Campbell's support in the recent coup. Also, his newly acquired rock-top castle at Dollar, conveniently close to royal Stirling, had its name officially changed from Castle Gloom to Castle Campbell.

John lingered on for another ten years, now so harmless that he was once allowed to wander back briefly to Islay. He died penniless in about 1494 and was buried according to tradition in his Stewart mother's family vault at Paisley Abbey.

As one unique Scottish institution died another was born, for about this time we have the first written record of the monastic movement's involvement in the distilling of strong spirit, *aqua vitae* or whisky. A Friar John Cor was provided with eight bolls of malt for the purpose. Another new fashion arrived during this period. It came from Germany and was to change the style of Highland fighting for the next two centuries. It was the larger two-handed sword, known from this time on as the claymore.

8

THE PRISONER, BLACK DONALD

The death of Earl Colin Campbell in 1493 and the demotion of John of the Isles occurred within twelve months of each other and within four years of the murder of the colourful Angus Og. It was thus a turning point and left the stage open for a whole new cast of players.

For nearly the next twenty years Scotland was for once under a strong and energetic monarchy, with James IV paying serious attention to the pacification of the Scottish west coast. The MacDonalds were divided and badly led. The Campbells were headed by a new Earl Archibald who was to die as he had lived – conscientiously in the service of his king.

The first of the Islesmen to react against the harsh new discipline was Sir John MacDonald of Dunyveg and the Glens, son of Donald Balloch, who headed the branch of the clan with estates in both Islay and Ulster. Therefore, he was theoretically a subject of both James IV and Henry VII of England. He had been knighted by the king during the peace processes of 1493, but objected strongly soon afterwards to the king's seizure of Dunaverty Castle, which John regarded as still MacDonald property, as he did the traditional family seat at Dunyveg, Airds Castle at Carradale and Island Muller Castle south of Saddell. Not only did he then storm Dunaverty on its precipitous rock, but he also hanged the royal governor from the ramparts in full view of the departing Scottish navy. So while the other island barons submitted again to the king's peace at Mingary Castle, Ardnamurchan, in 1495, the Dunyveg family was outlawed. Sir John and four of his sons were eventually captured by a member of their own clan, MacIain of Ardnamurchan who had married a Campbell and was from this point on regarded as a turncoat

by the rest of the MacDonalds. The five captives were tried and executed
in Edinburgh. Many years later MacIain himself was tracked down and
killed by Donald MacDonald of Lochalsh. His beautifully carved
memorial slab on Iona shows him still in the traditional armour of the
west coast. Indeed, the two decades either side of 1500 seem to have
seen a remarkable new flowering of sculpture skills on the west coast,
for the great disc crosses, like that of Oronsay dated 1510, the
MacMillan Cross of Kilmory Knap with its superbly carved scenes and
the wonderfully decorated Maclean Cross of Iona, all date from around
this period.

Alexander of Lochalsh, who had taken up the challenge of fighting
the MacDonald cause, was also knighted in 1490, but a year later he
was defeated by a force of Mackenzies without royal intervention.
Alexander headed southwards to try to organise a general MacDonald
rebellion, but was caught and killed on the island of Oronsay by the
bounty-hunting MacIain in 1497.

Meanwhile, the focus turned back to the most extraordinary
character of the entire period. Donald Dhu, the teenager who had half
Campbell and half MacDonald blood, could claim with at least some
credibility to be the new Lord of the Isles, but was still held in close
confinement in the dungeon of Inchconnel Castle, the damp and
gloomy former home of the Campbell chiefs. The authorities, who began
in these days to include a posse of legally trained Campbells, had seen to
it that Donald Dhu was deprived of any inheritance that might have
been due to him. The undoubtedly legitimate son of the legitimised
bastard Angus Og MacDonald and of his wife Lady Isabella Campbell
was himself quite unfairly declared a bastard. His potential as a
troublemaker was too great. That was why he had been kidnapped as a
young child and kept in captivity by his grandfather ever since.

At long last, in 1501 after some fifteen years on the island castle of
Inchconnel Donald Dhu, aged about eighteen, was rescued by a band of
disgruntled Glencoe MacDonalds. The reason for their remarkable
attack on the island prison was what they considered massive
provocation by the Campbells. Since the break-up of the Lordship the
Campbell leaders had been taking advantage of the power vacuum and
royal favour to extend their territories more aggressively than ever
before. This was particularly true of Duncan of Glenorchy, head of the
second main branch of the Campbells based at the great castle of

Kilchurn (these days a lightning-split ruin). In 1498 he was made baillie of the Tay region with the remit to improve order. He proceeded to exploit the nearly forgotten marriage of one of the family to a MacGregor wife in order to thrust his authority into the weaker clan's territory of Glenstrae. At the same time he was pressurising the same clan southwards from Loch Tay towards Balquidder, pushing the last Stewarts westwards out of Glenlyon and the MacDonalds of Glencoe back into the least fertile parts of their own glen.

After a few years of this Campbell aggression the MacDonalds and MacGregors erupted and broke Donald Dhu out of his prison to act as their figurehead, perhaps even to become the new Lord of the Isles. All then joined up with Torquil MacLeod of Lewis and together, despite James IV's efforts, they undertook a winter invasion of Gordon and Badenoch, mainly to wreak revenge on the Earl of Huntly who in their eyes was classed alongside the Campbell Earl of Argyll as a major oppressor of the west. As was customary, once the MacDonald host had enjoyed a few weeks' plunder it disappeared back to whence it came.

Royal retaliation was massive – if slow to mobilise. The Earl of Argyll was put in charge of Kintyre and surrounding area, including control of the royal castle at Tarbert (still to this day an imposing ruin) and a newly built castle at Kilkerran (later renamed Campbeltown), which has now almost totally disappeared. Meanwhile, in 1504 a large fleet was assembled at Dumbarton and set off up the west coast under its experienced admiral, Andrew Wood of Largo. The MacLean part of the rebel army had shut itself up in the most remote of all the old Lordship castles – Cairnaborg on the tiny Treshnish Islands west of Mull. Given the treacherousness of the surrounding anchorages they would normally have expected to be immune from any attack, but for perhaps the first time in the history of the region the ships converging on Cairnaborg carried artillery. Thus, this occasion may well have marked the death knell of the galley that had for the previous five centuries been the proud badge of every family in the area. Within a short time of Wood's arrival the MacLeans were pulverised into submission.

Donald Dhu had still evaded capture and sought safety with Torquil MacLeod in Stornaway Castle, but there too Wood's fleet was able to demonstrate its artillery power: stone castles now seemed to have no other purpose than to be short-term refuges or prisons. Donald was taken back first to Stirling Castle, later to Edinburgh, where he was to spend the next forty-odd years before being allowed to escape one final time.

Meanwhile, the relentless Campbell expansion continued. As a result of the 1502 expedition the castle at Skipness south of Tarbert was added to the group of castles – Sween, Tarbert and Kilkerran – which they now held in order to dominate Kintyre. They now also re-acquired Dunstaffnage at the mouth of Loch Etive, which guarded the channel up to Mull. Duncan, the aggressive son of Colin of Glenorchy, resumed his attrition against the MacGregors and built Finlarig Castle on Loch Tay; it would eventually be the centre point of the new Campbell earldom of Brea d'Albane (Breadalbane). He also pressed his younger sons into lovely Glenlyon where their descendants were later to suffer such torment from marauding Glencoe MacDonalds and to develop such a grudge against them. But Duncan of Glenorchy, like his cousin Earl Colin, was to be killed fighting for their impetuous king, James IV, ten years later.

The most remarkable Campbell character of the period was certainly John, the earl's brother. A few years before the recapture of Donald Dhu this middle-aged widower chose to take sixty of his men to seize Muriel Rose, the redheaded three-year-old heiress of the Thane of Cawdor, by force. According to legend, she had been branded with a red-hot poker to make sure that no spurious little redheads were produced as false claimants to the thanedom. (Argyll did arrange for a few spurious little redheads of his own when the real one had a spot of illness and there were fears for her life.)

Naturally, the men of the Rose family objected strongly to the abduction and in the pursuit that followed all of John's seven sons by his earlier marriage were killed. But not in vain. After a ten-year wait the insatiable John Campbell married his young heiress. The Campbells were on their way to another major addition of territory that in due course was to turn into the fourth of their four earldoms, Argyll, Breadalbane, Loudoun and Calder. John took over the magnificent castle of Calder or Cawdor, with its recently added fortifications. The castle had been originally built over 100 years earlier on a site chosen by a donkey, where an ancient hawthorn tree still stands in the vaulted basement. Outside it was guarded by a dry moat with drawbridge and the Campbells were to enlarge and embellish it still further over the next 200 years.

John Campbell of Calder's other claim to fame was the murder of his brother-in-law, Hector MacLean of Duart. This was an act of revenge, acceptable in Highland tradition. MacLean had grown tired of his wife Catherine, John's sister, and left her stranded on the tidal skerry off Lismore now known as the Lady Rock. Instead of drowning as intended she was picked up by some passing Campbell fishermen and taken to Inveraray where she was reunited with her father, the 3rd Earl of Argyll. When MacLean turned up soon afterwards to report his wife's sad demise, she was produced from behind the curtain to his serious embarrassment, but following the rules of Highland hospitality he was allowed to leave the castle unscathed – only to be murdered by John of Calder six months later in Edinburgh. The widow Catherine's choice of second husband was somewhat safer – a Campbell of Auchinbreck, soon to be a prominent branch of the family, the new guardians of Castle Sween.

There was also another Campbell murderer at this time: in 1527 Sir Hugh Campbell of Loudoun killed Gilbert Kennedy, Earl of Cassilis, in one of the many on-going feuds that were a feature of Ayrshire and Galloway.

The disastrous battle of Flodden on 9 September 1513 was the result of James IV's misguided effort to create a diversion to help his French allies in their fight against the English. It ended in a humiliating defeat for the Scottish army by a smaller force sent by his brother-in-law, Henry VIII. James himself was killed, leaving the crown to yet another child successor. Furthermore, it was a calamity for the Campbells: the chiefs of both Inveraray and Glenorchy were killed along with a number of their followers, including the MacNaughton chief from Dunderave. The MacDonalds, few of whom were likely to have been present, could perhaps now see some light at the end of the tunnel. With a one-year-old king, James V (1513–42), on the throne, now, if ever, there was an opportunity to restore their fortunes.

The first to proclaim himself the Lord of the Isles in the new reign was Sir Donald Galda MacDonald of Lochalsh who had spent some of his childhood at court as a kind of hostage for his father's good behaviour and was knighted by the king at Flodden. He was now based at Strome Castle, nursing an almost pathological hunger for violence. He led the invasion of Inverness-shire in the usual MacDonald way and captured Urquhart Castle. Then he ravaged Ardnamurchan and destroyed Mingary Castle as revenge against a MacIain bounty-hunter who had killed his father Alexander and caused the death of MacDonald of Dunyveg. Eventually he caught up with MacIain himself and his followers at Craiganairgid or the Silver Crag. In the subsequent slaughter MacIain, his two sons and many others of his sept were killed. Not long afterwards Donald Galda himself died of an unknown cause probably at Cairnaborg Castle. He had no children so the Lochalsh branch of the MacDonalds died with him. Similarly, the MacIains never recovered from their decimation at Craiganairgid and within a few years the Campbells had taken advantage of the chief MacIain's marriage to a Campbell girl to start claiming ownership of Ardnamurchan for themselves.

Meanwhile, Colin, 3rd Earl of Argyll (d. 1530) had been given commission of fire and sword to deal with the MacDonalds and grasped the opportunity with enthusiasm. His actions included retaliating against an outbreak of MacLean marauding on the Campbell lands of Craignish and Rosneath, which followed the murder of their chief by John of Calder in Edinburgh. Black Duncan of Glenorchy made further heavy inroads against the MacGregors and Menzies round Loch Tay in 1519, reducing the MacGregors to penniless vagrants. The Campbells also managed to fit in some depredations in Morvern, Tiree and Mull before young King James V decided he had come of age and instructed a change of policy.

For the first time a Stewart king actually seemed to prefer the now underdog MacDonalds to the all-powerful Campbells. Two senior Campbell lairds had to go as hostages to Edinburgh to guarantee the good behaviour of Earl Colin. However, in 1530 Colin died and was succeeded by his son Archibald. The new earl was allowed to resume the somewhat overzealous pacification of MacDonald territory and began an almost personal vendetta against the latest MacDonald leader, Alexander of Islay. With exceptional shrewdness this gentleman managed to wrong-foot Argyll with the king, ingratiating himself with promises of undying loyalty and damning Earl Archibald as an overambitious and sadistic oppressor. The result was that Alexander MacDonald earned himself a lucrative campaign in Ireland to conduct devastations against the English, something that he and his men would happily have done for nothing, and Argyll was given a taste of prison to remind him that he was dispensable. It was enough to encourage him to keep a low profile for the rest of James V's brief reign. His uncle, another Archibald Campbell, of Skipness fared even worse, for he was a prisoner in Edinburgh Castle. He fell to his death while trying to escape and his even more unfortunate wife, the beautiful Lady Glamys, was burned at the stake on trumped-up charges of murder and witchcraft in 1537. She was said to have 'died with manlike courage'. Rather more placid was the life of another brother, Donald, who was made Abbot of Cupar and produced five sons.

Several years had passed in relative tranquillity until, perhaps encouraged by the eclipsing of the Campbells in royal favour, another aggressive new MacDonald leader tried to restore the Lordship. Donald Gruamach of Sleat, who also held Dunskeath Castle on Loch Eshort, had made a useful marriage to a MacLeod heiress from Lewis. This gave his branch of the family more land on Skye and backing in their feud with the other half of the MacLeods based at Dunvegan. Donald Gruamach's rebellion began promisingly in 1539. He marauded through MacKenzie territory and would probably have captured their castle at Eilean Donan quite easily, for it had only a tiny garrison. But Donald succumbed to overconfidence, refused to take cover and an arrow shot by the constable of the castle, a Macrae, wounded him in the leg. Even this need not have proved fatal, but in a fit of anger he pulled the arrow out himself and in doing so cut his own artery, dying soon afterwards on a nearby island. His followers took out their feelings on the surrounding Kintail villages and headed back to Skye, thus ending the rebellion.

A year later in 1540 James V set out on a major sea expedition to suppress all resistance on the west coast and unusually he asked for no help from the Campbells in this enterprise. Instead, with twelve well-equipped gunships he sailed from Leith north about, stopping at Orkney for supplies. Then he cruised down the west coast, graciously accepting voluntary submission from most of the various MacDonald chiefs, taking a few hostages and arresting only James MacDonald of Islay and the MacLean chief as the two most dangerous potential rebels still at large. He also put royal garrisons into Dunaverty and Dunyveg, with direct Edinburgh control of all the former lands of the Lordship. He even conducted the first coastal survey of Scotland and from a centralisation point of view it all looked very promising.

But within a few months all James V's plans turned to disaster. Henry VIII, who had declared himself king of Ireland and had just lost yet another wife, was in aggressive mood and resented James V's pretensions, particularly in Ireland. Both James's baby sons had died. As war threatened from England he found that his policy of divide and rule had left him with few friends. Just as his grandfather had suffered the indignity of mutiny at Lauder Bridge, so at Fala Muir, nearly sixty years later, James found that he could not count on the loyalty of his own barons when it really mattered and he was faced with an English invasion. His depression, perhaps hereditary, deepened and within months he was dead at the age of only thirty, leaving his crown, as so many of his forefathers had done, to a young child. But in his case the heir was even less satisfactory since it was a girl.

Yet again the prospect of a period of regency suggested that the embattled MacDonalds might make another bid for the restoration of lost territories and titles. They were helped by the dithering and divisions of the Scottish baronial class, splits now exacerbated by the first rifts between Catholic and Protestant. The remarkable Donald Dhu MacDonald, who for the last forty years had been a prisoner in Edinburgh, was either allowed or encouraged to escape by the regent, the Earl of Arran, perhaps to spite the Campbell Earl of Argyll, who was regarded as a dangerous opponent of his policies. Certainly Arran was responsible for releasing the other MacDonald hostages to go to join the battle against Argyll. Thus in 1543 a force of 1,800 MacDonald allies hit the Campbell heartlands with considerable loss of life. Clanranald was now under the able leadership of the illegitimate John Moydertach of Benbecula. He founded a new dynasty who styled themselves Captains of Clanranald and John himself became the senior MacDonald chief of the north. Together with the MacDonalds of Keppoch he invaded eastwards and as in previous MacDonald advances the key castle of Urquhart was captured. They then defeated the Frazers at Blar-na-line. The Campbells now found themselves in a wedge with the MacDonalds to the north and their enemy the Earl of Lennox backed up by an English fleet to the south. The ex-prisoner Donald Dhu, now amazingly hailed as Lord of the Isles and Earl of Ross, met with seventeen island chiefs at Knockfergus in Ulster. He would support Lennox and the English with a force of 4,000 men and nearly 200 galleys against Argyll and Mary, Queen of Scots' regents. In return he was presented with gold (1,000 crowns and the promise of a pension of 2,000 a year) and rich clothes sent by Henry VIII. Around 3,000 MacDonald adherents were put on the English payroll and plans were in hand for a joint MacDonald–English invasion of western Scotland to coincide with an all-English army attacking in the east. But there were the usual, inevitable delays and at this point the luckless Donald Dhu, still under sixty and having spent at least fifty of his years in prison, caught a fever, possibly measles which his long captivity had prevented him getting over in his youth. He died. He had outlived the first, second and third earls of Argyll, his hated relations. Rumour had it that he had produced a bastard, but this is by no means certain. There was a massive funeral befitting his high rank in the town of Drogheda where he died. So ended the last serious attempt to restore the Lordship of the Isles.

PART 2
CHANGE ENDS

'Tis distance lends enchantment to the view
And robes the mountain in its azure hue.

Thomas Campbell (1777–1844)

9
THE IRISH DIVERSION

With the death of Donald Dhu in 1545 the direct legitimate line of the Lords of the Isles had definitely become extinct. Thus the leadership of the MacDonalds fell by default to the half-Irish family of Dunyveg and the Glens, the descendants of John Mor Tanister. There had of course been a long Ulster connection going back to the days of Angus Og and his nephews, the sons of Alexander Og who fled to Ireland before Bannockburn. But it was John Tanister from his base castle at Dunyveg on Islay beside the superb anchorage of Lagavulin who lifted the Ulster MacDonalds from the level of hired gallowglasses to major landowners. He had begun this process by marrying an Antrim heiress, one of the Bissets. His son had continued the tradition with a wife from the O'Neills of Connaught and his grandson did the same again. Thus the MacDonalds – or MacDonnells as they were often known over there – soon became multiple estate-owners in Ireland with a significant military pool at their disposal.

The Tanister's son Donald Balloch had, as we have seen, played a significant part in the rescue of the 3rd Lord of the Isles and his descendants continued to take an aggressive role in Scottish politics. The Tanister's grandson John (d. 1499) was knighted by James IV and for the next four or five generations this remarkable family produced a succession of chiefs and their siblings who struggled, usually against impossible odds, to revive past glories with fights on both sides of the North Channel. They tended to have such a proliferation of sons that reckless bravery in the pursuit of property was a natural necessity and for some the potential stakes were high.

John's grandson Alexander MacDonald of Dunyveg took part in two Scottish rebellions in 1519 and 1529. The next generation, James (d. 1565), married a Campbell and stood aloof from the Donald Dhu rebellion of 1545, but once Donald was dead the pull became too strong and he changed sides to support the English and to take over his role as would-be Lord of the Isles with a salary of £2,000 a year. His stance was short-lived, however, and after brief defiance against the regency he settled back to the quiet life. His only subsequent military venture was back in Ulster where he did some fighting against the English and removed the MacQuillans from territory that the MacDonalds fancied on the Antrim coast.

When he died Agnes Campbell, his ambitious widow, remarried twice and set herself up in Strabane Castle which she planned to use as a base for building estates for her two MacDonald sons. Her daughter Finola MacDonald, with her blood half each from our two clans and known as Inion Dhu (Black Daughter), married an O'Donnell and was even more formidable, stopping at nothing to ensure the future of her son Red Hugh. Referred to as 'a cruel bloody woman who has committed sundry murders', she and her mother both acted as conduits for the hiring of Highland soldiers or redshanks (so called because of their bare knees) to upset the balance of Irish politics.

Meanwhile, Archibald Campbell, 4th Earl of Argyll (d. 1558), led the Highlands and islands contingent in 1547 at the disastrous battle of Pinkie against the English as Henry VIII stepped up the pressure on the lacklustre Scottish regency. Argyll also continued to support the French-born regent Mary of Guise in her efforts to suppress the clans of the west. The least popular of these at the time was Clanranald of Moidart and Argyll was given the commission to eradicate them, an act of mini-genocide: he never carried it out, though Clanranald's chief was caught and beheaded for an attack on the Frasers. Donald the Cruel, the Captain of Clanranald, was one of the more violent of a very aggressive branch of the MacDonald family. It was perhaps at this time that the Campbells managed to capture Tioram Castle by pretending to go away and then sneaking back behind the island fortress when the doors had been opened. Most of the other MacDonald septs accepted the fact that for the time being Edinburgh was too strong for them and submitted.

The second most senior branch of the Campbells was also active. Grey Colin Campbell (d. 1583) of Glenorchy quietly continued the erosion of

MacGregor territory and in 1552 invited the clan's two senior chiefs to Finlarig Castle at Killin. Once they were in he had them both beheaded. The young chief next in line was then parcelled off to a Campbell guardian in Glenlyon, so that he would never be able to build any loyalty base in the future. Colin also built part of Taymouth Castle where he executed Gregor Roy MacGregor in 1570.

So the desultory struggle, in which the Campbells continued to expand and the other clans mostly lost out, continued. But then in 1558 came a major turning point, the beginnings of a total realignment of the two clans. In that year Archibald, the 4th Earl, died and was succeeded by his son, yet another Archibald (d. 1575). But this one, significantly, had joined the Protestant church. This made him unpopular both with the regent, Mary of Guise, and later to some extent with her daughter Mary, Queen of Scots (still at this time married to the dauphin of France) when she at last arrived back in Scotland. Like her dead husband, Mary of Guise now swung back in favour of the still Catholic MacDonalds as a counterweight to the huge power of the increasingly alien Campbells. She even arranged for John MacDonald to marry an exceedingly wealthy MacLeod heiress, a plan that fell through when Mary died but would have massively restored the MacDonald hold on the west.

The year 1558 also brought another event of major importance in our narrative: the death of Bloody Mary, Queen of England, and the succession of the Protestant Elizabeth I. It was initially religious differences that led to the reversal of clan allegiances, so that the Catholic MacDonalds who had opposed the Stewart dynasty for more than 200 years came in the end to be its last defenders, while the Campbells, who had supported it loyally for just as long, came to be its greatest enemies.

Nothing, though, was straightforward in the next period of Scottish history. When the widowed but still very young Mary, Queen of Scots sailed back to Leith to take up her Scottish crown she soon found that she had to compromise her Catholicism, while the Earl of Argyll, despite his Protestantism, spent most of his time supporting her. He was, in fact, her half-brother-in-law, for he had married Janet Stewart, an illegitimate daughter of James V, a lady of whom the new queen was very fond. This marriage, however, was not going very smoothly, for Janet preferred the jolly life of Holyrood to the austerity of Colin

Iongantach's tower on the Aray. Things were not too bad between the Campbell couple when they entertained the queen to a masqued ball at their Castle Campbell, the turreted pile perched on the rocks above Dollar Glen, where shepherds dressed in white damask played the lute. The couple doubtless also put a face on it when they entertained the queen for a few weeks' hunting at Inveraray in 1564. But Archibald and Janet, who had no children, soon fell out again and Mary was so anxious about the situation that she even asked her least favourite clergyman, John Knox, to try his hand as a marriage guidance counsellor. Knox's best efforts did not work and the Campbell couple eventually divorced. Castle Campbell still gives a vivid impression of the Renaissance splendour in which they lived.

Meanwhile, Earl Archibald was far from impressed by Mary's own marriage and her choice of male favourites. The first to excite his annoyance was David Rizzio and the earl may well have been involved with Mary's husband Darnley in the plot to murder the charismatic musician. Certainly quite soon after Rizzio's death he was involved in the plot to murder Darnley himself, for he signed the bond at Craigmillar, which resulted in the explosion at Kirk o'Field in 1567 that killed Mary's husband. In this act at least he may have pleased his sister-in-law, who had revealed her disgust with her syphilitic husband, but as she herself slid into terminal unpopularity Earl Archibald proved a somewhat ineffective ally. As leader of the largest private army in Scotland he took command of Mary's forces at the battle of Langside in 1568, just outside Glasgow. Facing another Scottish army led by Mary's half-brother, the Earl of Moray, Argyll's behaviour in the battle is one of many mysteries in the history of his family. There is, however, no doubt that his so-called fainting fit at a crucial point in the fighting was a significant factor in the heavy defeat, after which Mary felt she had no choice but to flee south to England, leaving Scotland as it had so often been before – with an infant as king.

In the meantime, the MacDonalds were culling each other in Ulster. In 1565 James of Dunyveg and the Glens was killed alongside one of his brothers, Angus, and a large number of their followers in a fight with the O'Neills and the English. This left two brothers, Sorley Boy (or Buie, i.e. fair-haired) who was to prove a great survivor, one of the truly remarkable MacDonald characters of his generation, and a fourth brother Alexander. This latter took it upon himself to avenge his two dead brothers by killing O'Neill, but he himself was killed a year later by O'Neill's brother. This left Sorley Boy as head of the family until James's sons grew up and, in the tradition of wicked uncles, he wanted to exploit his opportunity to the full. His ambition was to control the Glens of Antrim and the area called the Route, which had been acquired from the MacQuillans together with their massive castle on the Antrim clifftops at Dunluce. This, as we shall see, he was to achieve by fair means and foul.

Archibald of Argyll survived Langside by only eight years and died childless in 1575, leaving the clan to his brother Colin (d. 1584). Unsurprisingly, this was a period of haphazard rule with irresponsible regents desperately seeking to retain power. These regents failed to prevent a succession of ethnic atrocities in the Highlands, among both Campbells and MacDonalds. Grey Colin Campbell of Glenorchy had executed the MacGregor chief and continued to dispossess this unfortunate clan. Duncan Campbell of Auchinbreck had married the MacLeod heiress originally promised to the MacDonalds, and though he could not in reality take over such dangerous territory, he used it to lever himself up the ranks – he already had castles at Loch Gair (now almost vanished), Sween and Eilean Dearg on Loch Riddon. With no strong leader of their own the MacDonalds were riven with internal discord or were engaged in feuds with other clans that had traditionally been their allies. The disputes between the MacLeans of Duart and of Coll, between the MacLeods of Dunvegan and of Harris, between the MacDonalds and the MacKenzies, and between MacDonalds and MacLeans were semi-permanent and immensely destructive, albeit they were useful as a primitive substitute for population control.

In 1577 the well-known Eigg atrocity occurred when the MacLeods retaliated against the MacDonalds for an earlier depredation in which they had locked them up in their own church of Trumpan and burned it down – by no means the only example of such an incident. The Glengarry MacDonalds did the same to the MacKenzies near Dingwall. Despite being Justice General, Earl Colin Campbell organised an invasion of the island of Luing and without proper authority imprisoned John MacDonald of Castle Camus (Skye) in his private gaol on Inchconnel. At the same time Grey Colin Campbell of Glenorchy had taken it upon himself to execute another MacGregor chief without proper trial. In 1569 one half of the MacLeods of Raasay had wiped out the other after inviting them to a celebratory feast on Isay in Waterness. Also at about this time, the MacDonalds of Glencoe made one of their most famous raids on the Campbells of Glenlyon, when Mad Colin Campbell (d. 1597) the psychopathically violent laird of Meggernie Castle refused to be caught napping. He managed to catch thirty-six of the MacDonalds while they were trying to drive off his cattle. He shot their leader and hanged the rest from trees on the road over to Rannoch. Despite this warning the MacDonalds tried to raid again in 1583, this time with more success for they not only got away with most of Mad Colin's livestock and furniture but even had leisure, as Campbell put it in his official complaint, 'to dang the women'. But having taken the law into his own hands on the previous occasion Mad Colin got little sympathy this time. It should be mentioned that among his symptoms of madness, attributed to a blow on the head in childhood, Colin is one of the first Scotsmen recorded as actually having climbed to the top of one of the Scottish mountains, the Stuchd an Lochain, a grass-covered 3,000 feet mountain (a Munro in modern parlance) that looks down on the surprisingly elegant white tower of Colin's castle at Meggernie.

Back in Ulster the epic saga of Sorley Boy's fight for Antrim continued. In 1586 an English army expelled him from Dunluce Castle, but soon afterwards he contrived to get himself and some of his men back in again and killed the English governor. The English, however, soon retaliated and this time not only was he ejected from his castle, but he also lost two sons who were killed in the fighting and some 50,000 of his livestock. The animals were his chief source of wealth and influence, so without them he had nothing. Undaunted, he promptly surrendered to the English, prostrated himself before a portrait of Queen Elizabeth and begged for forgiveness in Dublin Cathedral. Having been graciously granted English citizenship he was – to most people's amazement – given back Dunluce Castle. Despite his new-found respectability and the fact that he was now in his eighties he did contrive one more fine piece of opportunism when a stray galleon from the retreating Spanish Armada called in on her way north. He helped the crew of the *Girona* to get to Scotland and exacted a handsome reward of gold and guns.

When Sorley Boy died, his eldest surviving son, Sir James MacSorley of Dunluce, took over briefly and joined the Tyrone rebellion against the English in 1597, capturing and beheading the governor of

Carrickfergus Castle. But it was the younger son, Sir Ranald, who eventually came through on top. His problem of deciding whether he was Scottish, Irish or English was now solved because in 1603 James VI of Scotland became also James I of England and Ireland. Ranald was made Viscount Luce and later Earl of Antrim. Thus, ironically it was in the least promising area and among the least likely sept that the MacDonalds regained an earldom after more than a century of trying. This family was also to play a significant role in the next major incident of the long feud and later still conducted the famous Jacobite attack on Londonderry, whose defence by apprentices acquired such legendary proportions in twentieth-century Ulster.

10

ARCHIBALD THE GRIM AND DUNCAN OF THE SEVEN CASTLES

Archibald Gruamach or 'the Grim' (1584–1638) was the first of three extremely complex men to hold the chieftainship of the Campbells and remarkably all three were eventually to be condemned as traitors. The main problem facing the family was that the Argyll inheritance had become so massive that it excited jealousies both within and outside the family. Thus when the teenage Archibald Gruamach succeeded his father, he was the object of numerous plots. The first was mixed up with regency politics and was intended to produce the murder of the Bonnie Earl of Moray and three senior Campbells. Moray was killed but only one of the Campbells, John of Calder, who was shot at Knipoch. The plotters, who by no means gave up, included the heads of two major Campbell offshoots, Black Duncan of Glenorchy (1552–1631) and Campbell of Lochnell. Black Duncan – also known as Duncan of the Cowl and Duncan of the Seven Castles – had already shown himself unusually ambitious, even for a Campbell. He had built and carved his arms on the new Black Castle of Barcaldine, near Loch Creran. He had constructed Achallader at the mouth of Glencoe, having tricked the Fletchers who owned the estate into killing one of his own ghillies and taking flight. He had refurbished Kilchurn, Finlarig and the island castle on Loch Dochart, built more of Balloch/Taymouth and extended Edinample on Loch Earn. But Glenstrae Castle belonging to the MacGregors he destroyed.

He was a man of huge drive and stamina who lived to the age of eighty-one and fathered eighteen legitimate children as well as at least two bastards. By encouraging his vassals to exterminate the MacGregors, he ruthlessly extended and consolidated the Glenorchy patrimony but he was also a major patron of the arts – hiring the painter George Jamesone for months on end, buying numerous Flemish tapestries to embellish his dynasty – and a pioneering tree-planter. He was knighted after James VI's wedding in 1590 but eleven years later he was locked up in Edinburgh for 'false and forged inventions' and had to pay a large fine. He knew how to grovel to his superiors, sent two eagles to the Prince of Wales and an offer of hunting his special white stags. He also subscribed to become a baron of Nova Scotia. Thus, with his wealth and great ring of castles to intimidate his neighbours, he deeply resented the superior status of his Inveraray cousin, whose guardian John Campbell of Calder became the first victim of his vendetta.

The other key plotter, Campbell of Lochnell, was a lesser figure and pursued a number of ideas for assassinating the young earl. The next plot also failed and John Og Campbell, its front man, was tortured till he confessed, then executed, while his wife Mary was convicted of witchcraft for the spells that she had been concocting to get rid of the Campbell chief. The guilty Campbell of Lochnell avoided a trial and had one last attempt to claim his victim. Archibald Gruamach, still only nineteen, had been given command of a force to attack the Roman Catholic earls and their MacDonald supporters in the north-east. Lochnell consorted with the enemy and told them exactly where one of their snipers could shoot the young earl on the day of the battle. The fight took place in Glenlivet in 1594 and went badly for the young Earl of Argyll, but it went even worse for Lochnell for he stood too close to the man he had betrayed and ironically it was he who died at the hands of the enemy sniper instead of his intended victim. Duncan Campbell of Auchinbreck, the Captain of the Castle Sween men, was also killed.

Meanwhile, Angus MacDonald of Dunyveg had not only been squeezed out of his Antrim inheritance by his uncle Sorley Boy but was even having difficulty holding on to his little bit of Islay, attacked by both the MacSorleys from Antrim and the MacLeans of Mull. This second feud proved particularly unpleasant and ultimately very damaging. In 1586 the naively trusting MacDonald had dropped in to Duart to see his violent brother-in-law MacLean, who had quite recently condoned the murder of sixty MacDonalds of Sleat by his henchmen on Jura. MacLean entertained Angus generously, then flung him and his followers into the Duart dungeon. He promised death unless Angus signed over the areas known as the Rinns of Islay, which the MacLeans had been claiming for some years. Angus had no choice but to sign and provide one of his sons as a hostage.

A few months later MacLean came with his men to Islay to claim the Rinns and set up home there in the ruined castle on an island in Loch Gorm. Amazingly Angus MacDonald invited him and his men to dinner at Mullintrea and even more amazingly MacLean, after asking for token assurances of safety, accepted the invitation. As at Duart the entertainment was generous and predictably as at Duart it was followed by a change of heart. Around 300 MacDonalds rounded up some ninety MacLeans and burned the two least popular to death. There was an even more macabre twist. One of the MacLeans who had taken a dislike to his own chief started a rumour that some remaining MacDonald hostages back at Duart had been executed. In retaliation one of Angus's sons executed two MacLeans each day until only the chief was left. He only survived because Angus MacDonald fell from his horse at the moment of execution.

At this point the government was so horrified by the violence that it stepped in and arranged for the Earl of Argyll to sort them out. Peace was briefly achieved but the next year the MacLeans conducted a ruthless devastation of Islay, killing every MacDonald they could find. In retaliation, Angus MacDonald, who had been in Antrim at the time, invaded Mull and Tiree, doing similar damage to land, livestock and clansmen. MacLean, not to be outdone, did a repeat performance in Kintyre. The authorities again attempted restraint, but the incorrigible MacLean, whose personal galley was painted white one side and black the other to confuse his enemies, now turned his attention to the MacIain MacDonalds of Ardnamurchan. Having – to their astonishment – blessed a marriage between his mother and their chief, he invited them en masse to the wedding on Mull and then, as was his habit, had them butchered – an incident known subsequently as the MacLean Nuptials. But for his mother's intervention the bridegroom himself would have died on his wedding night, but he was spared for a spell of torture in the Duart dungeon instead. There then followed a piece of opportunism which matched that of his remote cousin Sorley Boy of Dunluce. When the *Florida*, a survivor of the Spanish Armada, put into Tobermory harbour for supplies, MacLean would only provision her after the Spanish soldiers had done some dirty work for him and ravaged the MacDonald islands of Rum and Eigg, then the MacIain ones of Muck and Canna, then more MacIain land round Mingary Castle on Ardnamurchan. Ironically these crack troops of Philip II of Spain failed to capture the antiquated defences of Mingary itself (an area nearby is still known as Port a Spainndeach). MacLean only stopped when the MacDonalds invaded Mull and severely ravaged his own estates.

This debilitating destruction eventually exhausted itself and the two chiefs both submitted to Edinburgh. As usual they were let off quite lightly and certainly the MacLeans and a number of MacDonalds, but perhaps not Angus, were on the rebel side against Argyll at the battle of Glenlivet in 1594.

The remarkably dysfunctional family of Dunyveg now produced yet another character: Angus MacDonald's son Sir James had spent most of his early years as a hostage for his father's good behaviour and we have already seen a number of examples where this kind of treatment led, not surprisingly, to a streak of bitterness and perhaps some special resentment against the father who had agreed to use his child in such a way. Certainly James was a very complex character and seemed at first to have been well brainwashed by his Edinburgh gaolers. But when he was sent back to Islay to train his father in civilised behaviour he seems to have changed completely, resenting deeply the fact that his father's erratic career had seriously eroded his own inheritance. In 1598 he set fire to the house of Askomel (now part of Campbeltown) in which his parents had sought refuge, and when the badly burned Angus at last emerged James put him in irons for a few months in the shoreline castle of Island Muller at Smerbie, which could only be reached by causeway. Having proclaimed himself chief, he now proceeded to the kind of violent behaviour that was almost guaranteed to bring about further losses. His father's old enemy Lachlan MacLean renewed his demand for the disputed Rinns of Islay. Sir James refused to hand over, despite MacLean's superior forces, and won a remarkable victory at Loch Gruinart on Islay. The MacDonald used the classic ploy of pretending retreat, but actually was moving on to higher ground from which he gained the momentum to unleash a crushing charge. The MacLean chief and nearly 300 of his followers were killed. But it all did James very little good, for the MacLeans were soon back with reinforcements, beat the MacDonalds in a rematch and totally devastated Islay. Sir James now tried to obtain a pardon from the government and surrendered Dunyveg. He attempted to negotiate to regain some of his estates legally, but this did not suit the Campbells. The Campbell Earl of Argyll, who wanted full control of Kintyre, and the new John of Calder, whose sister Sir James had just married and who himself wanted Jura, seem to have egged him on to further intransigence so that he would be removed from the scene altogether.

James MacDonald was eventually condemned to death in 1609, but not actually executed. His beloved castle at Dunyveg was captured by government forces in his absence in 1614 but then recaptured by his bastard brother Ranald and handed over to a new MacDonald hero. This man was one of the Colonsay branch of the Dunyveg line and was known as Coll Keitach (Kolkitto) or Left-handed Coll (d. 1647) on account of his ambidexterity with a claymore. Coll and his even more famous son, often also nicknamed Kolkitto, were to be the two most remarkable MacDonald warriors of the Stuart era. Kolkitto had support from Sir James of Dunyveg himself – the latter had managed to talk his way out of prison in Edinburgh – but he was driven out of Dunyveg by the superior artillery of John Campbell of Calder, who executed twenty of the fortress's defenders and another half-dozen men who were holding the little castle on Loch Gorm. The 'Pibroch of Dunyveg' or the 'Lament for the Castle' may date from this time.

Kolkitto got away partly through bargaining for his own escape by agreeing to surrender some of his allies, but the truce did not last long. Kolkitto escaped with great difficulty in a leaky boat and was hunted from island to island by the determined Campbell of Calder. During a brief stay at home on Colonsay he murdered the prior of Oronsay Priory. In the course of subsequent wanderings he effectively became a pirate and captured at least three merchant ships, one of which he sailed to St Kilda where he rested for a few months. He even thought of setting up home on the almost vertical Stack of Borary. Eventually he had to escape to Ireland with his young son and made one more brief appearance in history some thirty years later (see p. 76).

Sir James MacDonald, who had now lost everything, also escaped and had to go abroad to eke out a living as a mercenary in Spain. He died childless and alone in London in 1626, the last of a remarkable, if self-destructive, line and still too dangerous to be allowed back into Scotland.

Meanwhile, the departure of King James VI to London in 1603 had presented the Earl of Argyll with a real problem. To continue enjoying the benefits of close contact with royalty he had no choice but to set up a second home in London and this caused considerable expense. He also seems to have got into financial difficulties with his vast expenditure on the building of Campbeltown and while he had to bear the cost of patrolling large new tracts of Kintyre the income from them was probably negligible due to frequent depredations over previous years. It is probable that many of his somewhat devious hirings of other clansmen to conduct raids, for example his encouragement of the MacGregors to attack and kill the Colquhouns of Luss in 1603, also required cash payment.

At the time of the 1614 rebellion headed by Kolkitto he was summoned up from London to lead a major force to pacify the west and it is likely that he also had to do this at his own expense. It led to further territorial gains and as he executed some nineteen minor chieftains in Kintyre and Islay he was ethnically cleansing the area of many MacLeans and MacDonalds ready for further Campbell colonisation. Specifically he turned on the wretched MacIains of Ardnamurchan, who had suffered so much for marrying a Campbell 100 years earlier and had already been half-destroyed by the MacLeans. Now Donald, a bastard son of Campbell of Calder, was set loose on them, succeeded in capturing Mingary Castle where the Spaniards had failed, and drove the remaining MacIains into piracy. He later showed particularly ruthless ambition, swindling Castle Stalker out of its slightly unintelligent Stewart owner by swapping it for a fast galley in 1627. He founded the Airds branch of the family and made himself respectable with a Nova Scotia baronetcy. His grand-daughter Janet, known as the Black Bitch of Dunstaffnage, marooned groups of Islay MacDonalds on small rocks to get rid of them.

The Campbells had also done better than the MacDonalds, as one might expect, in the fruits of dissolving the monasteries, though none of those in Scotland was desperately rich. When Saddell was closed and passed to the Campbells it had an annual income of only £9. At Ardchattan Priory yet another spare son of the prolific Campbell of Calder had been made the Commendator, and despite promotion to the Bishopric of the Isles, he still managed to father a son who succeeded him and then quietly turned the priory into his private estate.

The bishop's castle at Carnasserie became a Campbell tower house when Bishop Carswell's daughter married a Neil Campbell who took over Kilmartin Church and the castle. Their three sons all inherited positions in the church, Neil as Bishop of the Isles and John as Bishop of Argyll, though John had to accept demotion back to a mere minister of Campbeltown when bishops were abolished in 1642. Even a grandson became minister of Inishail, so there was a whole dynasty of Campbell clergy in the area, four generations who between them translated the Old Testament into Gaelic. In an even more blatant example of making profit from the church, Alexander Campbell, Bishop of Brechin (d. 1608) converted to Calvinism and then took it upon himself to transfer huge tracts of land from his diocese to his kinsman, the Earl of Argyll, leaving only a tiny parcel to sustain the parish of Brechin. In the previous era there had been numerous examples of family inheritance of bishoprics: for example, Angus MacDonald (fl. 1426–38), Bishop of the Isles, had a son who took over the same post in the 1470s. Later MacDonald clergy on the other hand, particularly if they stayed Catholic or neglected to attend a Lowland university, lost out on ecclesiastical posts and their lay cousins gained very little from the Reformation.

Despite his aggressive display of support for King James, Archibald Campbell, the Earl of Argyll, was himself a mass of contradictions. The year before the king endorsed the new translation of the Bible into English, the widower Argyll picked a very unfashionable type of new wife, a fervent Catholic. This Lady Ann Cornwallis was obviously a woman of great strength, for the earl, despite all the disadvantages and his own Calvinist upbringing, soon converted to her faith and it is significant that all four of their daughters became nuns. Archibald, whose cash-flow position was seriously out of control and whose new religious conviction made life increasingly difficult in England, now deceitfully requested a passport to visit a foreign spa and once there promptly headed for Spain where ironically he met up with his fellow exile Sir James MacDonald. Like his old enemy and many other vagrant MacDonalds he joined the Spanish army under Philip III and served against the Protestant rebels in Holland. As a contemporary satirist put it rather wittily:

> Now Earl of Guile and Lord Forlorn thou goes
> Quitting thy prince to serve his foreign foes
> No faith in plaids, no trust in highland trews
> Chameleon like they change so many hues.

He was declared a traitor in 1619 and never returned to Scotland, though he was eventually allowed back into England where he died in 1639.

It had been a bad three decades for both clans, but it was worse for the MacDonalds. They had devastated each other's territory, bringing widespread poverty and misery. This was all basically due to the feckless heads of families producing more children, legitimate and otherwise, than was prudent. A MacDonald of Benbecula took the right to put aside three of his five wives without any resort to lawyers and it was commonplace, despite the tough environment, for families of a dozen children to survive to adulthood. The proud fathers were expected to find little baronies or sinecure church jobs for all of their sons so that they could maintain a baronial lifestyle without resorting to menial labour. The one acceptable outside source of employment was mercenary fighting, often in Ireland, increasingly in Spain and France. We even hear of a Captain Kammel at the siege of Stralsund in 1714 by Charles XII of Sweden and of a Thomas MacDonnell who served in the Russian navy in the Smolensk campaign of 1630. Matthew Campbell of Loudoun settled in Livonia in 1603, changing his name to Loudoun and was probably the ancestor of Field Marshal von Laudon (see p. 92) of the Austrian army. Those who missed out in this career path, including some of the Glencoe men or the MacGregors, became professional cattle thieves or pirates like Old Kolkitto and the displaced MacDonalds of Ardnamurchan. Many soon began to drift into the cities as whores, horse-thieves and pickpockets. Strong spirits, the early forms of whisky, may also have started to play a significant role at this time. For example, Old Kolkitto was certainly fond of a dram and the Statutes of Inchcolmkill imposed on the Highlands by the government demanded more moderation in the buying of wine, thus to some extent encouraging production of the much stronger native beverage. They also imposed a severe reduction in the size of private armies and private fleets of galleys and in the hiring of poetic harpists to incite them all to battle. Undoubtedly the vast progeny of MacDonalds, and to a lesser extent Campbells, had a low regard for human life, including their own, and a low work ethic except for when it came to fighting, but they also had a great admiration for expensive wine, clothes and the elaborately carved tombstones that are still scattered in vast but nameless numbers all over the west coast. These recumbent stone warriors still people many now almost empty islands that were teeming with thousands of real people in their day.

By contrast, one expatriate Campbell dynasty of unknown provenance – at this time living in Foulsham, Norfolk – was making its fortune in the iron trade. Thomas Campbell, son of Robert, became sheriff of London, was knighted in 1603 and made Lord Mayor in 1609. His son Sir James was also sheriff, alderman of Billingsgate, then in 1629 Lord Mayor of London and a director of the fabulously rich East India Company. He left no family but his money went to the 'redemption of poor captives in Turkish slavery'.

11
KING CAMPBELL VERSUS MACCOLLA

The long feud which had already lasted 350 years was at last reaching a climax. The MacDonalds had been pushed relentlessly to the poorest extremities of the west coast or into their new enclave in Ulster. Many hundreds had died and many more been reduced to abject poverty. The Campbells had gone – with only a few minor aberrations – from strength to strength, taking over huge tracts of territory that had once been MacDonald or MacGregor. But the moment for revenge was at hand.

There had already been signs of role-swapping in the age-old triangle of Campbell, MacDonald and Royal Stewart. One reason had been that it was now the Campbells rather than the MacDonalds who were so powerful as to be a threat to the government. Perhaps, too, the MacDonalds liked the Stewart – by this time Stuart – dynasty better now that it was based a bit further away in London. The other reason and ultimately the main one was that apart from the 7th Earl and John of Calder, most of the Campbells were strenuously Presbyterian, whereas the Royal Stuarts were high Episcopalian if not actually Catholic. There is not much evidence to suggest that the MacDonalds would have cared much either way, for the island churches had been largely moribund and the clergy poorly disciplined or even corrupt, but it suited them to stick with old-fashioned Catholicism and it certainly presented them with a great excuse for teaming up with the Stuarts against the Campbells. As it happened Pope Urban VIII had made the religious difference more intense by establishing new Franciscan mission stations in Ireland as a base for winning back the British. This had the effect of polarising the Irish, the MacDonalds and other Catholics at one end of the sectarian spectrum and the extreme Protestants at the other, particularly in Ireland itself.

Ironically it was the religious intransigence of the last Stuart monarch born in Scotland, Charles I, that created the climate for the greatest and bloodiest series of confrontations between the Campbells and MacDonalds. The period during which the English fought their Civil War was the one in which Scotland produced its parallel and more complex civil war with the royalist side dominated by MacDonalds, and the Campbells as the backbone of the Covenanters – Scotland's equivalent of Roundheads.

There could have been no greater contrast than existed between the two men who became figureheads of the two clans at this time. Archibald, 8th Earl and shortly to become Marquess of Argyll (1598–1661 and sometimes called Gruamach like his father), took over the theoretically bankrupt estates from his disgraced parent when Old Gruamach slipped off to join the Spanish army. There was no love lost between father and son, especially after the old earl's remarriage and change of faith. Perhaps this bitterness contributed to the fervour with which Argyll saw the light and embraced the Covenant in 1638. But as it happened this conversion made him a leading candidate for the crown of Presbyterian Scotland if he could get rid of Charles I. This King Campbell idea was put about with the dubious claim that Argyll was descended from Robert the Bruce and an obscure prophecy from Thomas the Rhymer: 'That of the Bruces blood shall come' – a new king eight generations after the first.

Alastair MacColla MacDonald (*c.* 1605–48) is also sometimes called by the same nickname as his father, Kolkitto, but unlike the two Campbells, the father and son MacDonalds of Colonsay were kindred spirits. Alastair had all the demonic courage that was typical of the house of Dunyveg and the Glens, although the two Kolkittos came from a branch that had settled in Colonsay. Throughout the Civil War Alastair was renowned for his amazing strength and physical bravery, whereas Archibald of Argyll was portrayed, perhaps a little unfairly, as a physical coward who let his henchmen take all the risks. But Alastair too had been known to sacrifice comrades to save his own skin, and while Argyll was not in the same class as a military leader he had certainly fought a duel. Nevertheless, it was Alastair who became the stuff of legend, the 'Achilles of the North', the subject of numerous poems as both war hero and lover.

Young Gruamach had lost his mother at an early age and saw little of his father, who married again when the boy was only three. He studied at St Andrews, won a medal for archery and as a teenager took part in the suppression of the MacIain MacDonalds of Ardnamurchan. As he grew up Archibald began to work obsessively to clear the family name and restore its bank balance. At least Alastair MacColla MacDonald had learned to read, unlike his father, but this may have been because he was actually tutored for a while by a Campbell; otherwise he had few periods of settled home-life as Old Kolkitto, an illiterate, moved from one bolt hole to another.

The two protagonists' first conflict was indirect and due to the plottings of Alastair's cousin, the MacDonnell Earl of Antrim, grandson of Sorley Boy. This gentleman had already toyed with the idea of acquiring the MacDonald lands in Scotland for himself and as a staunch Catholic found himself in an awkward position in the civil war between Irish Catholics and the Stuart King Charles I. Naturally Argyll objected hugely to the MacDonell plot to take back Islay and Kintyre from him and also to the killing of Irish Protestants, many of whom were of Scottish extraction. So he sent his henchman Duncan Campbell of Auchinbreck, laird of Castle Sween and Loch Gair, over to Ireland with a force that massacred a significant number of MacDonalds on Rathlin Island and then captured the MacDonnell stronghold of Dunluce with the Earl of Antrim himself inside it.

In the course of this Irish conflict Alastair was severely wounded and both he and the MacDonnell Earl of Antrim were more motivated to fight than ever when the emergent English Civil War gave them the excuse for an officially blessed counter-attack against the Campbells. The situation was slightly embarrassing for Alastair because he had recently betrayed the Catholic side to obtain his freedom and had made a brief attempt to serve on the Protestant/Campbell force before recanting again. But he had begun to prove himself a remarkably able soldier. David Stevenson's excellent biography gives him substantial credit for developing what came to be known as the Highland charge. The novelty of this method of attack lay in the fact that the combatants no longer wore heavy armour and used a single-handed rather than a two-handed sword, leaving the other hand free to carry a targe or buckler. This light weaponry gave them a huge speed advantage. When they had fired one musket volley they dropped their guns and ran forward with blood-curdling yells in a wedge formation. This tactic proved able to break any but the most determined enemy.

In 1641 Alastair set out on his first expedition to Scotland with a couple of hundred men. He skirmished on Colonsay but 150 of his force were trapped and massacred on Islay by Campbell of Ardkinglas.

Undeterred by this loss of life, the next year Alastair MacColla set out with a much bigger force, perhaps 1,600 men, equipped by the Earl of Antrim and with the blessing of Charles I. He landed on Morvern and captured two Campbell-held castles, Kinlochaline and Mingary. From this base he attempted to attract local MacDonald recruits, but without much response. Even when he sent out the fiery cross, a sign that any who did not answer the call would be condemned to death, only the Keppoch MacDonalds and a few others joined him. As he marched eastwards he met with little success and by the time he reached Atholl he had run out of ideas about what to do next.

At this point Alastair MacColla MacDonald was joined by the Marquess of Montrose, the senior royalist general in Scotland but one with no army. He and MacColla made a brilliant team – Montrose with continental experience and a fine strategic sense, MacColla with his undoubted personal courage and opportunistic flair. Moreover, while potential recruits had held back from joining MacColla, whose half-Irishness rendered him suspect, Montrose had the credibility to widen the royalist appeal.

The history of the amazing campaign conducted by these two leaders has been extremely well told by Sir Walter Scott, John Buchan and most recently David Stevenson. The battles of Tippermuir and Aberdeen in 1644 were fought against mixed ability but much larger Covenanter armies and were major victories in terms of morale for the Stuart and MacDonald cause and for the effectiveness of Irish troops in Scotland. But it was the next stage of the campaign that brought the MacDonalds and Campbells into direct confrontation on a bigger scale than ever before. After the sacking of Aberdeen Alastair MacColla led his men down through the Tayside territory of the Glenorchy Campbells towards Argyll. In his absence the Campbell Earl of Argyll (now a marquess) for once took personal charge of an army but he failed to make any impact on Montrose, even though the latter was without his Irish ally, and he retreated.

Now that the Campbells were no longer seen to be invincible some of the underdog clans began to have the courage to turn against them. The MacNabs, for example, organised the capture of Eilean Dochart Castle, whose island cannon guarded the main roads west from Tayside. Thereafter, a mixture of Irish MacDonnells and Scots MacDonalds began burning and looting, releasing years of pent-up jealousy and hatred. A figure of 895 is given for the number of Campbells killed and 18 parishes were said to have been destroyed. Archibald, Marquess of Argyll, escaped by galley from Inveraray, where his town and castle were burned to the ground, and headed for his fortress at Rosneath. There he was quite badly injured in a fall from his horse and was temporarily out of action, but his reputation as a man able to defend his clansmen and their farms had taken a massive tumble. He mustered all the troops from his subsidiary septs and camped beside Inverlochy Castle in Lochaber, threatening MacColla's line of retreat. But laden with loot and satiated by destruction MacColla and his men headed back east to join up with Montrose at Atholl again.

The campaign that followed is one of the great classics of military history. Montrose was, as usual, outnumbered and outgunned and the Campbells were rested and waiting for him in a secure position. But with his flare for doing the unexpected, taking unorthodox risks to improve the odds when facing superior forces, Montrose did the unthinkable. Using local MacDonald guides he led his army from Roy Bridge up the Spean, through steep, snow-covered mountain passes to come down on Inverlochy from the least likely angle, thus taking the Campbells off guard. In early February 1645 with just oatmeal and water for sustenance this was a remarkable feat of endurance.

The Campbell army that awaited Montrose's forces was under the command of the experienced Duncan Campbell of Auchinbreck, master of Castle Sween, as Argyll himself was probably not fully recovered from his accident and anyway was a less effective field commander than Auchinbreck. This gentleman had already made himself extremely unpopular with the MacDonnells because he had led the massacre on Rathlin, commanded the force that occupied Antrim and possibly been involved in an earlier plot to kill MacColla himself. In his own day Auchinbreck was described as 'a stout sojer but a very vitious man' and it is clear that he was no soft opponent. Despite being tired and hungry after their dangerous night march through the wintry mountains, Montrose's men, with the MacDonnells on the right and the Scots MacDonalds in the centre, charged the Campbells ferociously and after heavy fighting reached Argyll's standard bearer. With the standard captured Campbell resistance became less confident and the battle soon turned into a rout. Seventeen Campbell chiefs were killed, including Auchinbreck himself. According to the bards, the general was offered a choice of methods of excecution by Alastair MacColla, perhaps a sign that there was a particular grudge between them, and when he made his choice Alastair cut him down in cold blood.

Hundreds of other Campbells were massacred trying to get into Inverlochy Castle after the battle. Ian Lom, the bard of the Keppoch MacDonalds, for whose head Argyll had offered a handsome reward, wrote rhapsodically in his 'L'atha Inbhir Lochaidh' (The Victory at Inverlochy) about the quantity of Campbell blood spilt, the red on the green tartan. For him this seemed to be a climactic turning point after years of Campbell oppression. As the Napier translation puts it:

> Though the braes of Lochaber a desert be made
> And Glen Roy may be lost to the plough and the spade
> Though the bones of my kindred unhonoured, unurned,
> Mark the desolate place where the Campbells have burned –
> Be it so. From that foray they never returned.

The Marquess of Argyll had been sitting out on Loch Linnhe in his birlinn, waiting for the result and at the first hint of defeat he made a rapid departure, just as he had from Inveraray, thus further damaging his reputation. One Campbell survivor, Campbell of Skipness, announced that he would have changed sides if he had known that his chief was such a coward. Other Campbells were pursued and killed up to 9 miles from the battlefield and the total estimated losses were around 1,500. Taken together with the executions during the earlier period of depredations in Argyll, this suggests that between 2,000 and 3,000 Campbells were slaughtered within a three-month period, a massive revenge for Rathlin, Islay and more than a century of getting the worst of it from the Campbells. The brutality was more or less normal in this period. A number of both the Irish McDonnells and Scots

MacDonalds such as Donald MacRanald of Glengarry had fought in the Thirty Years War in Flanders and Germany and there too the savagery had been exacerbated by the religious divide and hysterical propaganda.

John Moydart (d. 1670), Captain of Clanranald, now terrorised southern Argyll and his son, Donald Dhu (d. 1686, known as The Cuckoo because he called his favourite gun his cuckoo), gained an unsavoury reputation for he condemned his own chief to hang and later locked up his wife on the island of Canna on a trumped-up charge of adultery. He also nursed an obsession with monster toads that lived in his dungeon and chased him over the sea.

After Inverlochy the triumphant progress of Montrose and Alastair MacColla continued with victories at Auldearn in 1645, where Mungo Campbell of Lawers was the main Covenanter commander and was killed with many of his Campbell regiment. Then came Kilsyth where Argyll was once more on the losing side and after which MacColla was knighted by Montrose in the king's name. In delight the Argyll MacDonalds pronounced that 'they were King Campbell's men no more'.

Before the disastrous 1645 battle of Philiphaugh, however, when Montrose's brilliance and luck both seemed to desert him, MacColla had left to pursue his own vendettas further in the west. His colleague O'Cahan did stay to the end and many of the Irish and their camp followers were massacred during and after the battle.

Sir Alastair MacColla now headed first to Glasgow and Ayrshire where his ravaging took in the southern Campbell earldom of Loudoun. Then he spent nearly two years in further massive depredations of Campbell territory. A Campbell force under Ardkinglas was badly mauled in Perthshire. The one frustration MacColla had to endure was his general inability to capture castles like Skipness, Kilberry and Dunstaffnage where near-starving Campbells still held out against him. Even Duntrune resisted him, according to legend warned of his approach by a sympathetic piper who paid for his music with the loss of both hands (a handless skeleton was apparently later unearthed at Duntrune to confirm the story). The one castle that seems to have succumbed was Castle Sween, home of the hated Auchinbreck, but by then it was nearly too late to help the Royalist cause.

MacColla had vented his fury on a group of Campbells controlled by blue-eyed Campbell of Lochnell and burned two dozen of them to death at Lagganmore in Glen Euchar, Sabhal nan Cnabh, the Barn of Bones. But nemesis was at hand. The Earl of Antrim at last brought reinforcements, but just at that moment Charles I, having lost his war against Cromwell, surrendered to the Scottish Covenanters and ordered his generals Montrose and MacColla to lay down their arms. This also meant that the main Scottish army under Leslie could return from England to deal with rebels.

MacColla knew there would be no mercy for him. He was a superstitious man and fortune tellers had warned him to beware of a place called Gocam Go and of the Red Baron of Dunavich. Gocam Go was probably near Loch Eredine and the barons of nearby Loch Avich traditionally had red hair. Certainly he seems to have regarded these omens as fatal. Meanwhile, the Campbells had organised their first brutal retaliation, massacring the Lamonts of Cowal, who had deserted them to join MacColla. Some 200 were killed in cold blood beside an already prepared mass grave. After a final great burning in Knapdale MacColla retreated down Kintyre and fought an apparently careless rearguard action at Rhunahaorine Point opposite Gigha – but perhaps this action did allow more than 500 of his men to retreat first to Islay, then back to Ulster. About 300 stayed behind in Dunaverty Castle, probably because they belonged to Kintyre and had nowhere else to go. But Leslie captured the rock-top castle with ease. Then, egged on by the Marquess of Argyll and attendant Presbyterian clergy, he had virtually all the male defenders massacred. There was further minor slaughter on Islay where MacColla had put his geriatric father Old Kolkitto in charge of Dunyveg Castle once more. The old man seems to have been divorced from reality and amiably surrendered as if this were still the age of chivalry. His men were all executed and according to legend he was hanged from the mast of his own galley at Dunstaffnage Castle. At least two other sons were killed at about the same time, leaving only Alastair still alive. But he did not survive them long. He was killed fighting alongside Scottish MacDonald and Irish redshanks at the battle of Knocknanus, near Cork, and was buried at Clonmeen nearby in 1647.

Marquess Archibald lasted somewhat longer but also met a violent death. Though he changed his allegiance back to the Stuarts and organised the coronation of young Charles II at Scone, he had served as MP for Aberdeen in Cromwell's Westminster and was regarded as hopelessly compromised. He was condemned as a traitor in 1661, beheaded by the Maiden in Edinburgh and his head was placed on the spike previously occupied by that of the Marquess of Montrose. The total losses suffered by the two clans under Alastair and Archibald must have been in the region of 10,000, with massive devastation of their homes and land from which perhaps they never totally recovered. On balance the Campbells had suffered substantially more than the MacDonalds, but the island clan had achieved no permanent recovery of lost lands and the dead Campbells would soon be replaced by new offspring.

One other remarkable Campbell died at about this time, young Gruamach's half-brother, the Catholic James Campbell, Earl of Irvine (1611–46). This extraordinary man captured a pirate ship at the age of twenty and later raised a regiment of over 4,000 men to take to France. His Regiment des Gardes Ecossois fought for Louis XIII and Cardinal Richelieu until he died bankrupt in his early thirties – a tale worthy of Alexandre Dumas.

Ironically, the Campbells and MacDonalds had united briefly in an effort to defeat Cromwell. Many men from both clans fought bravely, if ineffectively, at Dunbar and Worcester and it was after these two battles that the first forced transportation of Scottish prisoners of war to plantations in New England, Carolina and the West Indies took place. For example, the ship *John and Sarah* took both MacDonald and Campbell prisoners to Boston, Massachusetts, in 1652. The lairds, of course, suffered less, but even they had to put up with destruction of their homes. Several Campbell castles like Dollar and Loudoun were very severely damaged by Cromwell's armies.

12

TARTAN AND ORANGE

The Restoration period was like an Indian summer for the MacDonalds. It began with the beheading of a Campbell chief and twenty-four years later this extraordinary event was repeated, as the third in three generations of Campbell earls was condemned as a traitor.

Archibald Campbell, 9th Earl of Argyll (1629–85), was more a man of principle than either his father or grandfather. Yet he fitted into neither the low Anglican, republican camp of Cromwell nor the high church authoritarianism of the later Stuarts. As a young man he fought bravely in the Scottish army against Cromwell at Dunbar and again for the royalists at Worcester, alongside both other Campbells and MacDonalds. John Campbell of Lawers (1598–1663), now Earl of Loudoun, was also at both battles. The two earls got away, as did young Charles II, but many clansmen from both our families suffered transportation to the plantations of Jamaica and Carolina.

Argyll spent the next twenty years in relative obscurity, no doubt shocked by the execution of his father in 1661 and struggling to rebuild the fortunes of the Campbells. In the meantime, the more aggressive extension of Campbell fortunes was undertaken by his distant cousin Grey John Campbell of Glenorchy (1635–1717), six years his junior and described as 'cunning as a fox, wise as a serpent and slippery as an eel'. This Campbell turned a new technique of acquisition into an art form. This consisted of buying up the IOUs of other less provident landowners so that, like a primitive building society, he could then foreclose on the debts and take over the property at a knock-down price. His main target was the earldom of Caithness and by 1672 Grey John had legal ownership of its estates and was angling for the title too. Not long afterwards the bankrupt earl died and John, a mere baronet, declared himself Earl of Caithness and for good measure Viscount Breadalbane and Lord Sinclair. He then took 700 of his men and marched into Caithness to the newly composed tune of 'The Campbells are Coming', beating the Sinclairs in what has been described by Smout as 'the last major pitched battle between two clan armies' at Altimarlich, near Wick, in 1680. Charles II, who disliked subjects who awarded themselves titles, cancelled all three of Grey John's, but compromised by creating a new one: Earl Breadalbane and Holland (perhaps some consolation for John – his wife Mary Holland had died some years before and their eldest son was mentally retarded).

Thus, after long years of rivalry the Glenorchy-based Campbells had at long last caught up with the senior clan at Inveraray. But soon afterwards Earl Archibald, a very different character from Grey John, decided to risk everything. Twenty years after his father's death the 9th Earl also became a traitor. He objected to the harsh persecution of Covenanters by James, Duke of York, the king's brother and heir. The dirty work was being done by Black Jack Graham of Claverhouse, who seven years later as Viscount Dundee was to be a key player in this episode of the long feud. For his pains Earl Archibald was incarcerated in Edinburgh Castle, but managed to make a spectacular escape. His first wife, of whom he was extremely fond, had died a few years earlier and he had remarried, this time to the high-spirited Lady Anna Seaforth, and it was her daughter Sophia who was the major aid to his escape. She went to visit him in prison and took with her a page boy whose head was heavily bandaged. Once inside he swapped garb with the earl who then walked out of the main gate with his stepdaughter at the end of visiting hour. Once clear of the castle the earl dived into the nearest dark Edinburgh wynd and was next heard of lodging in London with a Mrs Smith, a rich sugar widow who helped fund his escape to Holland and his next act of rebellion.

When Charles II died with no legitimate offspring in 1685, Earl Archibald could not tolerate the idea of the Catholic James, Duke of York, succeeding and neither could the old king's bastard son, the Duke of Monmouth. Together they concocted a rather hare-brained joint invasion plan – Monmouth to land in the south-west of England and Campbell in Argyll. Using Mrs Smith's money Earl Archibald bought guns in Amsterdam, but like a number of subsequent invasions by Scottish exiles, this attempt was woefully ill-prepared. He landed at Campbeltown and announced that James II was guilty of murdering his own brother, Charles II. Meanwhile, Archibald's younger son Charles garrisoned Carnasserie Castle and Sir Duncan Campbell held the other arsenal at Eilean Dearg Castle on Loch Riddon by the Clyde. But not all the Campbells joined the cause, not even Argyll's own elder son and especially not Grey John of Breadalbane. Argyll's standard with the legend 'For God and Reform Against Poperie, Tyrannie, Absolute Government and Erastianism' was hardly catchy and failed to attract widespread support. The garrison at Eilean Dearg fatally deserted him. It and Carnasserie were both blown up. His eldest son Archibald went grovelling to the king and volunteered to hunt down his own father. After fording the Clyde and fighting against great odds Argyll was arrested by St Conval's Stone, near Renfrew, taken in chains to Edinburgh and died with considerable dignity under the blade of the Maiden.

Argyll's execution was the signal for another great Highland invasion of Campbell territory and the MacDonalds naturally played a major part in this. Three more castles – Dunstaffnage, Dunoon and Carrick – were sacked. Massive quantities of livestock were removed from south Argyll to restock Islay, Glencoe and Keppoch. Numerous Campbells were hanged from their own Gallows Tree at Inveraray, many more had their ears cropped and were sent to plantations in Jamaica and North Carolina. The MacDonalds exacted a major revenge for their sufferings of 1647. In despair the dead earl's brother, Lord Neil Campbell, led a large group of survivors over to America to found a new Campbell community in East New Jersey. The ship *Henry and Francis* carried a further large group of Covenanters, including some more Campbells, to New Jersey in 1686 although many died on the voyage.

While the majority of the previous Earls of Argyll had been ruthless and often devious, Archibald, the 10th and last (d. 1703), was probably one of the most charming but least principled. In 1685 he had offered to fight against his own father and even to become a Catholic to please James II, but when this grovelling was spurned he helped to initiate a series of events that to some extent might appear to have avenged his father's execution and also triggered off yet another Campbell/MacDonald confrontation. Outwardly good-looking and polished – he had done the Grand Tour – he was described by a contemporary as 'addicted to a lewd and profligate life' and though never condemned for treason like his three predecessors, he was in the end very much a traitor.

When he realised that King James II was not going to give him any special honours he went off in dudgeon to Holland to cultivate the king's son-in-law and possible heir, William of Orange. So Archibald, 10th Earl of Argyll, became one of the prime movers in the revolution that swept James off the throne and William onto it. In fact, he personally administered the coronation oath to William. In an irony of fate, a MacDonald was one of two sea captains who organised the sloop that took the panic-stricken James II from Rochester into exile.

The MacDonalds in both Scotland and Ireland were for various reasons displeased by the Glorious Revolution of 1688 in which William of Orange and his wife Mary were installed as joint monarchs. For a start many of them were still Catholics like James II and if the Campbells were pro-Orange it was natural for the MacDonalds to be Jacobite. To some extent there was a basic alignment of the late Stuarts and the Highlanders, encouraged by their being used to help suppress the Lowland Covenanters in 1671, 1681 and 1685.

In Scotland at this time, however, the MacDonalds produced no natural leader of their own and this role was now performed by the remarkable Ian Dhu, erstwhile Black John Graham of Claverhouse, persecutor of Covenanters, now recycled as the ex-king's champion Bonnie Dundee. Like Montrose (whose family surname he shared) Dundee was a charismatic professional soldier who was able to lead the Highland clans to a memorable victory at Killiecrankie in 1688, albeit fighting for the moribund cause of James II against a Scots force supporting William of Orange. At Killiecrankie, Dundee made dramatic use of the Highland charge as developed by Alastair MacColla. On his left wing he had 700 MacDonalds of Keppoch led by their chief Coll of the Cows (a reference to his penchant for removing other people's cattle), whom Dundee had just restrained from burning the city of Dundee. Coll was described as carrying 'a shield studded with brazen knobs and all plaided and plumed in his tartan array'. He had taken over the clan after the MacDonalds of Sleat had helped kill the usurper who had murdered the previous two young heirs of Keppoch. The heads of the seven murderers were put in a barrel, an event commemorated by the Seven Heads Well that still stands by Loch Oich, now a section of the Caledonian Canal.

Alongside Keppoch were the MacDonalds of Glencoe under their massive chief, Alastair MacIain, and the MacDonalds of Sleat under Sir Donald MacDonald in his scarlet cloak. To the right were the MacDonalds of Clanranald under their chief Allan and Glengarry whose chief Alastair Dubh MacDonell appeared 'mounted on a foaming steed . . . clad in glittering armour and cloth shining with gold'. But leaving kilts and plaids behind, for it was a summer's day, the Highlanders charged about six deep in their yellow shirts. Though around 600 were killed they did not stop to shoot until they were a mere 30 yards from the enemy, then they fired, dropped their muskets and headed straight into General Mackay's waiting regiments.

It was a remarkable victory, much romanticised as if it were a Scottish victory over the English, which was not the case, and made more dramatic by the ruthless Dundee dying at the moment of victory so that he became a sanctified Scottish martyr. But the victorious Highland host dominated by MacDonalds now had no acceptable commander-in-chief and no strategy. So after a brief attack on Dunkeld it vented its frustration in the customary way by devastating Campbell territory, particularly Breadalbane, Glenlyon and Kintyre. This achieved little more than the temporary alleviation of poverty in the west and left a massive residue of bitterness and desire for revenge among the injured Campbells.

In Ireland during the same period the MacDonalds also fought for James II. Most spectacularly Alexander MacDonnell, Earl of Antrim (d. 1696), had been summoned by the Jacobite side to take over the defence of Londonderry from a commander who was regarded as too conciliatory to the Protestant–Orange cause. Famously, thirteen apprentice boys slammed the gates in his face. Antrim was more a restoration rake than an effective officer and had once before been deprived of his estates for rebellion, but he could still raise some 600 men, many of them MacDonald descendants, to fight for James II against William of Orange at the battle of the Boyne. They were put to flight by Nassau's regiment. Antrim was captured by the Anglo-Dutch forces and lost his estates yet again, dying a poverty-stricken old roué in London. The Boyne marked not just the beginning of the Protestant ascendancy in Ulster but the end of the MacDonald clan as a serious power broker in Ireland.

13
GLENCOE AND GLENLYON

As we have seen, the fifty years before the massacre of Glencoe in 1692 witnessed numerous, much bigger massacres of Campbells by MacDonalds and vice versa. We have also seen that the MacDonalds in general were frequent disrupters of the peace in central Scotland as the pressures of a rising population without much of a work ethic forced the clan to resort to cattle thieving and mercenary soldiering as its main means of earning extra income. The Campbells had, if anything, been more aggressive and acquisitive but by putting many of their sons into the legal profession they had made sure that their increased wealth was both more permanent and more respectable.

The MacIains of Glencoe and the MacDonalds of Keppoch, Sleat, Clanranald and Glengarry stood out as the most disruptive families. For example, in 1690 men from one of King William's ships landed men on Skye to burn down Armadale Castle but when they tried to do the same at Camus the MacDonalds counter-attacked and hanged the sailors from gibbets made out of their own oars. The MacDonalds were thus still seen as semi-barbarian and the Glencoe branch of the family was particularly unpopular for its frequent raids on Glenlyon and Inveraray. What, therefore, began as a fairly understandable and normal government attempt to bring law to the western Highlands came in the end to be seen as centralist repression of an ethnic tradition, and the massacre of Glencoe receives far more attention than all the massacres that went before or came afterwards. With a mere thirty-eight killed its toll was tiny by comparison with Inverlochy or Dunaverty yet its peculiar circumstances, and the fact that it made good propaganda material for the anti-Orange parties in Edinburgh and London, meant that it became far better known. In fact, the events of Glencoe represent a whole series of odd coincidences and more or less deliberate misunderstandings.

Alastair MacIain MacDonald, 12th Chief of Glencoe, was the direct descendant of Ian Fraoch, bastard son of Angus Og, who aided the survival of Robert Bruce (see p. 10). He had spent some time acquiring polish in Paris, a standard practice for a Highland chief despite the fact that other members of his large extended family had to make do with relatively small and infertile pieces of land, and produced too many children to survive in any style without conducting cattle raids on wealthier neighbours. The Glencoe MacDonalds had joined in virtually every raid southwards or eastwards since Alastair MacColla first mobilised the MacDonalds in 1645. Particularly popular had been the attacks on Glenlyon to the east, where the MacDonalds had virtually ruined the Campbells of Meggernie, whose chief, Robert Campbell of Glenlyon (1632–96), was now an ageing but cash-starved regular with Argyll's Regiment. The Glencoe men had their Hidden Valley (Coire Gabhail) into which they could drive vast numbers of stolen cattle well out of sight of the main glen.

Numerous mysteries still surround the massacre, not least with regard to the behaviour of the 12th Chief. Described as having long white hair and a spiked moustache, dressing in tartan trews and often carrying both large broadsword and blunderbuss, he was regarded as honourable within the code of Highland gentlemen, for whom theft from other people was a natural activity. However, he had been accused of murdering some of his own men. He had been arrested in 1673 and imprisoned at Inveraray but then escaped.

The other mystery about Alastair MacIain is why he made such a mess of his capitulation. He was an experienced campaigner and not a stupid man. Soon after the end of August 1691 he must have received the offer of pardon extended to all Highlanders by William of Orange so long as they reported to their local sheriff by 1 January of the following year. He knew that for him it meant a trip down to Inveraray, yet he left everything to the last minute and then reported in the wrong town, Fort William. Even the Glengarry MacDonalds, who along with Glencoe were perhaps the least popular with the authorities, had managed to sign the capitulation on time, yet MacIain sauntered along to the wrong town with only days to spare. Then after a slow midwinter journey from Fort William to Inveraray he arrived too late and because it was the new year holiday had to wait another three days before being allowed to sign. Since the Sheriff, Colin Campbell of Ardkinglas, had been a heavy recent sufferer from Glencoe depredations it was not surprising that he made Alastair sweat it out.

At this point MacIain's capitulation was accepted, albeit technically he was five days overdue. Whether the technicality was exploited as an excuse to 'root out that damnable sept', which the authorities and the Campbells undoubtedly wanted to do, or whether Campbell clerks made sure the paperwork was not properly processed in Edinburgh, is not clear. Certainly a week later, when he still thought that MacIain had signed the documents on time, Stair, the Secretary of State, wrote on the king's behalf to Sir Thomas Livingstone, senior officer in Scotland: 'You are hereby ordered and authorised to march our troops which are now posted at Inverlochy and Inverness and to act against these highland rebels . . . by fire and sword and all manner of hostility: to burn their houses, seize or destroy their goods and cattle, plenishings or clothes and to cut off the men.' This order was signed by the king. Three weeks later Stair wrote also to Livingstone having heard the news that MacIain had been late: 'I am glad Glencoe did not come in the time prescribed . . . it were of great advantage to the nation that thieving tribe were rooted out and cut off. It must be quietly done.' Livingstone in turn wrote to Hamilton, the officer commanding Fort William, 'here is a fair occasion for you to show that your garrison serves for some use. . . . Begin with Glencoe and spare nothing which belongs to him, but do not trouble the government with prisoners.' Hamilton in turn passed on the orders to Major Duncanson of the Earl of Argyll's Regiment on 12 February 1692: '. . . pursuant to the commander in chief's orders for putting into execution the service against the rebels in Glencoe the orders are that none be spared'.

That same day Duncanson wrote to Captain Robert Campbell of Glenlyon, the last link in the chain, 'you are hereby ordered to fall upon the rebels, the MacDonalds of Glencoe and to put all to the sword under seventy. You are to have a special care that the old fox and his sons upon no account escape your hands. This you are to put into execution at 5 of the clock precisely.' Thus, like so many war crimes over the centuries, the guilt was spread thinly from top to bottom.

Some things about Robert Campbell are straightforward, others less so. Given that he was a professional soldier, virtually bankrupt, an alcoholic and, at sixty, well past normal retirement age, it is hardly surprising that he obeyed his orders. His obedience is even less remarkable when we remember that it was mainly the Glencoe MacDonalds who had caused his ruination by so many raids on his farms. They had also recently burned down the castle at Achallader, south of Glencoe, which belonged to his cousin, Campbell of Glenorchy. What is more surprising – and this is the main reason why Robert Campbell's reputation has remained so black – is that if he was aware of the purpose of his expedition to Glencoe for the ten days between arriving there and receiving his final orders, how could he bear to enjoy the MacDonalds' hospitality so hypocritically for all that time? This dishonesty was made even more objectionable by the fact that his own niece was married to one of Alastair MacIain's sons and was living in the glen.

The final mystery about Glenlyon is, given the fact that he did so totally deceive the unsuspecting MacDonalds and therefore take them so utterly by surprise, why did he not do a better job of exterminating them? Despite Glenlyon's huge advantages of trained soldiers and complete surprise, only about 38 MacDonalds were killed and at least 300 escaped over the hills. (Some died of exposure.) He had not obeyed his orders very thoroughly; indeed, he had left alive people who could act as witnesses of the way he had behaved. And he managed to lose three of his own men as well.

Of the roughly 150 men who took part in the massacre, under 10 per cent were Campbells, but these included the commanding officer, two junior officers and a corporal. There is no doubt that several other Campbells contributed to the atmosphere that led to the massacre: Archibald, Earl of Argyll, Grey John, Earl of Breadalbane, and Colin Campbell of Ardkinglas, Sheriff of Argyll. But at least one MacDonald had also contributed to it: Alastair, 12th Chief of Glencoe, with his forty years of plundering and a last piece of very careless paperwork.

Paul Hopkins has summed it all up very well. 'The massacre was carried out by one group of highlanders on another upon orders given by a Scottish secretary of state, countersigned by a Dutch king.' The big difference between this and numerous other massacres was that for political reasons it was well publicised and subsequently, for different motives, sentimentalised, as the self-pitying element of Highland culture came to replace the vigour and bravado of earlier years.

14
THE BATTLE OF TOUBACANTI

For twenty-three years after the mass capitulation of the various MacDonald septs to William of Orange in 1692 the clan kept a relatively low profile. On the other hand, the Campbells, though their reputation had been severely damaged by the massacre of Glencoe and though they had seen their rivals very much weakened, now started to cast their avaricious eyes over the world outside Scotland.

The most ambitious and least successful example of this was the Darien Scheme, a plan for a Scottish colony in the Panama area, where members of the Campbell clan formed the majority of shareholders and provided many of the actual colonists. The originator of the scheme was William Paterson (1658–1719), who had probably first met the Earl of Argyll in Amsterdam when they were both working there for William of Orange. The basic idea was to set up a Scottish colonial trading post on the Isthmus of Panama so that goods from the Pacific coast could be transmitted across the narrow strip of land for shipping over the Atlantic to Scotland. Other nations had colonies in exotic locations, but as yet Scotland had none. The only obvious obstacle to the plan was that Darien was then in Spanish territory, and King William had no intention of supporting the Scots in a war against Spain. It was also an area of tropical forest, unhealthy and to this day without roads.

For a private company with its own small army, but with backing only from the Scottish parliament, not London, to install a new colony in a remote tropical region already belonging to a much larger imperial power, was by any standards foolhardy. But despite the massive culling of Campbells that had taken place over the past fifty years the family was still producing plenty of apparently expendable offspring and some at least had money to speculate. Archibald, Earl of Argyll, was the second largest shareholder with £1,500, his brother James had £700 and with another twenty Campbells the clan members had between them £9,400. The shareholders included the Campbells of Ardkinglas, Aberuchil, Succoth, Monzie, Boghott, Calder, Cessnock and Kinpoint plus a number of the clan who had moved to Greenock and Glasgow to set up as merchants. The company's London agent was John Campbell and many of the military staff were seconded from Argyll's Regiment, which had taken responsibility for Glencoe. There were at least six Campbell army officers, two of them captains, a Campbell mate on the ship *St Andrew*, a midshipman and several sailors on the *Rising Sun*, plus a trainee seaman, Colin Campbell of Monzie who, luckily for posterity, kept a journal. Even the Bibles and prayer books for the voyage were provided by a Campbell printer. So far as we know there was only one solitary MacDonald and he was an ordinary seaman.

From almost the first moment that the colonists set sail the expedition started to go wrong. Over 100 died on the voyage from Rothesay to New Caledonia. Once they arrived in Darien their food stores rotted rapidly and deaths continued. The first expedition ended in disaster and when all the sea-going officers of the *St Andrew* had died it was a military captain, Colin Campbell, who showed great determination and courage in sailing the group of survivors to Jamaica. There they arrived yellow with fever and almost starving, only to be refused any assistance by the British senior officer on the island, Admiral Benbow.

The second attempt to colonise Darien produced an even more remarkable Campbell hero. When this colony too was close to disaster because of disease and Spanish attacks, Colonel Alexander Campbell of Fonab was sent out to take over command of the defences. This officer had actually been a friend and colleague of Robert Campbell of Glenlyon, fought with him at Dottignies and Dixemude in western Flanders, then attended the funeral of the wretched man when he died in Bruges. Fonab arrived on a Barbados sloop with only one aide on 11 February 1700, exuding confidence and resplendent in his scarlet coat. He immediately took command of the demoralised garrison. Within a day of arriving he decided not just to sit and wait for the Spaniards to attack, but to take the initiative. He then led a party of 200 Scots and about 30 friendly Indians on an arduous three-day march through mangrove swamps, over the River Sancta Maria, through the mountains to attack the Spanish fort of Toubacanti. Despite having nothing to eat but rotten biscuits and near rotten fish his men stormed the star-shaped stockade and captured it. It was a remarkable victory and caused almost hysterical joy when the news at last reached Edinburgh, although ironically by that time the Scottish colony of Darien had long since surrendered to the Spanish army. Campbell of Fonab, despite being wounded in the attack on Toubacanti, tried hard to maintain resistance to the very end, but his men were dying of disease at the rate of around a dozen a day. They had even melted down all their pewter dishes to make shot and at last, after heavy bombardment by Spanish troops, the surviving 300 surrendered to the local Spanish governor, Don Melchior de Guevara. Young Colin Campbell the diarist was put into a Spanish prison, Fonab headed home via New York. The little town of New Edinburgh and its Fort St Andrew, on a promontory where the Campbells had cut a trench to make it an island, were soon covered over by the luxuriant jungle and forgotten: apart from an exploratory expedition that located the sites in 1979, they have stayed that way ever since.

A few colonists stayed on in the Caribbean, like John Campbell (1674–1711) of Inveraray who settled in Port Elizabeth, Jamaica, and rose to be on the island's council. A merchant called John Campbell is also mentioned as sending his son back from Jamaica to Glasgow University in 1720 and there were Campbells in Tobago in 1700. Perhaps there were still quite a few Campbell and even MacDonald survivors from the punishment transportations organised by Cromwell and James II.

There is evidence that Greenock Campbells were by this time trading with the sugar plantations of the West Indies. Daniel Campbell (1671–1753), later of Shawfield, Glasgow, who made his first fortune as a distiller built a new sugar house in the city in 1700 and he sent his brother to Sweden to look after the Baltic end of his business a year or so later. Campbell and his colleagues were also beginning to develop the lucrative tobacco trade between Virginia and Glasgow, on which the latter city's subsequent prosperity was based. Several Campbells had their own ships: George Campbell was master of a Greenock ship in 1685. Hew Campbell sailed on the *Walter of Glasgow* to the West Indies in 1683 and two other Campbells were captains of the frigates *Elizabeth of Argyll* – 68 tons and 5 guns – and *William and George of Glasgow* – 180 tons and 16 guns – in 1692.

There were now Campbells and MacDonalds resident in Boston, New York, New Jersey, the Carolinas and Jamaica. In Barbados the Scots settlers were known as 'red legs'. There was a Captain Campbell in Crawford's regiment of the Tsar of Russia's army in 1690. There was even a Campbell sergeant who retired at York Fort, Bencoolen, in Sumatra and married a Portuguese Indian. There was a shipwrecked Campbell settled in Lapland whose son Duncan, though reputedly deaf and dumb, became a very expensive and successful soothsayer or fortune-teller in fashionable London. Colen Campbell (1679–1726) from the Cawdor branch of the family became a successful architect. He helped rich Daniel Campbell, the Glasgow merchant, build his new mansion at Shawfield and then became a fashionable designer of Palladian mansions in England – he was the architect of Burlington House, London, and Prime Minister Robert Walpole's home at Houghton Hall, Norfolk. Campbell and MacDonald mercenaries were fighting for the Russian, French, Spanish, Swedish, Danish and Dutch armies. Such was the energy and initiative of these two families as they tired at last of fighting each other for a few impoverished islands and crumbling castles and began to look further afield.

As the last stragglers from Darien returned home, Archibald Campbell, 10th Earl of Argyll was made a duke for his services to the House of Orange. Also around this time Campbell of Ardkinglas, the sheriff who had been so unhelpful to MacIain of Glencoe, used devious means to acquire another castle. The last MacNaughton heir of Dunderave was in love with Campbell's pretty, younger daughter and a marriage was arranged. But in the confusion of the party Ardkinglas switched daughters, palming the bridegroom off with an older ugly one. Next morning MacNaughton took this very badly, eloped to Ireland with the pretty daughter and left his castle to his wife and Ardkinglas.

15
RED JOHN AND GREEN KELP

For nearly sixty years after Darien, affairs in Scotland were dominated by two brothers, sons of the 1st Duke of Argyll. In different ways both John, the elder, and Archibald were extremely able men; both successively became Dukes of Argyll but both died without producing legitimate male heirs. In contrast the MacDonalds produced a number of colourful offspring, but none of them had the judgement or persistence to make any real impact as political or military leaders.

Red John of the Battles, Ian Rudach Campbell, 2nd Duke of Argyll (1678–1743), was born at Ham House, London, and was twenty-five and already pursuing a successful career as a professional soldier when he took over the title from his father. He was officer commanding the 10th Regiment of Foot at the siege of Keyserswaert in Flanders. Having lost money in Darien and with the old family tower house in distant Inveraray severely damaged by Highlanders at least four times in the previous half century, he probably regarded England as his natural home, even if Scotland was still his power base. For this and other reasons he was a strong supporter of the Act of Union between England and Scotland in 1707, helping its passage through the House of Lords and suggesting to Queen Anne the appointment of Commissioners, including several Campbells, to supervise the union of parliaments.

By this time Red John was a brigadier-general serving against the French under the Duke of Marlborough whom he regarded, possibly with some professional jealousy, as a bit of an upstart. He played an important role in the victories over the French at Ramillies and Oudenaarde, captured Ostend and commanded at the siege of Ghent in 1709. By the time of Tournai in that same year he was a lieutenant-general and displayed considerable personal courage at Malplaquet, sustaining several musket holes in his cloak and hat. He seems to have been quite popular with his troops as one not above sharing the hardships and dangers of the ordinary soldier. He was also on good terms with the Tory literary set, Alexander Pope and particularly, for a while, Dean Jonathan Swift. Red John sympathised hugely with the latter's pamphlet *On the Conduct of the Allies* and its searing attack on the arrogance of Marlborough. The last straw for Argyll in his relationship with the duke seems to have been Marlborough's request to be appointed Captain-General for life, but Red John's own military career now went downhill. For two years after 1712 he was sidelined as Governor of Minorca, but arrived back in London in 1714 to join in the welcome for the Hanoverian George I as the new king.

In thus supporting both the Act of Union and the Hanoverian succession Argyll might seem the antithesis of a patriotic Scot, but this impression is partly due to the subsequent sentimental confusion of the, by this time, anglicised if not Frenchified Stuart dynasty with the Scottish identity, ignoring religion and many other political facts of life.

Certainly when the Stuart heir James, known as the Old Pretender, began to organise a rebellion in 1715, Argyll, by this time a field marshal, was the natural choice to be commander-in-chief in Scotland to repel the Jacobites. Prominent Campbells who served under him included his brother Archibald Campbell, Lord Islay, who had also fought on the continent under Marlborough. Islay arrived half an hour before the battle of Sheriffmuir and was twice wounded. There too were Red John's cousin, later to be the 4th Duke, Colonel Jack Campbell of Mamore and Hugh Campbell, Earl of Loudoun. Another Campbell who had done well in the British army was Loudoun's brother Sir James Campbell of Lawers (1667–1745), a colonel in the Scots Greys, who fought at Malplaquet, was personally commended by Prince Eugene for leading the charge of dragoons at Blenheim and had his legs blown off at Fontenoy. He is sometimes confused with the James Campbell, Colonel of the Russian dragoons, who fought at Lesnaya against the Swedes and was made a tsarist brigadier.

There was, of course, also at this time that other descendant of the Loudoun Campbells, Gideon Freiherr von Laudon (1719–90), grandson of Sir Matthew Campbell who had settled in Livonia (see p. 67). He joined the Russian army in 1732, failed in an attempt to transfer to the

Prussian army and took a post with the Austrians in 1741 as captain of a Croat platoon. He married a Frau von Hagen and settled on the Croat border. Despite a diffident personality and small stature, he rose steadily up the ranks and led 2,000 Croats and 600 hussars at Kolin, rising to become a field marshal under the Emperor Joseph II. His greatest triumph was to help defeat Frederick the Great of Prussia at Kunersdorf in 1759 and to capture the fortress of Schweidnitz in Silesia. King Frederick was so impressed that later at a peacetime banquet he invited Laudon to sit beside him, saying he preferred that situation to being on opposing sides. The emperor rewarded Laudon with two houses in Vienna and a castle at Hadersdach, but he came out of retirement to repel the Turks from Bosnia and actually captured Belgrade for the Emperor Joseph in 1787.

There were also Campbells, but not so many, on the Jacobite side at Sheriffmuir. The most motivated were probably the two sons of Robert Campbell of Glenlyon, still trying to live down the stigma of Glencoe. But there were also two sons of the Grey Fox of Breadalbane, though he was in his late seventies and stayed at home waiting to see who would come out on top. Perhaps the most famous was that half-Campbell, Rob Roy, who had a Campbell mother and a Campbell wife and used the name Campbell because the name MacGregor was still attainted. Ironically, Rob Roy's personal problems stemmed from the disappearance, voluntary or otherwise, of an assistant called MacDonald who was carrying £1,000 in borrowed cash, the float for a cattle-drive. In fact, Rob was actually away on a scouting mission at the time of the main battle at Sheriffmuir, though there was no doubt about his skill as a warrior.

If the Campbells provided the senior general, some very experienced officers and a good number of the soldiery on the Hanoverian side at Sheriffmuir, the MacDonalds did not provide the leader of the Jacobites, nor did they have any one man recognised by all septs as the senior chief. Nor, of course, did the Royal Stuarts provide a leader, for the Old Pretender, though still then quite young, made only a brief, belated appearance, was struck down by illness, took no part in the fighting and departed ignominiously as soon as the first battle proved indecisive. The leadership of the Jacobite cause in Scotland was instead provided by the self-appointed, very recent convert to the Stuarts (because King George I would not give him a job), Bobbing John Erskine, Earl of Mar.

The MacDonalds did supply three out of the six battalions in the front line of Mar's right wing, who fought beside one battalion of Glenorchy Campbells. The three were Clanranald under Alan, Captain of Clanranald, who had burned down his own castle of Tioram before leaving in case it proved of use to the enemy, Glengarry with Glencoe under Alastair Dubh MacDonald and Sleat under the chief's son Donald.

As it happened most of the Campbells were on the Hanoverian right wing where their chief positioned himself, so since the MacDonalds were on the Jacobite right wing there was little direct fighting between the two clans. It could be argued that both the Campbells and the MacDonalds won their part of the battle, for the Jacobite right wing under General Gordon scored a charging victory over General Whitham's mainly English battalions, while the Hanoverian right directly under Argyll severely defeated the Jacobite left under General Hamilton, albeit after a struggle. If the Highlanders on the Jacobite right wing had been better controlled they could have been redirected to assist the flagging left wing, but instead they were allowed to drift off in pursuit of the fleeing Hanoverian left. Thus, despite the fact that overall he had superior numbers and better troops Mar failed to capitalise on the success of his right wing and the battle was a stalemate.

Argyll had avoided defeat when faced by superior numbers but he was still heavily criticised in London for not scoring an outright victory. However, it was soon evident that a stalemate was good enough. The Jacobite invasion of central Scotland had been stopped before it reached the Forth and it was effectively over. The rest of the rebellion in Scotland consisted of no more than burning a few Perthshire villages and a rather disorderly retreat back to Badenoch. Then came dispersal of the clansmen, mostly just to their homes, a few key rebels like Clanranald's brother and MacDonald of Keppoch by ship to France and a few prisoners who were sent to Carlisle for trial. The punishment of Highland rebels was by custom not severe, a tradition largely created by the virtual uncatchability of fugitives once they disappeared into the mountains. But this last great natural defence of the old order was about to be severely degraded by General Wade and his road system. By the time of the next serious rebellion in 1745 a network of new roads, bridges, barracks and forts had been constructed, which meant that punishment next time would be much more efficient. In 1715–16 the more obvious rebel leaders, like Clanranald, Keppoch and Glencoe, forfeited their estates, but most soon got them back. However, the net result of the '15 was certainly a further erosion of the land-base, wealth and dynastic integrity of several MacDonald branches and a further increase in the bitterness that they felt towards the southern establishment.

There can be little doubt that, so far as the MacDonald group of clans was concerned, the '15 was not really about the restoration of the Stuart dynasty and it certainly was not about Scottish nationhood, freedom or self-determination, for the Old Pretender stood for none of those things. It might have been partially about restoring the Roman Catholic church, as had also been true to some extent at the time of Alastair MacColla, but this is unlikely to have been a major motivation. Much more it was to do with a last ditch attempt to regain the lusher pastures of Ross and Argyll, which the MacDonalds had lost to the Campbells and others over previous centuries, in order to restore the power and glory of the ancient chiefdoms now that castles and galleys were no longer such useful tools of warfare. The MacDonalds had only one significant asset left: manpower coupled with the concept of the Highland charge. At Sheriffmuir it very nearly came off, but if it had and the Stuarts had by some fluke been restored it can be imagined that the MacDonalds would soon have outlived their usefulness to James VIII and the Campbells, yet again, would have contrived to change sides.

Meanwhile, there was a reprise of the rebellion in 1719. Again it might have gone the full distance if there had been vigorous leadership, but there was not. This time the impetus came from a small boatload of returning exiles, one of them Clanranald, backed up by two Spanish frigates. But the island castle of Eilean Donan, which had been chosen as a supply base, was no match for the Royal Navy and the invaders blew up their own second ammunition depot further up Loch Duich in case it fell into government hands. There was a good turnout of MacDonalds – plus the inevitable Rob Roy – at the battle of Glenshiel which followed, but the Highland charge was completely wasted and the battle ended in a fairly pathetic if not too bloody defeat.

Red John, Duke of Argyll and Duke of Greenwich, never quite recovered from his disgrace after Sheriffmuir but became a respected member of the bitter opposition to Sir Robert Walpole. He retired to his Surrey mansion of Sudbrook House, died two years before the '45 and was buried under a superb tomb created by the sculptor Roubiliac in Westminster Abbey, leaving five daughters. His brother Archibald, 3rd Duke (d. 1761), however, remained very much in favour with the government and dominated political life in Scotland for forty-odd years after Sheriffmuir, inheriting the dukedom in 1743. He had a long-term relationship with a Mrs Williams, which resulted in an illegitimate son, Colonel William Campbell, but no heir to the dukedom.

In addition to Wade's new roads there were other long-term economic factors that hastened change in western Scotland after 1715. Black cattle had been both the main export and the main focus of Highland crime, as exemplified for around 100 years by the Glencoe MacDonalds, by Colin MacDonell of Barisdale, who was reduced to living off protection money from drovers taking their cattle south from Skye, or even Rob Roy, though he was a professional drover. The Jacobite period saw its increasing regularisation as populations grew and the whole business needed to be put on a proper footing. It also saw the introduction of both a new industry and a new staple food crop to the islands. The new industry began in about 1726 when Alexander MacDonald of Boisdale introduced the idea of kelp seaweed collection and burning to North Uist from Ireland. The growth of the seaweed was encouraged by placing stones in bays along the coast and the ash was sent south mainly as a catalyst for use in glass, linen and soap manufacture. The new staple food was the potato, which arrived in the Hebrides in 1743 and was to become the cheap food for cheap labour for the next 100 years – until the blight cataclysmically removed it. The introduction of the potato also meant that less barley was needed for food and the surplus could be used for distilling whisky, another industry that now began to grow. The kelp and the potato between them generated a kind of economic Indian summer which for a short time hid the basic problems of the west coast.

There was, of course, another export that had been departing for centuries; it now started to become more obvious. While there was a slight influx of cheap labour to harvest the kelp, there was also a continuous exodus of talent to the colonies and to foreign wars. Among the captured rebels of 1716 there were a number of both MacDonalds and Campbells, but more of the former were transported from English ports on the *Wakefield* and the *Susannah* to South Carolina, on the *Friendship* to Maryland, on the *Two Brothers* to Montserrat and on the

Scipio to Antigua. Those who survived the journey worked as indentured slaves on plantations and those who survived the work in some cases provided permanent new families for the new world. In the circumstances the two clans intermarried quite happily and sometimes they married into the black African population.

Back in Scotland, in 1739 there was an early example of what was later to be called a clearance, though at this point it was not for the sake of freeing up land for sheep. MacDonald of Sleat and MacLeod of Dunvegan together organised the sale of a significant number of their people to South Carolina as indentured servants. There were already other MacDonalds and Campbells settling in Bladen County, by the Cape Fear River in North Carolina.

Overseas military service also continued to grow as an outlet for clan energies. There were MacDonalds serving in the French, Spanish, Swedish and Russian armies and a few in the British army. Naturally, the Campbells were quicker than the MacDonalds to sign up with southern regiments or found their own but in 1725 the government raised six independent companies as a watch; since the men wore dark tartan it soon acquired the nickname of Black Watch and was formed into a regiment in 1739. As the 43rd Highland Regiment of Foot under Colonel Campbell of Fonab, Duncan Campbell of Lochnell and John Campbell of Lawers, it fought the French at Fontenoy in 1745 when a James Campbell killed nine Frenchmen before losing his arm. A number of prominent Campbells fought at Dettingen in 1742 and the Black Watch marked the first coordinated use of Scottish regiments to assist in the assertion of British power overseas. The diaspora had indeed begun.

16

THE WHITE ROSE AND THE WHITE HORSE

Without question it was the 1745 Jacobite rebellion that provided the MacDonalds and other Highland clans with their last reasonable chance to reverse the rise of the Campbells, of the Lowlands and of the Whig so-called idea of progress. It was another great culling, the worst since 1647 and also the last, but this time the Campbells played a relatively passive role and neither of the two great clans provided any of the top leadership.

The frustrations, stupidities and might-have-beens of the '45 have been told well and often by many historians, but from the point of view of this narrative certain facts are especially relevant. Most writers agree that without the MacDonalds it is almost certain that the rising would never have got off the ground; it might even have been successful if they had been given their head and the Campbells, after 1715, were regarded by London as insufficiently motivated or trustworthy to suppress it.

Bonnie Prince Charlie's badly prepared and fairly irresponsible landing in Scotland was supposedly intended to resuscitate a dynasty that had already been rejected by the British people at least three times, had a reputation for autocratic obstinacy and Catholicism which did not suit the times and, what is more, had long since lost any roots or credibility in Scotland itself. Despite his Italian upbringing and half-Polish ancestry Bonnie Prince Charlie certainly did show great talent in rapidly turning himself into a kind of Scottish icon; like a chameleon he tartanised himself to merge with the area where his rising had to begin and provided yet another outlet for the long-lingering resentment of the MacDonalds and their cousins.

Of the so-called seven men of Moidart – Prince Charlie's sole companions when he arrived – two were MacDonalds, Aeneas of Clanranald, the Paris-based banker, and Sir John, an Irish professional soldier who had served in the Spanish army. Significantly, the prince's confessor was also a MacDonald.

One of the first to agree to fight for Charles was Ronald MacDonald of Kinlochmoidart, a South Uist laird whose father had been at both Killiecrankie and Sheriffmuir. He is reputed to have sneered when he saw Clanranald senior and some of the other chiefs hesitating to join the standard and said: 'Tho' no other men draw a sword, I am ready to die for you.' In fact he was to live to a reasonable old age, father twenty-one children, most of whom went to America. Others of his sept, however, were executed at Carlisle. MacDonald of Boisdale, on the other hand, was one of the first to refuse outright to support the prince and the Catholic bishop of the Highlands, Hugh MacDonald, was the first to have the nerve to tell Charlie to head back to France.

The emblematic first white rose was plucked and the standard was first raised on MacDonald land at Glenfinnan, the estate of Alexander MacDonald of Glenaladale, himself also one of the first to volunteer and one of the last to give up, while the first clan leader to join with his men was young Clanranald, whose great-uncle had been the most prominent fatality at Sheriffmuir. The first to draw blood was Donald MacDonald of Tirnadris who used his wits to capture two raw companies of Scots Guards at Laggan Achadun. Later, he took a wrong turning at Falkirk, was captured and executed.

The first senior chief to refuse outright to join was Alexander MacDonald of Sleat, a member of a family that had provided a contingent in 1715 but this time regarded the rebellion as too ill-prepared. Thus there were to be three MacDonald regiments in the campaign: Keppoch, under its chief Alexander; Glengarry, led by Angus Og MacDonell (the chief's son); and Clanranald also under the chief's son Ranald (the father refused). With about 900 men between them, the MacDonalds made up around 40 per cent of the total Jacobite army.

The first two people to raise the alarm of invasion were Lachlan Campbell, the Church of Scotland minister at Kilmore, and Campbell of

Auchindoun (near Cawdor), the Duke of Argyll's factor in Ardnamurchan and his governor of Mingary Castle. Among the first to start organising the defence of the Lowlands were three senior Campbells: General Jack Campbell of Mamore, himself later the 4th Duke (1693–1770), was an experienced soldier; his son Colonel Jack ran the eight companies of Argyll militia; John Campbell, 4th Earl of Loudoun (1705–82), had raised his regiment two years earlier and as colonel was adjutant to Sir Johnnie Cope. Almost his entire force was to be wiped out by the Jacobites at Prestonpans. It would be some time before Loudoun was able to return to his massively imposing mansion in Ayrshire and the ancient family yew tree that grew beside it.

Among the first to agree to fight for the opposite side to their fellow clansmen were Ranald MacDonald of Scotas in Knoydart, who fought for the Hanoverian King George II, and Sir James Campbell of Auchinbreck, who supported Jacobite rebels but was arrested before he could get far. The Glenlyon Campbells also supported the Stuarts once more.

One of the first regular army officers to desert a government regiment and transfer to the Jacobites was Donald MacDonald of Lochgarry. But though the MacDonalds provided the backbone of Prince Charlie's army, none of their chiefs was in the high command: the nearest to the top was Colonel Sir John MacDonald, Inspector of Cavalry. There were three Drummond generals, two Murrays, a Forbes and a Gordon. And while the Campbells provided the backbone of the Hanoverian defence in Scotland they were somewhat sidelined in the main campaign. The duke himself was past fighting age and had severe rheumatism. He had only recently visited Inveraray for the first time in thirty years and been appalled by its delapidation, commissioning an architect to replace the badly damaged old castle with a completely new one. His heir, General Jack Campbell of Mamore, garrisoned the ruins with his Scots Fusiliers while Mamore's son Colonel Jack raised the local militia. Surprisingly, a Campbell, John, the bastard son of Campbell of Ardmaddy and a grandson of the Grey Fox, was a key figure in Jacobite finance. As cashier of the Royal Bank of Scotland he put up the money for invading England.

As before at Inverlochy, Killiecrankie and Sheriffmuir the Highland charge worked excellently when the two armies met at Prestonpans on 21 September 1745 and the Jacobites achieved rapid success beyond all expectations. The rebels turned south but a lack of confidence and of ruthlessness at the top led to the hesitation at Derby when London appeared to be within their reach. It was almost a repeat of the situation after Sheriffmuir: once a rebellion shifts from attack to retreat it is doomed. It was Clanranald who had the thankless and difficult task of covering the retreat from Derby and dragging the artillery back over Shap by brute force in dreadful conditions.

When the forces met at Falkirk on 17 January 1746 the Highland charge again worked well and George II's army was partially defeated but greater results would have been achieved from the battle if the MacDonald follow-up had been more disciplined. In addition, the accidental shooting of Angus Og Glengarry by a fellow MacDonald was a severe blow to morale.

Prince Charles's army had retreated north and by every standard the Jacobite generals made a mess of Culloden when battle came on 16 April 1746. They chose unsuitable terrain, tired out their own troops by ill-thought-out manoeuvres and vacillation, and failed totally to make proper use of their greatest asset, the Highland charge. This particularly affected the MacDonalds who to their disgust were given the left wing instead of their customary right. This condemned them to a 600 yard run over rough ground and totally exposed them to enemy fire. Furthermore, a number of Clanranald had left in protest at the execution of one of their number who had accidentally killed Glengarry at Falkirk. Generally morale among the men seemed to sink rapidly and only the officers made much effort to fight. So it became more a slaughter than a battle. But from our point of view it was the last occasion when the MacDonalds and their allies fought against the non-Highland clans, the Lowlanders and the English in a final despairing effort to win back what had been taken from them. The age of private armies, personal fiefdoms and freedom to fight each other for land or goods stood against the discipline of government, the comfortable squirearchy of the south, the lawyers, the merchants and the reformed church. Bonnie Prince Charlie just happened to turn up as a rallying point for the old ways: if he had ever become a king it is most unlikely that the symbolic would have become real.

Examining the Jacobite army at Culloden it is surprising just how many Campbells had now also fallen below the resentment line and thus chose to identify with and fight for the underdog Jacobite cause. In the Atholl regiment there were eleven Campbells, including three officers, and fourteen MacDonalds, also including three officers, mostly from the Rannoch–Glenlyon area where the two families had mixed and intermarried. The two brothers MacDonald of Dalchosnie were both killed at Culloden. Of the other ranks two MacDonalds and two Campbells were transported to the colonies after the battle. In the Cameron regiment there were two Campbells and no MacDonalds. The Earl of Cromarty's regiment had eight Campbells and four MacDonalds and six of the Campbells suffered transportation. There were even three Campbells in the Glengarry regiment, as well as 103 named MacDonalds, of whom two Campbells and thirty MacDonalds were condemned to transportation. With Keppoch there were six Campbells and the four sons of Rob Roy, known for a while as MacGregor-Campbells, but quite a few Keppoch MacDonalds had stayed in Lochaber after the siege of Fort William. There was even one Campbell in the Clanranald regiment, a herdsman from Eigg who was killed. Thus there were scatterings of both families throughout the regiments, though the bulk of MacDonalds were with their three chiefs and the bulk of the Campbells were on the Hanoverian side with the Fusiliers or the Argyll militia.

It is hard to estimate the total casualties but the MacDonalds must have lost several hundred men, including six executed, and many more died soon afterwards of privations in Scotland itself or in the heat of the plantations. The Campbells must have lost at least half this number but only two were executed, both deserters, and not so many transported. Two Campbell redcoat officers were killed, Captain Archibald of Ballimore and Captain John of Auchnabar. Significantly, transportation was a punishment for other ranks only and the officers, except for a select few, got off quite lightly. Two of the three main MacDonald leaders who took part were killed – Glengarry in the friendly fire incident at Falkirk and Keppoch with two of his brothers at Culloden. Other senior figures like MacDonald of Lochgarry went into exile with Prince Charlie. Several of the great MacDonald families, such as Keppoch and Knoydart, suffered irreparable damage, losing castles, heirs and estates so that the survivors were virtually forced to seek a livelihood abroad. However, the general culling of the MacDonalds and other Jacobite clans fell far short of the ethnic cleansing that the Duke of Cumberland undoubtedly had in mind. Their political and military power had certainly now been broken – a task that kings of Scotland had been trying to achieve since James I in 1425 if not earlier.

Significantly, just as two of the seven men of Moidart who accompanied Prince Charles were MacDonalds, so two of the seven men of Glenmoriston who helped him to escape were also MacDonalds. Yet undoubtedly the most famous MacDonald of this entire period was not a soldier or a committed Jacobite but Flora from South Uist. Having lost her father at an early age Flora Macdonald (1722–90) was adopted by Lady Clanranald, the chief's wife; meanwhile, her mother married a Hugh Macdonald of the Sleat branch of the clan, a serving officer in the royal army who was in Benbecula when the fugitive prince found the net of Cumberland's men closing round him. It may or may not have been on her initiative that the prince was disguised as her maid 'Betty Burke' and taken by boat over the sea to Skye. After a difficult crossing and one attempted landing that had to be aborted because of hostile fire, they landed on the Trotternish peninsula of Skye, near the house of Macdonald of Kingsburgh, Flora's future father-in-law. The twelve-day partnership added greatly to the prince's image even if it did not immediately lead to his rescue, but it cost Flora some eighteen months on a convict ship at Leith and in the Tower of London. General Jack Campbell, the future 5th Duke of Argyll, was one of the most prominent people to speak out against her execution.

The most puzzling character of the episode was Alastair Ruadh MacDonell (1724–61), a captain in the French Scots Brigade and later 13th Chief of his sept. He had fallen into English hands in 1745 and spent the years of the rising in the Tower of London. Thereafter he was a courier of Jacobite funds that mysteriously disappeared and was accused after his death of being the English spy known as Pickle.

The most confusing yet typical player in the whole drama was the fine Gaelic poet Alexander MacDonald (1700–80). Originally a teacher and elder in the Church of Scotland he gave this up to become a Catholic and supported Hugh MacDonald, Bishop of the Isles, in his complaints about a Francis MacDonald. Francis's crime was to have left the Catholics to join the Church of Scotland.

PART 3
THE DIASPORA

We plough the seeds and scatter
The good seed on the land,
But it is fed and watered
By God's almighty hand.

Jane Montgomerie Campbell (1824–1905)

17

THE SUN NEVER SETS

We know of at least five ships that took both Campbell and MacDonald prisoners in their holds across the Atlantic in 1746: the *Gildart* landed at Port North Potomac, Virginia, the *Frere* on Barbados, the *Johnson* at Port Oxford, the *St George* on Jamaica and the *Veteran*, after being captured on its way to the Leewards by some friendly French, landed instead on the latter's island of Martinique. But this was part of a much larger exodus of both our clans for whom kelp, potatoes and thin black cattle represented a very unattractive future. Many chiefs had begun to make their homes in the south like the Dukes of Argyll, though the Campbell dukes had also started to build themselves a new baronial château at Inveraray, demolishing the old castle and the old town to make way for it and rebuilding an elegant new town beyond the garden wall. They even set up a job-creation programme with a new spinning business to revive the fortunes of the burgh which was now no more than their occasional holiday home. Colonel Jack Campbell, the 5th Duke of Argyll, was now also Baron Sunbridge of Coombank in Kent, married to the beautiful widow, Elizabeth, Duchess of Hamilton, but all their wealth could not prevent the loss of their first child as a baby in Rosneath Castle in 1759. Two other major Campbell chiefs also moved south, Roy of Glenorchy as MP for Oxford, ambassador to Russia and a Lord of the Admiralty, Campbell of Cawdor to his wife's seat at Stackpole Court in south Wales. The Macdonalds of Sleat, the only major branch of the MacDonalds not to support Bonnie Prince Charlie and the first to start organised clearances, also went south for a good English marriage and later built themselves a new Gothic mansion at Armadale on the proceeds of their kelp business and the good marriage.

Almost in a reverse of the fashionable trend, the Campbells of Glasgow returned to their roots, bought back Islay and built the new town of Bowmore in 1768, like the new Inveraray a model of its kind.

The battle of Culloden was a major turning point, not just because so many felt that they now had to seek their fortunes overseas but even more because their chiefs now knew that they could never again win wealth or position by domestic violence and theft. They had to find other means to improve the viability of their over-populated estates. It was also the end of the great feud, for the differences between the profitability of island and mainland estates had become much less marked. Both Campbells and MacDonalds had mingled, intermarried and over-bred in remote glens that could not support them.

We have already seen the steady flow of transported prisoners, both civilian and military, to America and the West Indies from 1647 onwards. There had also been the founding of the colonies by Lord Neil Campbell in East New Jersey, south of Newark, and by Sir George Campbell of Cessnock near Port Royal, South Carolina, both in 1685 in the aftermath of the suppression of Covenanters. There were a few Darien survivors too, enterprising Campbell traders who had settled in Jamaica and elsewhere. In fact, in 1762 it was estimated that nearly two-thirds of Jamaica was owned by Scots. The Campbells of Glassary had a big sugar plantation at Orange Bay and there were Campbells with interests in sugar, rum and the black slave trade throughout the Westmorland, Hanover and St Elizabeth districts of western Jamaica. John Campbell (1674–1740) of Inveraray survived Darien and settled by the Black River, Jamaica. John Campbell Senior & Co. of Glasgow had two estates on Grenada and five in Guiana. The MacDonalds, though slower to take an interest in trade, did begin to catch up, for the linked companies of John MacDonald & Co., New Providence, and Roderick McDonald of Glasgow jointly traded with Trinidad and Demerara. There was even a new Darien, a Scots outpost with a sprinkling of Campbells and the odd MacDonald who had been recruited by James Oglethorpe in 1735 to pioneer the southern section of his dangerous new colony in Georgia.

In addition, there were remarkable individuals like the John Campbell who went to Boston in 1695 and founded the *Boston Newsletter* a mere nine years later, the first successful newspaper in North America. In 1738 Captain Lachlan Campbell of Islay brought eighty-three Islay families, mostly Campbells, to the Lake George area north of Albany. Then came the first big MacDonald influx in 1739 and the settlement in the ironically named Cumberland County, North Carolina, in 1746. Twenty years later came the even more dramatic purchase of the Island of St John (now Prince Edward Island) off Nova Scotia by the Catholic John MacDonell of Glenaladale in 1767 and the colonies of Tracadie and Scotchfort. The emigration was caused partly by the penal rents imposed on Catholics in South Uist by the Protestant Colin MacDonald of Boisdale and negotiations for the new colony were helped by Bishop John MacDonell of the Isles. Meanwhile, the nearby Campobello Island colony was founded by the Campbell adherent Captain Owen in 1766 and three shiploads of assorted members of the two clans came from Kintyre in 1774. The whole process was accelerated by the increasing number of sheep being brought into the Highlands and the resultant decrease in arable land for crops.

Thus came a steady trickle of rich and poor from both clans: convicted whores like Janet Campbell of Edinburgh, MacDonald ship-looters from the north coast, pickpockets, Jacobites, sheep thieves, infanticides, beggars and traders added to the overall twin clan migration. Some Irish of both clans also now began to arrive in areas such as the aptly named Orange County, North Carolina. There were at least three Campbells acting as factors in Maryland and Virginia for Glasgow tobacco lords while in Glasgow John Campbell of Clathic and John Coats Campbell were both extremely wealthy tobacco merchants.

But in addition to all these forms of migration was another old favourite which now rapidly became much more popular – professional soldiering. The 88th Campbell Highlanders fought in Germany 1756–61 and took heavy losses at Warburg. Both clans had a tradition of providing mercenaries for foreign armies and even before Culloden both, but more especially the Campbells, had provided recruits for British regiments. John Campbell of Loudoun (see p. 100) was briefly commander-in-chief in America in 1756 but failed to impress. It was the rapid expansion of the British Empire under William Pitt from 1758 onwards that provided far more opportunities for long-term foreign postings and it was generals like Wade and Wolfe who recommended the recruitment of Highland soldiers.

Thanks mainly to Robert Louis Stevenson the battle at Fort Ticonderoga (now in New York State) in 1758 has come to symbolise the transformation of Scottish clansmen into empire builders in the most exotic corners of the earth:

> Through Asiatic jungles
> The Tartans filed their way
> And the neighing of the war-pipes
> Struck terror in Cathay.

Major Duncan Campbell of Inverawe had a dream that he would die at a place with such a strange foreign name and his dream was fulfilled:

> O you of the outland tongue
> You of the painted face
> This is the place of my death
> Can you tell me the name of the place?

And he did indeed meet his death at Ticonderoga, shot by the French. His son was badly injured there too, as were several other Campbells, including Captain John Campbell who died, and there were certainly a number of MacDonalds fighting alongside them.

In this and several other battles against the French for control of North America the Highlanders played a part and many who survived stayed on in the new world. There were both Campbells and MacDonalds in significant numbers with General Wolfe on the Heights of Abraham when Wolfe's men captured Quebec. John MacDonell of Leek on Loch Oich joined the French army after Culloden, but changed sides back to a British force under Campbell of Loudoun at Bergen op Zoom, Holland. He now saved the life of the French General Montcalm when British troops tried to murder him in revenge for the death of their own General Wolfe. As one of the Mohawk colony founders he went on to command the veterans in Newfoundland and his son was to lead the Glengarry Light Infantry in 1812 (see p. 125). At least two other MacDonalds were killed at Fort Duquesne (now Pittsburgh) and two at Quebec. Members of both clans fought and died together in the 42nd and other Highland regiments throughout the campaigns of the Seven Years War against France. And, as a less dangerous pastime, members of the two clans at this time introduced the sport of curling to Canada where it thrived.

But only sixteen years after Quebec and a mere thirty after Culloden came the most extraordinary sign of change in the attitudes of the Highlanders. Given the anti-Hanoverian tradition of the MacDonalds and the Whiggish tendency of the Campbells it is remarkable that most of the settlers in America from the two clans fought against American independence between 1775 and 1781. In the case of some of the MacDonalds it is slightly more understandable in that many of them were Catholic and regarded the Boston liberals as fanatically Protestant. Alexander MacDonald had left the army after the Seven Years War and settled in New York as a wine merchant and organ seller. He brought 100 men from Staten Island to fight against independence and joined up with 200 MacDonell immigrants on the Mohawk River. John MacDonell of Scotas, who had done a stint in the Spanish army before coming west, had risen to be a director of the Hudson's Bay Company and now fought with the Loyalists. Once defeat was inevitable he moved his tribe out of Mohawk Valley where they had settled after landing from the *Pearl* in New York. Now, like Moses, he led them to a new promised land in Canada and they settled at Glengarry, north of the St Lawrence River. His cousin, MacDonell of Aberchalder, was in the King's Royal Regiment of New York and led a mixture of 300 Tories, Indians and Dutch at Schoharie Creek. He was accused of atrocities but later settled at Charlottenburg, Cornwall, and became first speaker of the Upper Canada assembly. Less fortunate were Colonel Mungo Campbell, who was killed in the attack on Fort Montgomery by the Popolopen, and Donald Macdonald, who was shot in the raid at Schell's Bush, had his leg amputated but died soon afterwards. Brigadier John Campbell, who halted a rebel attack on Staten Island, lived to tell the tale.

Another Loyalist, Brigadier Donald McDonald, led 7,000 men to fight (at the last minute he fell ill and handed over command to his deputy) for George III against Washington at the battle of Moore's Creek Bridge in North Carolina, but was badly defeated and retreated by a strange irony to a town called Campbelltown (where Hugh Campbell had settled in 1733 – since renamed Fayetteville). He had been given highly unreliable advice by Farquhar Campbell, the Cumberland County delegate who managed to stay friendly with both sides in the War of Independence until it was clear which one was going to win. Significantly Farquhar Campbell owned fifty black slaves – most of the Scots in the area tended to have at least a few, so this helps to explain the number of black Campbells and MacDonalds who have become prominent in more recent times. North Carolina was at this time the home of the most famous living Macdonald, Flora, who had emigrated with her husband Allan Macdonald of Kingsburgh. He too fought for King George in the North Carolina Volunteers and was captured at Moore's Creek. Thereafter the couple found life difficult and decided not to settle in America but to return to Skye. Meanwhile, the Macdonald Highlanders, raised by Macdonald of Sleat, came out to New York to fight for the king in 1779, but too late to stop the rot and eventually they surrendered at Yorktown in 1781. There were also a number of MacDonalds in the 84th and William MacDonald who served in the 79th Foot later went on to be governor of Jamaica.

There were two Campbell governors in America at this time. Lord William Campbell, a Royal Navy captain and the 5th Duke of Argyll's brother, had volunteered to take charge of South Carolina since he had married a Charleston girl. Unfortunately he became involved in what the Patriots regarded as dirty tactics, encouraging black slaves and native Americans to side with the British, and he had to flee almost immediately. Soon afterwards, despite his rank, he volunteered to act as gun captain on the dangerous lower deck of a frigate in the sea battle off Charleston. He was severely wounded and died. The other governor was Alexander Campbell of Barcaldine in charge of Boston who stayed to fight at Bunker's Hill and later joined MacLean's Regiment. Another Alexander Campbell from the same area came to Boston as a grocer in 1775, joined the army, later won several lucrative army timber contracts and ended up with two large properties in New York. The most obviously successful Campbell on the Loyalist side was General Archibald who had been wounded at Quebec. He was sent out as a trouble-shooter, only to be captured immediately when he landed at Boston, but he organised his own release and went on to capture Savannah and Augusta – rare Hanoverian successes. Much less reputable was the tale of the irascible Colin Campbell of Kilberry who killed a brother officer in a quarrel, escaped punishment but spent his declining years as an ageing bachelor fop in Edinburgh.

There were also a few from both clans on the side of the revolutionaries. Nicholas Campbell was one of the plotters in the Boston Tea Party and it was Daniel Campbell who admitted George Washington to the Freemasons in 1752. It was at a Mrs Campbell's Virginia Coffee house in Williamsburg that a number of important Patriot meetings took place in 1776. Colonel William Campbell (1745–1811), an

Inchconnel Castle on its island in Loch Awe, first home of the Campbells of Argyll. (Author)

Old Inveraray Castle, demolished in the mid-eighteenth century to make way for the new one below. (Pernant)

Inveraray Castle, seat of the Dukes of Argyll. (Author)

Taymouth Castle, Perthshire, seat of the Campbell Earls of Breadalbane. (Author)

Loudoun Castle, Ayrshire, seat of the Campbell Earls of Loudoun. (Author)

Cawdor Castle, near Nairn, seat of the Campbell Earls of Cawdor. (Author)

Duntulm Castle, Skye, original home of the MacDonalds of Sleat. (Pernant)

Mingary Castle, Ardnamurchan, which changed hands from MacDonald to Campbell in the sixteenth century.

View of the islands on Loch Finlaggan, Islay, where the Lords of the Isles had their headquarters. (Dr David Caldwell)

Black Duncan of the Seven Castles,
Campbell of Glenorchy. (Scottish
National Portrait Gallery)

Archibald Campbell, Marquess of Argyll, executed in
1661. (Scottish National Portrait Gallery)

Red John Campbell, 2nd Duke of Argyll,
victor against the Jacobites in 1715.
(Scottish National Portrait Gallery)

Captain Robert Campbell of
Glenlyon, who carried out the
orders for the Glencoe massacre.
(Scottish National Portrait Gallery)

Field Marshal Sir Colin Campbell, later Lord Clyde, leader of the 'thin red line'. (Contemporary lithograph)

Sir Henry Campbell-Bannerman, Liberal Prime Minister of Britain, 1905–8. (Author's collection)

Flora Macdonald, rescuer of Bonnie Prince Charlie. (Scottish National Portrait Gallery)

General Sir James MacDonell, hero of Waterloo. (Scottish National Portrait Gallery)

Sir Hector Macdonald, 'Fighting Mac', faces disgrace. (Author's collection)

Sir John Alexander Macdonald, founder and first Prime Minister of the Dominion of Canada, 1867–73 and 1878–91. (Author's collection)

Ramsay MacDonald, the first Labour Prime Minister of Britain in 1924. (Author's collection)

ex-Cherokee fighter from Tennessee, came up the Holston Gorge and led the rebel Virginia Militia, a near rabble of backwoodsmen, at the battle of King's Mountain by the Watauga against another expatriate Scot, Colonel Ferguson who was killed in the battle. The sharp shooting of the irregulars caused a surprise defeat for the professionals and Campbell's victory was regarded as a turning point in the war.

There was also a MacDougall who had come across with the Islay Campbells and rose to be a Patriot general under Washington. One of the few MacDonalds fighting for Washington was Charles of Kinlochmoidart who by an extraordinary coincidence was involved in organising an exchange of prisoners when his own brother was the negotiator for the British army. In order to meet his brother he had to be blindfolded and marched thus into the British encampment. Subsequently he did well enough in the French contingent to become a general and a count, but as the French Revolution followed soon afterwards this was far from a benefit and he was guillotined for his pains when he went back to France.

So there was a scattering of both clans on both sides in the American War of Independence, but more against the revolution than for it. This partly accounts for the fact that Canada, to which many Loyalists now migrated, remained a part of the British Empire and had a high concentration of Highland Scots. By contrast, when Florida was handed over to Spain after 1786 few Scots stayed on; however, at least two MacDonalds did. Meanwhile, in 1785 a ship called *Macdonald* arrived in Quebec with 520 clansmen crammed below decks, the start of a new wave of immigrants.

It is also to be remembered that by this time both clans were beginning to produce heroes of the American frontier. In 1774 Major Angus MacDonald led an expedition of 400 men from Fort Fincastle deep into hostile Shawnee territory in Ohio and discovered the Muskingum River. Then a year later Colonel Arthur Campbell of Holston, Tennessee – a friend of Daniel Boone and relation presumably of the Colonel Campbell who won at King's Mountain – crossed the Kentucky River and probed deep into uncharted territory, despite attacks by Indians. Five years later he took his revenge by burning and laying waste large tracts of Cherokee country so that in the winter the local population starved. Much more peace-minded was the John MacDonald who set up store in Chicamauga Creek in 1766, took a half-Cherokee wife and established good trading relationships with the tribe.

Further north in 1794 another John MacDonald helped to found Fort Augustus on the Saskatchewan River for the North West Company, right opposite the Hudson's Bay Company's new base at Fort Edmonton.

The Far East was the second main area where the two clans looked to new horizons, though the Campbells, as might be expected, found it easier than the MacDonalds in the early days. Campbell, Clark & Co. of Glasgow opened a Calcutta office. Daniel Campbell's bankrupt brother Colin was sent to Göteborg in Sweden in 1747 to manage the family's interests there and became a director of the Svenska Ostindiska Co – Swedish East India Company – before sailing to China and coming back with a fortune. There were also Campbell merchants such as Sir Robert, based in Madras in the 1770s, who became a governor of the East India Company and put all his sons into the Indian army. An Alexander Campbell who went out to Bengal in 1763 and returned home four years later with £30,000 was regarded as the worst kind of nabob. General Archibald Campbell, who had served at Quebec and Savannah, used his engineering skills to build the Calcutta docks and served as governor of Jamaica, then governor of Madras where he made a fortune. Roy MacDonald, who was in the East India Company in 1773, was not so lucky – he became bankrupt. Nor was Donald Campbell: serving in the cavalry of the Nawab of Arcot he was taken prisoner by Hyder Ali and spent an unpleasant period of imprisonment chained to a corpse in the cells of Seringapatam. John Campbell of Stonefield (1753–84), who had served in America 1775–7, went with the Seaforths to Bombay and succeeded in capturing Annanpore, then conducted a famously stubborn defence of Mangalore which was so strenuous that he died soon afterwards from exhaustion, still in his early thirties. In 1793 Colonel Campbell had the pipes played during a hard attack on the French in Pondicherry, south of Madras. But perhaps the strangest of the clansmen who did well in the East was John Macdonald, known as Beau (1741–78). Left penniless by a Jacobite father, this youngster from Urquhart made a name for himself as the perfect gentleman's gentleman in Bombay, later settled down with a wife in Toledo, Spain, and claimed fame as the first person to carry an umbrella in London.

While officers from the clan aristocracies quite enjoyed their military adventures overseas, the private soldiers were often reluctant recruits and their pay, if it turned up at all, was pitiful. Thus there were a number of mutinies, particularly among the Highland troops stationed in Edinburgh and Glasgow. Private John MacDonald was an example of a mutineer who was condemned to 1,000 lashes though his sentence was commuted to an even worse alternative, posting to the fever-ridden West Indies, where the survival rate for troops was extremely low. Another was Private John Campbell of the 43rd who leapt to his death from a cell in the Tower of London to avoid the cat. In addition to mutineers, there were still plenty of civilian criminals also being sent to the colonies. In 1783 James Campbell was sent to Africa for seven years for stealing 3 shillings and a year later Alexander MacDonald of Middlesex received exactly the same sentence for removing some silver buckles and cloth. Another Campbell from Southwark also got seven years for stealing clothes but he was sent to America.

The younger sons of the clans sometimes did well at sea. John Campbell (1720–90) from Kirkbean was almost certainly the first Scotsman to circumnavigate the globe when he served as a petty officer under Captain Anson during the latter's remarkable treasure-hunting voyage of 1740–4. He had been a press gang victim but won promotion from the lower deck, pioneered the use of the sextant and, but for a twist of fate, might have discovered Australia (see p. 140). Later, Campbell became the first captain of HMS *Victory*, then Vice-Admiral of the *Blue* and governor of Newfoundland, turning down a knighthood. Coll MacDonald of Dalness in Glencoe was captain of the *Hampton Court*. John MacDonald joined the Russian navy in 1783 and served in the Baltic fleet. Not quite so creditable was Captain James Campbell who commanded the *Stirling Castle* under Kepple in 1762 at the siege of Havanna. He showed what was politely described as excessive caution on two occasions, once in the use of his cannon to aid an assault and once in failing to rescue another navy ship in distress. He was dismissed from the service. More remarkable was the strange renegade Campbell who served the Sultan of Turkey and converted to Islam. Under the name of Ingeliz Mustafa he set up a mathematics course for Turkish navigators and helped organise a cannon foundry. At a more mundane, but nevertheless dangerous, level many Campbells were involved in whaling in the 1750s, sailing to Greenland from Leith and Campbeltown. Other seamen included the privateer Malcolm Campbell of Port Glasgow and George Campbell of Liverpool, whose *Brave Blakeney* captured a French sloop in 1755 and helped him set up his

St Domingo estate near Everton. Patrick Campbell, a Bristol skipper was in all probability a slaver in the 1740s. Given the Campbells' widespread interests in plantations as well as in shipping, a fairly substantial involvement in the slave trade must be assumed.

Appointments in foreign armies also persisted. Colonel Donald MacDonald served for many years in the Dutch army before returning to Skye in 1768 and Colonel John MacDonald had charge of a regiment in the Portuguese army.

Two economic changes affected our two clans during the decade of the American War of Independence. One, directly due to the war, was the collapse of the Glasgow tobacco trade in which a number of Campbells had been involved. The other was the introduction of the first sheep-walk (pastureland) in 1783, which began a major acceleration in the shift from arable to sheep farming and initiated the main period of forced emigration from the Highlands and Islands known as the clearances. Almost inevitably a Campbell has been blamed for starting the trend. It was the near-bankrupt Ayrshire farmer, John Campbell of Laguine, who moved with his sheep to a cheaper piece of land on Loch Fyne. He found by accident that they flourished there without effort or shelter and made far more money than cattle. So he soon started snapping up more cheap land in the Highlands and others followed his lead. In 1785 some 55 crofters and their families – around 300 people – had to abandon the Glengarry village of Daingean, where the rents had been put up to prohibitive levels. This pattern was repeated in many villages in Campbell and MacDonald territory and sheep were not the only threat. Also ominous was the first hint of a drop in the price of kelp, the industry on which so many island livelihoods now depended.

Two famous visitors went to the Highlands at this time. Dr Samuel Johnson stayed with the Macdonalds of Sleat among others on his famous journey and expressed disgust at their lack of enthusiasm for the old clan virtues. Robert Burns, visiting Inveraray, was also unimpressed.

> There's naething here but Hielan' pride
> An' Hieland scab an' hunger.

Doubtless he preferred Dunoon where Mary Campbell was one of his more delightful conquests and was immortalised as Highland Mary.

18
NAPOLEON AND THE CLANS

The Napoleonic wars provided massive employment opportunities for the fighting talents of our two clans. Though the wars and migrations of the previous fifty years had led to many premature deaths for their young men from battle and disease and many had died unmarried, the two clans still managed to produce far more men than they lost and continued to generate the vital energy that made them proactive all over the world.

With two or three well-known exceptions, all members of the two clans who fought in the Napoleonic wars were on the same side, but it is two MacDonalds who fought with the French that illustrate some of the most remarkable features of the race. Jacques Etienne Joseph Macdonald (1765–1840) was born in Sedan in the Ardennes, the son of Neil Macdonald, a South Uist Jacobite who had escaped with Bonnie Prince Charlie to France in 1746 and eked out a living as a schoolmaster. Jacques joined the French army in 1785, served in the legion of Maillebois in Holland, then after the revolution transferred to the Irish Regiment of Dillon as a royalist. Had he stayed a royalist his career might have languished, but he was in love with a Mademoiselle Jacob, referred to subsequently as the most beautiful woman in France, and she was a republican. Thus motivated he changed sides, married the girl and joined the staff of Dumouriez. He was a lieutenant by 1791 and a year later showed such outstanding bravery at Jemappes that he was made up to colonel in the field. He led the Picardy cavalry and as a brigadier assisted in the conquest of Holland for Napoleon in 1794, crossing the Waal on the ice and capturing Naarden. Two years later he entered the city of Rome with 12,000 troops and, though significantly outnumbered, he defeated the Austrian General Mack at Otricoli and Colvi. He won again at Modena in 1799 and, though still suffering from a nasty wound sustained in a friendly fire accident, he held his own despite heavy losses in the three-day battle of Trebbia against the Russian General Suvorov. Then came one of the most remarkable feats of the entire war.

Napoleon ordered Macdonald to march his army over the Alps in December 1800. Hannibal and Napoleon had both managed it in the summer but in winter it was regarded as impossible. Napoleon's orders to Macdonald were that an army could pass in any season when two men could place their feet one in front of the other. The guns were pulled on sledges by oxen. The Swiss guides refused to help, so Macdonald had to go on without local knowledge: the route to Rheinthal and Splügen in the Tyrol involved passing cliffs with a drop of 3,000 feet. Macdonald led from the front, braving avalanches, and told his men 'Your glory requires you should rise victorious . . . your destiny calls you.' At one point he lost 100 men who fell into an abyss, but with the rest he made it. This feat has been referred to as 'the most memorable, extraordinary undertaking in modern war'. Napoleon, however, was far from grateful, partly because he resented any other general staking a claim to hero-status and partly because Macdonald was not a good courtier at the Tuileries, did not join in the uncritical adulation of the new emperor – he acquired the nickname of 'His Outspokenness'. So for four years he was kept on the sidelines. Then in 1809 he was given back his command and captured the city of Ljubljana in Slovenia, taking 10,000 prisoners. At the crucial battle of Wagram he commanded eight battalions and pierced the Austrian centre 'pressing on with unconquerable resolution in a frightful storm of bullets', moving aside the wreck of guns, the dead and dying, winning the battle despite huge losses. Afterwards Napoleon held out his hand: 'Touch it, Macdonald, without any further grudge', and Macdonald replied 'Sire, we are now together for life and death.'

General Macdonald was briefly in charge of Vienna, received his marshal's baton and was made Duke of Tarentum. Then he had a year or so commanding the Calabrian front in Spain, probably the one occasion when he was actually fighting other Macdonalds and Campbells, before joining the ill-fated Russian campaign. There he commanded from Riga the Baltic States and managed an orderly retreat after Napoleon's own disaster in Moscow. He helped win the victories of Lutzen and Bautzen but was himself severely beaten by the Prussians at Katzbach, before covering Napoleon's retreat again at Leipzig and swimming the river after ordering the final bridge to be blown up. He was one of the last of Napoleon's marshals to desert him, but when the emperor made his comeback after the escape from Elba, Macdonald refused to help him and therefore took no part in the Waterloo campaign. His career revived under the restored Bourbon monarchy and both his son and grandson followed him in the dukedom. In 1825 he actually visited Scotland for the first time, taken to Benbecula by a British cruiser *Swift* and calling at other Macdonald villages on the west coast and in Northern Ireland.

The other MacDonald on the French side is rather less well known but nearly as remarkable. Francesco Macdonald (1777–1837) was an Italian general of Irish-Scots descent who became Minister of War under Prince Murat when he was King of Naples in 1808. By a twist of fate one of Macdonald's key opponents was a Campbell. Captain Robert Campbell RN of the *Tremendous* led a small fleet into the Bay of Naples in 1815 and threatened to bombard the city unless Napoleon's puppet regime surrendered. Macdonald handled the awkward negotiations that led to the handing over to Campbell of Murat's wife, Queen Caroline, who was also Napoleon's younger sister – she and her children were taken into exile in Trieste. Campbell was a married man but clearly fell victim to Caroline's considerable charms; after the six-week voyage from Naples they exchanged affectionate gifts and he accorded her, quite unnecessarily, a twenty-one gun salute.

Even more susceptible to Caroline's beauty was General Macdonald who had briefly left his desk to command an army, but lost in a battle with the Austrians at Mignano in May 1815. He made his escape and then had the unpleasant task of bringing Caroline the news that her husband Murat had faced a firing squad. His powers of consolation may be judged from the fact that the two seem quite rapidly to have become lovers and may even have been secretly married. Certainly Macdonald managed all Caroline's affairs until he died in Florence in 1837. She died a year later.

Of the MacDonalds on the British side the most notable was probably Sir James MacDonell of Glengarry (1781–1857), brother of the eccentric chief Alastair Ranaldson (see p. 126). Having served in Spain and Egypt by 1807 he became a colonel in the Coldstream Guards at Salamanca and Vittoria. His most famous exploit came in 1815 when he was ordered to occupy the Château Hougoumont with its walled garden on the night before the battle of Waterloo. The holding of this building became a crucial part of the victory that followed. MacDonell was commended personally by Wellington for using his great personal strength to shut the gates of the château. Later, he became a general, was in charge of Armagh 1831–8 and then served as senior officer in Canada during the crisis of 1838.

Other interesting MacDonalds involved in the conflict with Napoleon included John (1759–1831), the youngest son of the great Flora. This engineer served in India and Sumatra as a mapping surveyor, then did a survey of Boulogne ready for the proposed British invasion of 1801. He helped to develop the naval telegraph system which enabled orders to be transmitted faster and further than by the traditional flag method. He also served in Malta as a captain, in Egypt and St Helena, won a gold medal at the battle of Barrosa and became a great advocate of educational reform. His cousin Alexander was a lieutenant-general in the artillery. Also distinguished was Donald MacDonald of Dalchosnie who served in Egypt in 1801, at Copenhagen and Corunna, was shot through both legs at Arroyo dos Molinos but recovered to take part in the big charge of the 92nd at Waterloo where he had two horses shot from under him. He was awarded the Order of Vladimir and other decorations.

There was also Sir John MacDonald (d. 1850), who took part in the capture of Minorca and Malta in 1800, commanded the German Legion at Copenhagen, served also in the Spanish Peninsular War, at Badajoz and was wounded at Vittoria. He later held commands in Jamaica and Ireland. Alexander MacDonald of Keppoch was at the siege of Toulon, and was wounded in the battle of Aboukir Bay in Egypt (1798). He died childless in Jamaica, as did his brother who fought at Waterloo.

Much less orthodox was the career of Ronald McDonnell (d. 1847) who was in the Spanish army allied to the British in the Peninsular War. He later lost all his money at cards and joined the Portuguese army where he rose to be commander-in-chief, and defended the sadistic regime of King Miguel against his brother King Pedro, but was severely defeated at Vila Pouca. With the clans' usual duality there was also a senior Campbell officer in the Portuguese army, Major General

John Campbell (1780–1863) from Chatham, who ran the cavalry in 1809 and reorganised the army after 1814. He settled down in Lisbon with a Portuguese wife. He also took part in the wars of Dom Miguel. Another Campbell also briefly commanded the Portuguese navy (see p. 124).

Slightly unlucky was Colonel Duncan MacDonald of Dalness, who served with the so-called Die Hards* and was wounded at the River Nivelle. Accused of being too soft on his men with regard to the number of floggings he ordered, he committed suicide.

Of the Campbell participants in this war the greatest Campbell soldier perhaps in any century was only an ensign when first he served in Spain and as we shall see Colin was really only a Campbell on his mother's side. Almost his first action was a part in the disastrous Flanders diversion at Walcheren in 1809 where the main enemy was a kind of swamp fever that killed many and left others like Colin Campbell with recurrent bouts of the illness. John MacDonald, who was deputy adjutant-general there, had the same problem. Having recovered from Walcheren and now a lieutenant Campbell was one of the so-called Forlorn Hope in the storming of the fortified convent of San Bartolomeo beside San Sebastian and was twice wounded in a near suicidal attempt to mount the ramparts. In his own typically laconic words: 'On getting to the top I was shot through the hip and tumbled to the bottom. Finding on rising that I was not disabled I went back up to the breech, when I was shot in the hind part of the left thigh.' He then left hospital against orders to take part in the night attack on Bidassoa where he was wounded yet again.

The most successful Campbell in a senior position at this time was perhaps Sir James (1773–1835), who had served with the 42nd Black Watch in Minorca, Gibraltar and with the 94th in Madras, was at Trichinoply in 1803 when his introduction of the bagpipes helped terrify the enemy and he was famous for a march of 984 miles in the Indian campaign to attack Gawil Ghur. He won a significant victory against Mohammed Beg Khan at Timbudra. He then came back to fight in the Peninsular War with Wellesley as a brigadier at Ciudad Rodrigo, was wounded at Vittoria in 1813 and again severely at Salamanca.

---

* Regimental nickname given originally to the 52nd Foot in 1811.

Subsequently, he held a number of posts including governor of Grenada in 1831.

Also distinguished was Sir Archibald Campbell of Glenlyon (1769–1843) who did long service in India and Ceylon before transferring to the 71st Highland Light Infantry, serving at Vimeiro and Corunna, then commanding the 6th Portuguese Regiment at Arroyo dos Molinos, Vittoria and Nivelle River with the rank of major-general. In 1820 he was to move to Rangoon where he defeated the Burmese under Maha Bundoola, stormed the gold-covered Dagon Pagoda and led forty gunboats on the Irrawaddy.

General Alexander Campbell, a friend of the Prince Regent's, led the 4th Division at Talavera, Spain, in 1809 where he captured seventeen guns and impressed with his excellent control over his men, but he fell out of favour with Wellington for his lack of vigour in follow-up. Other Campbells prominent in the Peninsular War included Sir Guy (1786–1849), who had served in Canada in 1803, then Vimeiro, Corunna and the Pyrenees where he was badly wounded. He was on Wellington's staff at Waterloo, rose to be a general and commanded in Ireland in 1841, then in Jamaica, where like so many of this generation he died. Also noteworthy was Sir James Campbell (1763–1819), the last of the Inverneils, who after serving in America was an aide-de-camp to Wellesley in India in 1787, adjutant-general in the Mediterranean in 1805, led the attack on Messina and captured the Ionian Islands. Another Sir James Campbell, this one born in Calcutta (1745–1832), was Nelson's military liaison officer in the Greek Islands but later became eccentrically covetous when he inherited the Ardkinglas estates and fell out successively with three wives and a mistress.

Sir Colin Campbell of Melfort (1770–1847) had originally impressed Wellington in India at the siege of Ahmadnagar where he twice climbed the storming ladder on his own and twice was knocked down, but at the third attempt led a group over the rampart and 'hewed his way through the defenders'. He became one of Wellington's closest aides for the next sixteen years, leading the assault on Badajoz in 1812 where he won the ascent of the faussebrayes (artificial ramps), and commanding a regiment at Salamanca, then on to Waterloo. Amazingly he later bumped into his brother Sir Patrick the admiral in Kingston market, Jamaica.

Yet another Sir Colin Campbell (1754–1814), having served in America and the West Indies where he captured the island of St Lucia from the French in 1796, was sent to Ireland and beat the French there at Ballynahinch, before transferring to Gibraltar which, as Lieutenant-Governor he defended stubbornly against all attacks. Typical of the generation were the four brothers Campbell of Breadalbane, the first of whom died in Jamaica, the next as a captain in India, the third as an army doctor in Guadeloupe and the last again in India, all of them unmarried.

One Macdonald who did survive to middle age was Sir Godfrey (1770–1832), who had changed his name to Bosville when he inherited Thorpe Hall in Yorkshire and rose to the rank of general, but changed it back to Macdonald when he inherited Armadale. He wrote a poem to his wife Louisa from active service in Spain:

> If I fly dear Louisa 'tis not from thy arms
> It is glory which bids me depart
> For in peace or in battle alone can thy charms
> Give warmth to the throb of my heart.

Meanwhile, his brother was on a mission in Moscow where the tsar quizzed him about his family relationship with the Napoleonic Marshal Macdonald.

One senior Campbell who gained brief military glory without going far from home was John, Earl of Cawdor, whose Welsh estates in Pembroke were the scene of a raggle-taggle invasion by the Black Legion, a semi-criminal commando group sent as part of the advance guard of Napoleon's proposed invasion. Cawdor led his local militia against them and rounded up the whole legion without a problem.

The two clans also contributed to the naval war. Sir Patrick Campbell of Melfort (1773–1843), brother of General Colin and later a vice-admiral, was captain of HMS *Dart* in 1800, led two fireships into Dunkirk and destroyed four French frigates. He blockaded Venice in 1806, was sunk in the *Ariadne* and went on to be commander-in-chief on the Cape of Good Hope. Nelson's own secretary during the Nile campaign was John Campbell. He was wounded in the battle, but Nelson grew impatient with his slowness and he was transferred. Captain, later Rear Admiral, George Campbell of Calder (d. 1821) was reputedly one of Nelson's favourite captains in the Mediterranean. However, just before Trafalgar he showed signs of nervous breakdown, was recalled and several years later committed suicide. Another Campbell admiral whose career was cut short was Donald who had a promising start when he captured a French privateer in the West Indies. He later transferred to command the Portuguese navy. It was he who observed the French fleets heading off to the West Indies before Trafalgar and passed on this intelligence to Nelson on the *Victory*. The result was that the French ambassador insisted on his dismissal by the Portuguese and he died soon afterwards in poverty. Better fortune was enjoyed by Captain Colin MacDonald of the *Scylla* who captured a sixteen-gun French privateer *Le Grand Rodeur* in 1809 and a forty-gun frigate off Boulogne in 1813. His prize money must have been considerable.

Remarkably, there was at least one officer from one of our clans on the French side at Trafalgar. He was Commodore Enrique Macdonel of Irish descent, who commanded the *Rayo*, a rotting hulk of a Spanish warship, the only ship present in the battle which did not manage to fire a single shot.

Perhaps the most unfortunate Campbell in the entire Napoleonic period was Sir Neil of Duntrune (1776–1827) who actually saved Napoleon's life when the emperor was a prisoner and threatened by his own people at Orgon in 1814. Sir Neil was then appointed Napoleon's chief gaoler on Elba, where he shared breakfast and a morning stroll with the fallen idol, laying himself open to the charge that he might have been a little too lenient with him. He was then most unfortunately away on business when the ex-emperor succeeded in making his escape. This had the effect of plunging Europe once more into war and Campbell potentially into disgrace. However, he was cleared of all suspicion of bribery. In fact, his military record was otherwise very creditable. He had been a colonel at Salamanca and Ciudad Rodrigo. In 1814 he led a charge of the Russian cavalry and was accidentally wounded by his own side, but he received numerous Russian medals as compensation. In 1815 he led the capture of the town of Cambrai by escalade with the loss of only thirty-five men. He was to end his career as governor of Sierra Leone, trying to locate the missing explorer Mungo Park.

Strangest of the Campbells of this period was one who turned up in 1800 as a general of artillery in the Turkish army of Sultan Selim in

Egypt. He was a Kintyre man apparently exiled because of some murder but now described as a dignified Osmanli with a white beard and turban who burst into tears when he heard the bagpipes played by the banks of the Nile. Even sadder was Alexander Campbell who had soldiered well in Egypt but was executed in 1808 for fighting a duel with a fellow officer in America. More enterprising was the intrepid traveller Sir John Macdonald (1782–1830), sometimes calling himself by his mother's name of Kinneir. This ex-Indian army colonel from Linlithgow specialised in Middle Eastern diplomacy, going on a mission to Tehran in 1808 and Baghdad in 1810. By the usual clan quirk of fate he linked up with a Neil Campbell (1776–1827) to visit the tsar of Russia at Kilsitch to plan a new northern route to India. He died as a close friend of the shah who ordered three months' mourning for the distinguished foreigner.

There was, of course, another round of fighting in North America at this time since the United States supported the French during the Napoleonic Wars. The Glengarry Fencibles took to the field and young John MacDonell of Glengarry was killed at their head, while Colonel Red George MacDonell captured Ogdensburg in 1813 by pretending to hold drills on the frozen river and then turning them into a real attack.

Traditionally it had been the MacDonalds who were more enthusiastic about poetry than the Campbells, but in the Napoleonic Wars the Campbells produced one of the most popular poets of his generation. Thomas Campbell (1777–1844) was the son of a Glasgow tobacco merchant and was born just one year after the trade collapsed when his father was already sixty-seven. After attending Glasgow University he had his first success with 'The Origins of Evil'. Then came 'Lord Ullin's Daughter' and the popular 'Pleasures of Hope', though Campbell was at the time himself quite close to suicide. Later, he settled in Hamburg and Ratisbon, producing his war poems to suit the heroic mood of the time: 'Hohenlinden', 'Ye Mariners of England' and 'The Battle of the Baltic'. He was also a great supporter of Polish nationalism and when he was buried in Westminster Abbey a handful of earth from the Polish leader Kosciusko's grave was put into his. Another nationalist poet was Campbell of Ballymore, an Irish republican who fled to New York after the battle of Antrim:

> Then Campbell eagerly opened the door and boldly entered in
> And he grat with joy at the welcome he got from the kindly Antrim men.

The clans did not produce any specially notable politicians at this time though Sir Archibald Macdonald of East Sheen (1747–1826) did become Attorney General in 1788.

The most influential MacDonald of this period was really not a soldier, politician or poet but a poser – Alastair Ranaldson MacDonell of Glengarry (d. 1820), who became 14th Chief in 1794. Though he was a titular major in the Highland Fencible Infantry he did not see action. When the force was disbanded most of the men and their families went to Glengarry, Canada, in a ship called *Macdonald*, and the regiment was resurrected to fight the United States in 1812. Glengarry himself was vain, extravagant, and had a gang of retainers known as Glengarry's Tail. He was a pioneer of fashionable kilt-wearing as evening dress, of his eponymous hat, of Highland balls, of deerstalking as a rich-man's sport. He created an institution by staging Highland games with exotically ethnic events at Inverlochy. With these reinventions he provided the groundwork for the new Scottish shortbread-packet ethnicity that was promoted by Sir Walter Scott and that, despite its essential phoneyness, has helped quite a few industries to continue to exist. But despite having forced at least 500 of his clansmen to go to Canada and replaced them on his land with sheep, Glengarry's own finances remained in a parlous state. He was always on the verge of bankruptcy.

He was also a dedicated opponent of the new Caledonian Canal, which went right past his ancient castle. In fact, he met his end while trying to leap ashore from one of the new-fangled canal steamers which had hit a rock off Corran.

The Caledonian Canal itself was another by-product of Napoleon, for it was built to create a safe route for ships out of the way of the French privateers who patrolled the North Sea. Together with the new lighthouses it noticeably changed the landscape of the west coast. So did the new iron furnaces like those at Bonawe, the Duke of Argyll's joint venture at Furnace on Loch Fyne, the Campbell Earl of Breadalbane's massive slate quarry on Easdale and the new herring export industry centred on Ullapool. But still the people kept leaving and the sheep kept multiplying.

19
GREEN POTATOES AND THE THIN RED LINE

After the French Wars the clearances continued and indeed became more devastating when the kelp industry finally collapsed – there were now cheaper alternatives like soda ash. Then the onset of potato blight in 1846 decimated a vital source of cheap food. The southward move of the main landowners was also continuing as they found London life more interesting than the Highlands. Glengarry's heir emigrated to Australia, though he failed to make a go of it, and Ranald George McDonald, Captain of Clanranald, began selling off Arisaig and his other properties in 1813. Lord Godfrey Macdonald of Sleat made a gallant effort to help feed his people during the potato famine, but his debts mounted and his bankers warned him that he could not keep it up. Three years later he had to evict 600 people from Sollas, North Uist, and later he had to clear Suisnish and Boreraig on Skye. The Campbells too joined in the clearances. The Campbells of Islay went bankrupt in 1849 and the Breadalbane branch of the family evicted the MacNabs so that they could try to make a living from breeding capercailzie for sport. In 1842 the Marquess of Breadalbane entertained Queen Victoria and Prince Albert at the huge Gothic pile of Taymouth. A special launch was built to take the queen on Loch Tay, the trees were hung with lanterns and a huge guard of honour armed with Lochaber axes welcomed the royal guests. Four duchesses attended the ball and Prince Albert, after massacring a quantity of game, announced that he had enjoyed 'capital sport'. George William, the 6th Duke of Argyll meanwhile, a gambler of striking good looks, was known as the most dissipated rake in London. He reduced himself close to bankruptcy and neglected his Scottish estates. He left only bastards, but his hard-working younger brother succeeded him, married well and restored the family fortunes, helped to some extent by ruthless factors such as Big John Campbell of Tiree and Mull, news of whose death in 1872 was greeted with glee by many of his former tenants who were by then in Canada.

Despite the ethnic cleansing of the tenant classes and the freeing up of land that this was intended to achieve, the landowners among our two clans continued to find excitement and financial benefit from helping to build the British Empire. Of all the acts of war that typified the Campbell/MacDonald contribution no image is more powerful than that of 'the thin red line' at Balaclava. The fact that the line was red showed the extent to which the Highlanders had literally taken on the colour of their paymasters. The fact that the outcome of such a major battle depended on the grit of a Highland regiment showed how much Britain owed her status to the Scots.

Two particular figures, one from each clan, stand out as the great examples of Highland soldiering in the Victorian period: General Sir Colin Campbell (1792–1863 – Campbell was his mother's name and it was her brother who introduced him to the army so it was thought, not surprisingly, that Campbell was a better career name in the army than McIver) and Sir Hector MacDonald. We have already seen (p. 121) Colin Campbell's dramatic early career at Walcheren and in the Peninsula, which ended with him being invalided home in 1813. He recovered but by 1837 – a bachelor in his late forties – he was still only a colonel on garrison duty. Though recognised, as Veronica Wedgewood records, 'as the best administrator and soldier since Wellington' he could not afford to buy promotion and had to earn it. He saw further active service in the Sikh Wars, where he drove the opposing forces back at Chilianwala and Gujarat in 1849, and six years later was sent as a major-general to the Crimea. Despite the anger of other senior officers like the notorious Lord Cardigan, who regarded themselves as his social superiors, Campbell was given command of the Highland Brigade and played the key role in winning the desperate battles against the Russians at Alma and Balaclava. The thin red line was victorious and the Scottish component in it significant. General John Campbell of Glenlyon (1807–55), son of the captor of Rangoon, fought at Alma and Inkerman but was killed leaping out of the trench at the Great Redan.

Soon after the fall of Sebastopol the British faced another crisis when the native troops serving in the British Indian army mutinied against their white British officers. General Colin Campbell, now nicknamed 'Old Take Care', was a natural choice as leader to send out to deal with such an emergency and it was he who relieved the besieged British in Lucknow to the huge gratitude of the government. A popular Victorian painting captured the moment when a lady called Jessie heard the pipes playing 'The Campbells are Coming', proof that relief was about to arrive at last. Campbell was made a field marshal, created Lord Clyde and buried in Westminster Abbey as his reward.

The career of Sir Hector MacDonald (1853–1903) has a few similarities to that of Lord Clyde: he too had to make his own way up through the ranks by merit. He displayed the same total contempt for danger and placed the same low valuation of human life, born perhaps of generations in which only a minority expected to survive to middle age. MacDonald came from even humbler beginnings than Colin Campbell – a Dingwall tailor's shop. He joined the 92nd Gordons as a private in 1870 and over the next thirty years clawed his way up to become a general, an extremely rare feat. He was a sergeant by the time he went out to the Afghan War, where he performed so well at Kabul and Kandahar that he was commissioned in the field and was decorated at least three times.

MacDonald was next posted to South Africa for the first Boer War. In 1880 at Laing's Nek on the Natal border he held back a much larger Boer contingent with only twenty men – he was one of only two survivors. He also fought for a solid seven hours at Majuba Hill. A year or so later he was posted northwards to help in the relief of Khartoum. He was transferred to the Egyptian army as a captain and trained its forces in Highland fighting methods. He learned Arabic, was referred to as MacDonald Pasha and played a major part with Kitchener in the battle of Omdurman by brilliantly wheeling his entire brigade to meet the charging dervishes. Then he went back south again, spending virtually no time at home with his wife in these years, on to yet another war with the Boers. Wounded in the successful attack on the Boer laager at Paardeberg Drift, east of Kimberley, in 1900, he was still leading from the front – though by now he was a major-general.

'Fighting Mac' was a popular icon throughout the British Empire. Then suddenly, disaster. Just after he had taken up post as officer-in-charge of Ceylon in 1903 there came an allegation of indecent behaviour, apparently with a Ceylonese boy of noble birth. As the saying went he 'died like a gentleman'. He shot himself in the Hotel Regina, Paris, on his way to answer the charges. Despite his end, a handsome monument was raised to him outside Dingwall and a sealed envelope due to be opened in 2003 apparently contains some explanation of his final days.

If Colin Campbell and Hector MacDonald typified the remarkable extremes of physical courage that still persisted among the members of our two clans and many others, there were many further examples of subtler variations on the same theme. The MacDonalds picked up two Victoria Crosses at this time, the supreme award for bravery: one was for Colour Sergeant Henry MacDonald who continued sapping the ramparts of Sebastopol under heavy Russian fire; the other award was most unusually to a civilian, William MacDonell, a lawyer and Calcutta judge who took charge of a rudderless riverboat full of victims of the Indian Mutiny and brought them to safety at Arrah in 1857.

Sir Alexander MacDonald of Ardbrecknish served in the Kaffir War of 1846, led a battalion at Inkerman and Alma, and another in the suppression of the Indian Mutiny. Also in the Kaffir War, Major, later General, John I.G. Campbell stood on the roof of the school at Block Drift with four men to keep his rifle loaded and shot three kaffirs, earning the comment from one of his own men 'Weel done sodger.' Sir Arthur Campbell (1835–1908) was wounded at Sebastopol and went on, as a keen amateur scientist, to be a key supporter of the great physicist Lord Kelvin. Brigadier John Campbell (1807–55) displayed 'courage amounting to rashness' at Alma and Inkerman. Sir John MacDonald, the adjutant-general, gave Lord Cardigan and the other officers of the Light Brigade a severe lecture on working relationships, but as we all know it had no effect. An almoner called Mr MacDonald went out of his way to help Florence Nightingale obtain medical supplies.

In civilian life George Douglas Campbell, 8th Duke of Argyll, held government office for twenty-two years, mainly under William Gladstone. He supported the Crimean War in principle, but was totally opposed to the Afghan War and was so against Home Rule for Ireland that he fell out with Gladstone over the subject. He was also a major critic of Charles Darwin and his theories of evolution.

Also in cabinet was Lord Chief Justice John Campbell who became Lord Chancellor in 1857 and is most often remembered for his introduction of the Obscene Publications Bill. The nation, he thought, was being attacked by 'a poison more deadly than prussic acid' – pornography.

Several members of both clans played key roles in India in addition to Baron Clyde. Colonel Herbert Campbell led Hudson's Horse at the siege of Delhi in 1857. John Campbell of Melfort (1802–78), described as 'a man of outstanding perseverance and humanity', governed the Khonds of Orissa and did his best to get rid of both female infanticide and human sacrifice. So persistent was he that he became a hero in Khond legend known as the Great Kiabon Sahib. Sir George Campbell (1824–92) took charge of Lucknow after the mutiny, became an expert on Indian culture, stood up particularly for the rights of Muslims, and worked tirelessly to reduce the effects of famine. Similarly, the Catholic Baron John MacDonnell from Mayo (1844–1925) was exceptionally active in tackling famine relief and turned down the lucrative governorship of Bombay to help the starving in Bengal in 1898. Major-General James MacDonald (1862–1927) built railways into Afghanistan and Uganda and was a pioneer of balloons as observation platforms during the Boxer Rebellion in China in 1900. General Frederick Campbell (1860–1943) was one of the heroes of the North-West Frontier, serving for seven years with the 40th Pathans and taking part in the 1903 expedition into Tibet. Several other Campbells were involved in mapping and surveying Afghanistan and other remote areas. Colonel Robert Campbell of Barcaldine was not unusual in mastering three extra languages: Persian, Urdu and Hindi. His four brothers were all in the Indian army and his father had introduced the bagpipes to his Sikhs.

Several Campbells and MacDonalds were killed in the Indian Mutiny. Major MacDonald of Glenaladale was half scalped by one of his own sepoys and restored discipline by personally hanging the sepoy, using a moving elephant instead of the customary trapdoor. There were other by-products of Far Eastern service – Lieutenant J.G.C. Campbell of the Bengal Artillery was cashiered for drunkenness.

Perhaps due to the shortage of white women not a few Highlanders settled down with Indian wives. Colonel Archibald Campbell of

Dunstaffnage (d. 1912) had a wife called Golati and four Anglo-Indian children. There is a delicate reference to Mr Campbell, an Anglo-Indian officer, in other words one of mixed race, serving under Ranjit Singh, the Lion of Punjab. He showed great gallantry, was wounded at Kandahar and himself had an Afghan wife and daughter in Kabul.

Many Highlanders died young, like Colonel Alexander Campbell (1821–44), who had saved the life of a Lascar sailor in a storm and 'shot a tiger in circumstances showing great pluck'. He was killed in a skirmish at Savendroog and his body was saved by 'a plucky sepoy', an act rewarded by the appreciative citizens of Perth. The navy had less fighting to do than in previous generations but Admiral Sir Reginald MacDonell of Clanranald (1813–99) served worthily throughout the world.

The presence of the two clans was also evident in the Boer War, particularly in the person of Sir Hector MacDonald (see p. 128). Ivan Campbell was in the Scots Guards. John Campbell served in the Mounted Police of the Cape of Good Hope, but died in Burma.

Among other colourful characters was the amazing Lieutenant Ronald Campbell who ended up as the Baron von Craignish, a title given by the Duke of Saxe-Coburg Gotha. Half-Australian and half-Boer, he had joined the 7th Magdeburg Cuirassiers as a private and won his commission in the field at Sadowa fighting for Bismarck against the Austrians. He was probably the only Campbell to win the Iron Cross, which was awarded after he saved the life of his colonel at Vionville in 1871. As so often happened, there was at least one MacDonald on the other side in this conflict, for Alexander Macdonald, 2nd Duke of Tarentum, son of the Napoleonic marshal, was a member of the Corps Legislatif of Napoleon III and was sufficiently committed to have to go into exile with his master in 1870 when Bismarck toppled him from power.

Perhaps even more exotic was Arthur Campbell Pasha, yet another Campbell working for the Ottoman sultan, who claimed to have subdued the Serbs in 1877. He may have been the same person as the Camil Pasha who was governor of Belgrade in 1842. He was certainly not the same as the extraordinary journalist Alastair Campbell who in 1877 took charge of some wandering Turkish soldiers and defeated an invading Russian force in the Shipka Pass, earning himself several Turkish medals and the nickname Shipka Campbell. He was to die in dramatic circumstances two years later (see p. 143). More conventional but just as cosmopolitan was Sir Claude MacDonald who rose by his skill as a sympathetic negotiator with tribesmen to become the governor of Nigeria. It was he who employed Mary Slessor there as a missionary in 1876 and he was later the chief British diplomat in Peking at the time of the Boxer Rebellion.

But most symbolic in this period of the competitive and daredevil urge of the MacDonalds was Reginald McDonald who was the first to conquer the Jungfrau in 1864 – a pioneer wearing tweed jacket and stout brogues in the collection of inaccessible peaks. More poignant still was the life of the promising young novelist Harriette Campbell (1817–41) who died aged twenty-three just after the publication of her work *The Cardinal Virtues or Morals and Manners Connected*. Less sensitive was the thirty-year-old spendthrift Lord Macdonald of Sleat who tried to reduce his debts by withdrawing grazing rights at Braes on Skye in 1882 and caused a serious riot. In the end he backed down so as not to offend his shooting pals.

20

TAMING THE WEST

We have seen many examples of the parallel spread of our two clans and the strangely coincidental places where they sometimes still met on opposite sides. One of the most dramatic of these occurred in Canada in the 1870s. In 1867 John Alexander Macdonald became the first prime minister of the new Dominion of Canada and in 1878 Queen Victoria's representative as Governor-General of Canada was none other than John Douglas Sutherland Campbell, later the 9th Duke of Argyll. As we shall see, when it came to confrontation it was the grandson of a poor MacDonald emigrant who outmanoeuvred the aristocratic Campbell marquess.

John Alexander Macdonald (1815–91) was born in George Street, Glasgow, his grandfather having been evicted from Sutherland. In 1820 the family emigrated to Kingston, Ontario. John trained as a lawyer and quickly made his reputation with a vehement if ultimately futile defence of the Polish-American rebel Nils von Shoultz. By 1844 he was a Conservative member of the Ontario or Upper Canada Assembly. He was also a member of the Orange Lodge, positioned, therefore, as at least marginally hostile to French and Scottish Catholics whose bishop in Kingston at the time was a MacDonnell.

Three years later at the age of thirty-two Macdonald was briefly in the cabinet. Then he was out and back in again in 1854, briefly prime minister in 1857 and effective leader until 1862 when he was replaced for two years by the liberal John Sandfield Macdonald (1812–74), member for Glengarry. John Alexander then came back as attorney-general and began his main task: he first proposed the uniting of Upper

and Lower Canada as a single dominion, then when the opportunity
arose suggested that this should also include the colonies of Nova Scotia
and New Brunswick. The whole process was accelerated by the
pressures of the American Civil War with its threat to what was
regarded as British America and particularly the danger that the United
States might take over the whole Pacific coast.

Macdonald went to London to see that the act of union was passed
and, as a man who enjoyed a drink, had the misfortune to nod off over
his papers, upset his candle and set himself on fire. But undeterred by
his burns he still spoke the next day and the new Dominion of Canada
was created with himself as its first prime minister. Significantly, he
made sure that the key subsidiary job of premier of Ontario was given
to his old rival John Sandfield Macdonald whose presence there helped
attract Nova Scotia into the federation. Remarkably, Sir Alexander
Campbell (1822–92) from Hull was John Alexander's legal partner, took
part in the Charlottetown conference and became a pro-federal cabinet
member, though he later transferred to the opposition.

With one five-year break after 1873, Macdonald was prime minister
of Canada for the rest of his life, in total some twenty years. His most
distinctive characteristics were his conservatism and his Britishness and
it was essentially in this area that he fell out with the new Governor-
General John Campbell, Marquess of Lorne (1845–1914), who came
out to Canada from Britain in 1878 and who had been a Liberal MP.

Born in London, educated at Eton and Cambridge, Campbell was
rather in the shadow of a successful father for whom as Secretary of
State for India he acted as parliamentary secretary. At twenty-six the
young MP married the queen's daughter Princess Louise and this no
doubt helped his promotion to the job in Canada. The disagreement
with Macdonald was over the actions of the French-speaking Deputy
Governor of Quebec, Luc Letellier, who had dismissed Macdonald's
Tory colleagues from the administration of that province. Macdonald
thought the dismissals unjustified and asked for Letellier to be fired by
London. The mild marquess opposed this idea – as coincidentally did
Macdonald's old colleague Sir Alexander Campbell. The belligerent
Macdonald insisted that they consult the London cabinet, which
backed the prime minister, not the governor-general. Campbell had to
swallow his pride and the remaining five years of his relationship with
Macdonald seem to have been without mishap. Macdonald referred to

Campbell as 'a right good fellow and a good Canadian' but it is probable that the marquess, who preferred writing poetry and novels to the rough and tumble of politics, had to shut his eyes to the crudely commercial, nationalist aggression of Macdonald's government. In 1873 there had been a major scandal when it was discovered that the Canadian Pacific Railway Company had made a massive contribution to the Tory election expenses, and Macdonald, who was a master of the game of party politics, only just escaped censure.

Even less savoury was the policy close to ethnic cleansing that Macdonald encouraged in Manitoba where he wanted to marginalise the Metis, people of mixed European and Indian descent. These people included some half-Indian Macdonalds, and other Metis who had come to dominate that area but were now dispossessed by whites. It also included native Americans whose nickname for Macdonald was 'Old Tomorrow'. Macdonald's least attractive act was the hanging of the demonised Meti leader Louis Riel in 1885. In the same year the last ruthless spike was knocked into the Canadian Pacific Railway track at Craigellachie, British Columbia, thanks to cheap immigrant Chinese labour which Macdonald had encouraged to come to Canada for that one task alone. Certainly Macdonald created modern Canada, but at the cost of somewhat repressing some of its native peoples and to a lesser extent its French-speaking minority.

His first wife had been bedridden for many years and after her death he married a woman much younger than himself, saying that his new union symbolised the union of the new Canada. Regrettably their only child had severe brain damage. However, Macdonald never lost his sense of humour, once famously signing the visitors' book at Charlottetown with 'Cabinet maker' as his profession, and when he vomited in the midst of a political rally he quipped instantly 'The opposition leader made me sick.'

Meanwhile, there was another part of North America where the Campbells and MacDonalds played a significant role, sometimes on opposing sides. Not surprisingly there were members of both clans on both sides in the American Civil War (1861–5). One of the most interesting was John A. Campbell (1811–99), the Supreme Court judge from Alabama who tried his hardest to stop the war by negotiating with Secretary Seward over Fort Sumter. He was also the last member of the

Confederate cabinet to leave Richmond and the most persistent in trying to restore Virginia to the Union. Describing himself as 'the gentler gamester is the soonest winner', he met Abraham Lincoln for peace talks on the *Malvern* anchored off Rocket's Landing. Also opposed to the war was Joseph E. McDonald, an Indiana Democrat (1824–1908) who later sat in the Senate. Surprisingly, a black Campbell, Reverend J.P. Campbell of the Methodist Episcopal church from Trenton, New Jersey, attacked Lincoln as too warlike against the south.

In favour of secession was Charles J. McDonald (1793–1860), governor of Georgia, but he died before it began. Active in the Confederate army were Henry F. Campbell an Irish Virginian, James Campbell (1812–93) an Irish Pennsylvanian, and Josiah Campbell, a colonel who was wounded at Vicksburg. This last was later employed to help suppress the Ku Klux Klan but lost his job when his own Confederate past was revealed.

On the Union side was Brigadier William Campbell (1800–67), Republican governor of Tennessee, a hero of the Mexican Wars where his men of the 'Bloody First' had won at Vera Cruz. Lewis D. Campbell (1811–82), also a veteran of Mexico, was a colonel in the Ohio Volunteers. Allan Campbell (1815–94), who had built railways in Georgia and Argentina, organised the harbour defences of New York, while another railway pioneer, James H. Campbell (1820–95), fought against General Lee as a colonel in the 39th Pennsylvania Volunteers. Another John A. Campbell (1821–1905), who fought in Mexico, was later first governor of Wyoming, based in Cheyenne, and a pioneer of women's rights. But perhaps most remarkable of all was the black leader Tunis G. Campbell from Massachusetts who, at the outset of the Civil War, set up an independent black state on the Georgia Sea Islands. Another notable black Campbell was Lottie who pioneered human rights in Utah.

Among those who helped open up the frontier were many trappers and fur traders from both clans, about whom James Hunter has written in fascinating detail in his *Dance called America*. Miles Macdonell (1767–1828), son of Scotas (see p. 111) and an ex-captain in the Loyalist Royal Canadian Volunteers, was chosen by the Earl of Selkirk to develop the Red River Colony by Lake Winnipeg. In 1811 he founded Fort Douglas and was governor of the province of Assiniboia, but made himself unpopular by restricting exports of pemmican.

Archibald MacDonald from Glencoe joined the Hudson's Bay Company and as Chief Trader led a group of around ninety in horrendous conditions using heavy rowing boats like Highland birlinns to reach the mouth of the Red River and Lake Winnipeg in 1814. Later, he made a descent of the Fraser River and was in charge of Fort Colville on the Columbia River. Marjory Campbell, chronicler of the North-West Company described the 'singing of tender Scottish ballads and naughty French songs to the sensuous slip-slap of moccasined feet'. Finan 'Buffalo' McDonald from Garth was one of the first to explore the Snake River in Idaho and had to fight the Blackfeet there. Richard Campbell pioneered a new overland route to California, coming over the desert from Colorado in 1827. Robert Campbell (1808–94), a chief factor of the Hudson's Bay Company, explored the Mackenzie River in northern Canada, discovered the Pelly River, went down the Yukon, covered 3,000 miles of wilderness and escaped after being captured by Indians to reach the Pacific by the River Stikine. He founded Fort Selkirk in the Yukon and found gold but did not regard it as of great interest, a view shared by the Reverend Macdonald who also found the precious metal. Robert Campbell later retired to Manitoba.

Another Robert Campbell, this one from Ulster (1804–79), was sent to the mountains for his health and fought the Blackfeet at Pierre's Hole before setting up Fort Laramie on the Oregon Trail in Wyoming. Later, he established his own fur company and settled in St Louis. Angus MacDonald came to America from Glencoe in 1838, joined the Hudson's Bay Company and married the daughter of an Indian chief while involved in exploration of the Colorado River. McDonald Peak in Montana is named after him and Lake McDonald after his son, Duncan.

Ranald MacDonald (1824–94), the son of Archibald, the Hudson's Bay man who had married a Chinook or Nez Percé (pierced nose) princess in Fort George, went to sea as a whaler and had himself deliberately marooned on the coast of forbidden Japan. He survived capture and numerous adventures to become a pioneer of Japanese–American relationships and the first teacher of English in Japan. Later he was a gold prospector in Australia before returning to settle down in the USA.

Further south Thomas and Elizabeth Campbell of Skye lost thirteen of their children from smallpox as they headed in the wagon train to Salt Lake City. Then Thomas found a job in the stone quarry used to build the great Mormon Temple. Peter Campbell settled on some land 10 miles from Grand Island on the River Platte, Nebraska; two of his children were kidnapped by the Sioux. Little Dave Campbell served in G Troop, US Cavalry, with General Custer at the battle of Little Bighorn in 1876. He took a bullet in the shoulder but told his companions 'Go on boys. I can make it back some way', and he did.

Both Campbells and MacDonalds are found on both sides of the law in the Wild West of the 1870s. George Campbell was a trouble-maker in El Paso. He backed out of a fight but still managed to get himself shot and it is recorded that his dying words actually were: 'You big son of a bitch, you murdered me.' Deputy Sam Campbell in Oklahoma led a posse that failed to capture Nathaniel Wyatt. In 1879 William Campbell shot a one-armed lawyer in Lincoln, New Mexico. George McDonald of Buffalo Gap kept a bullet on his watch chain, but was shot down by a cattle rustler in 1888. Deputy John MacDonald of Abilene, Texas, was outnumbered in a gunfight in 1870. Rather more sophisticated was Big Mike Cassius McDonald (1837–1907), a professional gambler who became the underworld boss of Chicago from 1873 until his death. His first scam had been to claim bounty for recruiting Union soldiers in the Civil War, encourage them to desert and then claim a second bounty for recruiting them all over again. His ultimate rake-off was 40 per cent of all the profits from gambling and prostitution in Chicago, but he grew soft in old age and fell in love with a showgirl called Dora, thirty-five years his junior. When she went off with a sixteen-year-old McDonald became depressed and died.

Less antisocial was the work of Thomas (1763–1854) and Alexander (1788–1866) Campbell, a father and son team from Ulster. The two firebrand preachers could pull massive crowds and set up a variant on the Baptist church in Illinois that by the end of the century had over a million members, including the mother of future US President Ronald Reagan. Thomas and Alexander were both major opponents of slavery. Among their earliest disciples back in the old country were the Campbells of Rosneath and the McDonalds of Port Glasgow. Isabella Campbell of Rosneath, who was to die young of tuberculosis, became a well-known mystic with the gift of tongues. She was credited with the miracle cure of the crippled sister of James McDonald of Port Glasgow.

Francis J. Campbell (1832–1914), a blind man from Tennessee, became a pioneer of employment opportunities for the blind and himself climbed Mont Blanc in 1880 to prove that the disability could be overcome. Also more peaceful was John Campbell who moved to Little Scotland on the Wind River, Wyoming, and introduced the settlers there to ceilidh music on his melodion. In 1827 Duncan Campbell of Greenwood invented a stitching machine for shoes while John Taafe MacDonald became a successful chocolate-maker in Utah. George Washington Campbell (1817–98) moved from New York to Cherry Valley, then to Delaware, Ohio, where he became a hugely successful breeder of the Delaware and Campbell Early grapes. The Delaware subsequently became the leading grape variety in many other countries, including Japan.

In 1866 Alexander MacDonald (1821–81), born in New Monklands, Lanarkshire, the charismatic leader of the British mineworkers, came to America to visit the 12,000 Scots miners working in the United States. Eight years later he was elected the first so-called working-class (though not Labour Party) member of the British parliament. This was a momentous achievement and he showed his calibre by pushing through a bill to reduce the working day for young boys to ten hours. For the Fife miners he won an eight-hour day. As so often happens in our narrative, this Alexander MacDonald had a Campbell sparring partner – Alexander Campbell (1796–1870), an Owenite trade unionist from Skipness who was working on the *Sentinel* newspaper, a Glasgow-based organ for working-class improvement, when MacDonald took it over.

Meanwhile, Captain John Campbell RN (see p. 115) had come close to being the discoverer of Australia instead of his protégé Captain Cook. Campbell, an ex-collier skipper, was on the 1767 Royal Society committee that planned the *Endeavour* voyage and – as a very experienced navigator, an active supporter of John Harrison's new chronometer and himself a pioneer of the use of the sextant – was considered for the command. But he already had a larger ship and instead backed his junior, Lieutenant James Cook, who took the job and in gratitude named Cape Campbell after him.

Some American Scots moved on to Australia and New Zealand. Hugh Campbell travelled from Nova Scotia in 1845 to join the California gold rush before going on to make his fortune in the Australian gold fields. Other members of both clans were deported as convicts or travelled as emigrants direct from Scotland or England. In fact, it was a relation of Captain John Campbell, Duncan Campbell, a ship-owner and contractor in charge of prison hulks on the Thames (known popularly as 'Campbell's Academies'), who first worked out the logistics of sending convicts to Botany Bay in 1786. This remarkable, but little known, Campbell owned plantations inherited by his Campbell wife Rebecca in the West Indies. He was such a key figure in London's colonial trade that he was made chairman of the creditors who this same year negotiated with the future president of the United States, Thomas Jefferson, over the losses suffered by British landowners during the War of Independence.* But it was as a shipping contractor that he played a major part in the creation of Australia and the exploration of the Pacific (see p. 143) though his motives were purely financial. A civil servant of the time wrote 'the hulks in the River Thames under the direction of Mr Campbell are at present so crowded that any additions to their numbers would most likely produce disease'. However, when the first two transport ships put to sea the avaricious Campbell, who had been paid handsomely by the government, substituted rice for flour in prisoners' rations and in smaller quantities so that malnutrition and disease soon struck anyway.

Typical of this story, one of the first officers sent on Duncan Campbell's convoy and put in charge of a convict settlement at Sydney Cove and Parramatta in 1788 was a marine – Captain James Campbell – and one of the first convicts to be killed by Aboriginals was a MacDonald. An A.M. Campbell was one of the first to settle in Moonlight Creek, Australia, and was an early student of the Aboriginal language. The MacArthurs were also key figures among the early settlers and they were descendants of Arthur Campbell of Dunstaffnage.

Robert Campbell (1767–1846), son of the Greenock town clerk, Campbell of Ashfield, went out to join the Calcutta offices of Campbell, Clark & Co. in around 1797 but he rapidly moved on to Australia. Having arrived at Dawes Point on the *Hunter* in 1798, he set up an office at what is now Campbell's Wharf in Port Jackson, initially importing liquor, convicts and cattle. Soon realising the need to find a cargo for his homeward-bound ships, he encouraged sealers, such as William Campbell who by 1802 was the most successful of a number in the Bass Straits, and by 1810 they were in the Campbell Islands, New

* I am grateful for this information to Dan Byrnes of New South Wales.

Zealand. Thus Robert Campbell became the first man to send back a shipload of Australian merchandise to Britain direct, bypassing the East India Company monopoly. Soon afterwards he became the first shipbuilder in Australia and a founding partner in the first bank. Having initially made most of his profit from liquor imports, the poacher turned gamekeeper, standing by the unpopular new governor William Bligh, formerly master of a Campbell sailing ship (see p. 143), when he made his ill-fated attempt to crack down on the illegal rum trade, even doing a short spell in prison for his efforts and going temporarily bankrupt while involved in supporting Bligh's defence.

One of the first Scots in Tasmania was a convict – Archibald J. Campbell from the ship *Calcutta* – and he settled there with an Aboriginal wife in around 1819. Elsewhere on the continent, Robert Campbell, the son of the pioneer emigrant to Botany Bay, objected to the emancipation of convicts in 1837. Angus MacDonell, chief of Glengarry came to Gippsland early in 1841 with around thirty other Glengarry MacDonells, settling around Port Albert and Greenmount with 500 cattle, but he himself failed to make a go of it and went home after about a year. Regrettably, when he died eight years later he left such huge debts that his wife Josephine felt obliged to clear Knoydart and her factor ruthlessly emptied seven communities on that remote peninsula. Meanwhile, John Campbell from Tiree and Glencoe stayed on and had a run called Glencoe on the La Trobe River near Alexander McDonald of Skye who called his run Armadale. J.D. Lyon Campbell (d. 1844) was a well-known Melbourne snob while Archibald Campbell was a squatter in Port Philip as were some Campbells of both Kilberry and Lochnell.

A sawyer called Campbell built one of the first European houses in New Zealand in 1815 at Waitangi and the later Vice-Admiral David Macdonald of Kinlochmoidart, who had served up the River Yangtse in HMS *Hazard* was badly wounded at Korararika when he was involved in the Maori War of 1845. Afterwards he went on to put down the African slave trade and risked his life to rescue a drowning sailor. Captain Thomas MacDonell, known as 'Fighting Mac' for his earlier exploits against the Maoris, was appointed second British Resident in 1819 and forbade the sale of alcohol but he suffered a humiliating defeat at Titokowari in 1868.

John Logan Campbell (1817–1912) was one of the first entrepreneurs in New Zealand and started his business from a tent. He made his money out of brewing but preferred to drink burgundy himself. Known as the father of Auckland, he referred to Britain scathingly as 'ye milch cow John Bull' but still sent his children back there to be educated. And as a memento he left the parkland of One Tree Hill to the city of Auckland in his will. Robert Campbell, the Eton-educated son of an Australian sheep baron owned a million acres of New Zealand at one point – a reminder of older Campbell habits back in Britain.

One of the most remarkable of the wandering Campbells was Archibald who wrote his *Voyage Round the World 1806–12* and settled in Hawaii as a beachcomber, ending up with fifteen servants and a large area of land in his capacity as the king's chief sail-maker. But there were other Campbell connections with the South Sea Islands. Duncan Campbell, the ubiquitous master of the prison hulks, also owned three other ships trading in the West Indies. One of them, the *Bethia*, was captained by a mariner called William Bligh, who was married to Campbell's niece and had Fletcher Christian as his trainee midshipman. The irrepressible Campbell sold the *Bethia* to the Royal Navy, which changed her name to *Bounty* in 1787. Campbell then organised Bligh as captain of her mission to collect breadfruit plants from the Pacific so that they could be grown in the West Indian plantations, several still owned by other Campbells. There is no need to repeat the details of Bligh's famous voyage to Tahiti and, as we have seen, the unpopular captain also had Campbell connections when he became unpopular again as governor of New South Wales. William Campbell (1770–1827) was another remarkable sailor who spent some time as a pirate raiding the South American coast, then became the archetypal Tahiti schooner captain trading in pearl shells.

Southern Africa also attracted members of both clans from an early stage. One of the most unusual Campbells living in this area of the world was John (1766–1840) who had founded the Religious Tract Society back in Britain in 1793 and then became involved in the tricky task of rescuing prostitutes for the Magdalen Society of Edinburgh in 1793. Under the influence of the anti-slave trade campaigner William Wilberforce he travelled huge distances in southern Africa, a squat figure with a black umbrella, helping escaped slaves. He even discovered the source of the Limpopo River. Then in 1820 he helped to establish a mixed-raced community at Griqualand West, ruled over by Hottentot

Griquas with Boer names. The idea was perhaps a little ahead of its time, and regrettably it did not survive the massive influx of white diamond prospectors who began to descend on nearby Kimberley. Among these, needless to say, were at least two Campbells, the brothers of the famous 'Shipka' – but rather naively they sold their concession at Kimberley to Cecil Rhodes of De Beers whose fortune they consequently helped to make. Shipka himself, a mere two years after his Turkish adventure (see p. 132), became involved in one of the battles of the Zulu War of 1879 and, with yet another display of bravado, disappeared into a Zulu-held cave, never to be seen again. Among other Campbells killed in the same campaign was Lieutenant Ronald of Cawdor, who accused his colonel of cowardice for holding back and himself dashed against the Impis to certain death.

Rather more practically William Campbell from Uist pioneered the sugar beet industry in Natal. Another Duncan Campbell developed the wool industry and Hugh McDonald ran the only hotel in Durban in 1849. Meanwhile, George Macdonnell, a brilliant forger of American bank notes decided to try his hand at English ones, but was caught in London in 1873 and had to serve eighteen years in prison.

That very year the Campbells, who according to the up-and-coming politician Tom Johnston had a rather more sophisticated approach to illicit acquisition, owned between them 1½ million acres of Scotland as well as huge tracts of America, Australia, New Zealand and the West Indies. The MacDonalds had very little left in Scotland and except for Canada were well behind their old rivals in the possessions they owned in the empire.

21
ON THE LEFT WING AGAIN

Once again in the early twentieth century there came one of those remarkable coincidences that link the story of our two clans: a Campbell and a MacDonald each became prime minister of Great Britain less than twenty years apart and the MacDonald one was, of all things, brought down by an incident known as the 'Campbell case'.

As the new century dawned there were two Campbells in the government. Frederick, Earl of Cawdor (1847–1911) was First Lord of the Admiralty in Arthur Balfour's cabinet and together with the redoubtable Admiral Fisher played a significant part in the building of the first 'Dreadnought' class battleships that were a key part of British imperial posturing in the prelude to the First World War. This Wales-based Campbell was also a successful chairman of the Great Western Railway. The other Campbell in the Balfour administration was James, later Baron Glenavy (1851–1931), who was attorney-general for Ireland at the time of the Easter Rising and became Lord Chancellor in 1918. He was a staunch pro-Unionist, but when Ireland was released from the United Kingdom in 1922 he overcame his scruples and became chairman of the senate of the Irish Free State. Of not so very different persuasion in Irish politics was Anthony MacDonnell, later Baron Swinford (1844–1914), a Catholic from Lisburn who held office as Chief Secretary for Ireland. There was also 'Pom' MacDonell, Lord Salisbury's private secretary when he was prime minister.

Henry Campbell-Bannerman (1836–1908) was born plain Campbell at Kelvinside House, Glasgow – now the site of the BBC offices – to the merchant draper family of J. and W. Campbell of which he was a partner until 1868 when he entered parliament, two years after the

birth of Ramsay MacDonald. He added the maternal Bannerman to his
name in 1873 when the somewhat less privileged six-year-old Ramsay
(1866–1937), son of an unmarried couple (Anne Ramsay and a
Lossiemouth ploughman John MacDonald), was starting his basic
schooling. By a curious coincidence both men, therefore, used the
surnames of both their parents. In 1884 Campbell-Bannerman was
appointed Chief Secretary for Ireland (although not in the cabinet) by
Gladstone and he did well in a notoriously difficult post. As Charles
Parnell put it, 'as Irish Secretary he left things alone, a sensible thing
for an Irish Secretary' and unlike his clan chief the Duke of Argyll, who
resigned from the government, he accepted the principle of Home Rule.

In 1886 at the age of fifty Campbell-Bannerman was briefly Secretary
of State for War, about the same time as young Ramsay at twenty
moved to Bristol to run a boys' club and was editing a magazine called
Socrates. The MacDonald, like the Campbell, supported Irish Home Rule
and when he moved back to London as an invoice clerk he became a
party worker for the Liberals in the 1889 election. One of Campbell-
Bannerman's main achievements as war secretary was to set an
example by lowering the working week at Woolwich Arsenal to
48 hours. MacDonald, meanwhile, left the Liberals to join the
Independent Labour Party (ILP) and two years later married Margaret
Gladstone, who brought him emotional and financial security. He was
able to visit the United States for three months in 1893 and in 1898
founded the Society of Ethical Propagandists. Two years later he was
secretary of the ILP, though he had still not succeeded in getting into
parliament. Campbell-Bannerman on the other hand was now reaching
the pinnacle of his career, for in 1899 he became leader of the Liberal
Party in succession to Lord Roseberry.

These two politicians had one thing in particular in common – a
huge suspicion of and dislike for unnecessary wars. Campbell-
Bannerman risked accusations of lack of patriotism in 1900 when,
appalled by news of British ill-treatment of prisoners in concentration
camps, he called the Boer War 'a barbarity'. In just the same way
fourteen years later Ramsay MacDonald was referred to slightingly as
'the Kaiser's friend' for questioning some of the motives for First World
War aggressive posturing.

As party leader Campbell-Bannerman had a frustrating period of six
years in opposition until Balfour resigned and he at last became prime

minister, without a general election, in 1905. His cabinet included Herbert Asquith, David Lloyd George and Winston Churchill – all future prime ministers – and he began a series of radical reforms of taxation and the House of Lords. A year later he fought and won the 'khaki' election (so-called because the country had been at war) and at last Ramsay MacDonald also entered the Commons – as Labour member for Leicester, one of twenty-nine in the new parliament. Remarkably, Campbell-Bannerman supported MacDonald's private member's bill on trade union reform, surprising since the government had a similar bill of its own on the stocks.

However, despite his political success Campbell-Bannerman's private life was quite miserable. His wife had been unwell for some time and she died at Marienbad, while his own health was far from good. Nevertheless, for a further two years he continued to lay the foundations for reform and was an early supporter of women's suffrage. Described as modest and a lover of peace, he controlled the party with quiet humour rather than fiery rhetoric. He won round Edward VII to his liberal policies, met the French leader Georges Clemenceau and did his best to calm the Kaiser down, but after a serious heart attack he resigned in April 1908 and died three weeks later. Asquith, his successor, described him as 'not of a defiant and aggressive type, but calm, patient, persistent and indomitable'. But for the higher profile given by British history to the war leaders who followed him, his reputation would perhaps be considerably greater.

While it had taken Campbell-Bannerman nearly forty years to move from the back benches to Downing Street, it took Ramsay MacDonald less than twenty. A mere three years after the Campbell's death the MacDonald was leader of his party. When the Liberal Party disintegrated in 1922, the Labour Party became the official opposition.

Two years later Ramsay MacDonald was leader of the first Labour government, albeit a minority one. By one of those strange coincidences of which we have already seen numerous examples it was a Campbell who contributed significantly to this first Labour government's fall. John R. Campbell (1894–1969) was a Greenock Communist. Though he had an excellent war record and had been severely wounded in the conflict, he was a staunch admirer of the Russian Revolution which occurred in the penultimate year of hostilities. To the left of other Red Clydesiders like James Maxton and an embarrassment to a Labour Party taking its first faltering steps to governmental respectability, he wrote a so-called appeal to soldiers in the *Workers' Weekly*: 'Neither in the class war nor in the military war will you turn your guns on your fellow workers.' If the government had ignored such a piece of standard Communist rhetoric it would probably have been hardly noticed, but its legal officers made the mistake of first charging Campbell with incitement to mutiny and then dropping the charges. It looked as though MacDonald's administration had condoned Campbell's behaviour. In an atmosphere where the red menace was already causing panic and the Zinoviev letter, with its supposed threat of Communist expansion, was also being used to discredit Labour this mishandling of the Campbell case was the error of judgement that finally brought the fragile government down.

Ramsay MacDonald was to come back again for another controversial and difficult term from 1929 to 1931. John Campbell was to remain an active, if not hugely successful, Communist who supported the war against Hitler but never got into parliament. He became editor of the *Daily Worker*, in which he violently attacked the war against Korea in 1951. His own son had actually emigrated to Russia where he had an eventful career (see p. 155).

In terms of his reputation as a prime minister Ramsay MacDonald has suffered in some ways like Campbell-Bannerman for not being a great empire builder or war leader and even more for putting country before party. He lost his status as a Labour Party icon by helping to form the 1931 National government and like many other world leaders he failed to solve the problems of the 1930s slump. Nevertheless, his achievements were genuinely outstanding and he deserves better from history than has sometimes been his lot.

Despite the fact that our two clans' best-known politicians were proponents of peace not war the families still produced another crop of exceptional warriors when the First World War broke out. The Campbells were awarded their first three Victoria Crosses (VCs). Colonel John V. Campbell from Cawdor won the medal with the Coldstream Guards at Ginchy les Boeufs in 1916. With his hunting horn he twice rallied his men to the attack after his battalion had been decimated by machine-gun fire. Eventually he routed the Germans from what was known as the Brown Line. The second VC went to a Canadian lieutenant, Frederick Campbell, in similar circumstances. The third VC was awarded to Lieutenant-Commander, later Vice-Admiral, Gordon Campbell, the pioneer captain of Q-Ships or Mystery Ships. These vessels were converted tramps used as decoys but given enough armaments to sink unsuspecting U-boats once they had been enticed close enough by the sight of a tramp's crew taking to the lifeboats. As commander of the *Farnborough* he sank U68 in March 1915, the beginning of a counter-attack against German submarines. His VC was for his second submarine destroyed, the U83, also sunk by the *Farnborough* in 1917, though her decks were red hot and she was so badly damaged that even under tow she barely made it back to port. Campbell then had a third kill, UC28, in the collier *Vittoria* and his methods used by other commanders also resulted in a number of sinkings.

Several MacDonalds were prominent at the battle of Jutland including a cook who put out the fires on his ship, a commander who won the tsar's Order of St Anne on the *Jupiter* and two stokers who died on the *Queen Mary*. Rear Admiral H.H. Campbell commanded a cruiser at the Heligoland Bite in 1914, Commander G.W. Campbell sank a German destroyer at Jutland, Commander V.L. Campbell (who had been to the Antarctic with Captain Scott) won the Distinguished Service Order (DSO) in 1915.

On land Major-General James Alexander Campbell (1886–1964) commanded the East Lancashires in 1917–18, was twice wounded and won the DSO with bar. The Canadian General Archibald MacDonell of Ontario was killed by a sniper in France in 1916 and a Brigadier Leslie Campbell was wounded leading the 89th Punjabis in Mesopotamia in 1914.

In the air Lieutenant Douglas Campbell from California, aged twenty-two, was the first member of the US Air Service squadron to shoot down five enemy aircraft. He was grounded after a severe wound sustained during his sixth kill. I.D.R. McDonald of 24 Squadron RFC was an ace pilot at the age of twenty while Stuart Campbell of 56 Squadron was told to take up a BE12 for night combat having never flown in the dark before. The Campbells produced also at least two wartime inventors: C.D.M. Campbell who, with Brabazon, designed a new reconnaissance camera and Captain C. Campbell who invented a cipher for spies behind enemy lines.

Phyllis Campbell was a young girl attending a Paris house party in 1914 when war broke out. She immediately volunteered to train as a nurse. A year later she wrote a book recording the atrocities she had witnessed committed on Belgian women and children by German troops. It caused widespread horror. Less controversial was the best-known Macdonald nurse, the Canadian Margaret, who was chief matron of the 'Bluebirds' nurses in 1917.

The early decades of the twentieth century also saw a number of other interesting descendants from both clans in most parts of the world. Thomas C. Campbell from Palestine, Texas, was a noteworthy governor of his state in 1906, a major reforming liberal who found that convicts in Texas were still whipped to death for petty crimes. He arranged for the practice to cease. Henry Webster Campbell was a pioneer of agricultural improvement in Illinois, doing his best to prevent the area turning into a dust bowl, while John B. McDonald (1844–1911), a former Tammany Hall employee, was a major railway and tunnel builder on the American east coast. His work included a 2 mile tunnel under Baltimore. Sir John H. Macdonald (1836–1921) was Lord Justice Clerk of Scotland, an excellent shot and a pioneer of motor car driving. Sir Schomberg 'Pom' Macdonell (1861–1915) had been parliamentary private secretary to Lord Salisbury when the latter was prime minister and was a consummate event organiser. He was killed in Flanders in 1915. Charles McDonald (1861–1925) became speaker of the Australian parliament, while Colonel Eric Campbell, a retired AIF (Australian Imperial Force) officer, was a major upholder of the 'Digger' tradition in Australia and founded a new party to get rid of 'commos' and other undesirables.

George Campbell of the Democratic Unionist Party in Northern Ireland was an ardent Loyalist and advocate of something close to ethnic cleansing while on the opposite side Joseph Campbell (1879–1944) was a poet member of the Irish Republican Army who was sent to Mountjoy Prison in 1916. He later moved to New York but returned to die in Glencree. Canada produced both a Campbell poet and a Macdonald painter. The first, Wilfred Campbell, was xenophobically anti-French while J.E.H. Macdonald was an early advocate of the protection of the wilderness and environmentally friendly journeys by canoe.

Among a number of British artists from the two families were the two remarkable Macdonald sisters, Frances and Margaret, pioneers of art nouveau. Margaret (1865–1933) is now chiefly remembered as the wife of the architect Charles Rennie Mackintosh with whom she shared a tempestuous creative partnership. Both clans continued to produce a quota of sculptors, writers, archbishops, entrepreneurs and petty criminals. William Wallace Campbell (1860–1938), the Ohio astronomer, worked out the velocity of stars in 1930 and pronounced unequivocally that there was no life on Mars. Melville Campbell was the first Canadian to be convicted of burglary on fingerprint evidence in 1932 and Dr Henry Campbell was a New Jersey bigamist who killed his first and third wives before going to the electric chair in 1930.

22

BLUEBIRDS AND GOLDEN ARCHES

From the point of view of our two clans, the mid-twentieth century was dominated, at least superficially, by a pair from each family – a father and son Campbell and two brothers McDonald. Neither pair was at the forefront of military or political life but both still showed the frenetic competitive urge that had typified the two families in the past.

Malcolm Campbell (1855–1948) and his son Donald (1921–1967) between them dominated the world of land and water speed records for about half a century. Malcolm came from Kent and made money by selling libel insurance policies to newspapers. Then at Brooklands race track in 1908 he bought a Darracq, which he renamed *Bluebird*, and won his first race. Subsequently, despite numerous horrendous crashes, he won another 400 races, interrupted only by the First World War when he spent two years with the Royal Flying Corps. Then in 1925 he achieved his first world land record with a run at 150 mph on Pendine Sands in Wales. He lifted this to 246 mph at Dayton, Ohio, and then to 300 mph in 1932 at Bonneville, Utah. At this point he turned his attention to water and broke that speed record at 141.74 mph in 1939. Though well into his fifties he volunteered for service in the Second World War and ran a motorcycle unit. Thereafter, his son Donald, who had done war service in the RAF took up the challenge of the water speed record. Six years after his father's death he broke the record at Ullswater, Cumbria, in 1955 travelling at 202.3 mph in a turbojet hydroplane named *Bluebird*. He broke his own record again annually until, in 1964, he reached 276.33 mph on Lake Dumbleyung in Western Australia. He tackled the land speed record again in the

same year with the *Proteus Bluebird* and achieved 403.1 mph at Lake
Eyre salt flats in Australia. A couple of years later a further attempt
on the water speed record at Coniston Water, Cumbria, ended in
disaster. His latest *Bluebird* turbojet boat somersaulted. Campbell died
instantly. Elsewhere, another, unrelated Campbell – Tom Campbell
Black – became joint winner of the 1934 London to Auckland flying
race in a de Havilland DH88, travelling at an average speed of 158.9
mph.

In 1999 the Russian people, struggling with some difficulty to create
a new national identity for themselves, complained about what they
called the 'McDonaldisation' of Russia. Remarkably the name McDonald
had become symbolic of Western or American culture, better known
even than Coca Cola. The first McDonald's restaurant had been opened
in 1948 in San Bernardino, California. The founders of this business
were Dick McDonald (1909–98) and his brother Maurice or Mac. Not
much more than a dozen years later they sold the business to a Ray
Croc for £2.7 million but the concept was theirs. The golden arched M-
symbol became a recognised icon in virtually every city in the world. By
the end of the century the company had nearly 24,000 restaurants and
was the world's largest non-state employer with 220,000 people on its
books and a turnover in excess of $20,000 million.

McDonald's also fought and won the world's longest ever libel case: it
began in 1994 after the company was accused of destroying rain forests
and lasted for three years. The company is now based at Oak Brook,
Illinois.

The next largest commercial concern founded by either of the two
clans began in 1939 when an engineer named James Smith McDonnell
aged forty from Little Rock, Arkansas, set up his own business,
McDonnell Aircraft Corporation, in Lambert Field near St Louis. He had
previously worked at Ford and had earlier designed a Doodlebug
aircraft. Now he began to build fighters and bombers for the US Air
Force, including the highly successful Phantoms and the first jet to land
on an aircraft carrier. In 1959 the company built the Mercury
spacecraft for NASA and eight years later took over the struggling
Douglas Corporation. The new group had around 70,000 employees
and turnover around $15,000 million.

The best-known commercial contribution from our other clan was
the Campbell Soup Company, founded by a fruit merchant called Joseph

Campbell in 1869 in Camden, New Jersey, which as we have seen was an early Campbell mini-colony (see p. 80). The company is now based at Modesto, California, has interests in a wide range of snacks and soft drinks, as well as soup, has over 40,000 employees and a turnover of around $10,000 million.

Turning, inevitably, back to warfare we find that during the Second World War both clans made substantial and memorable contributions. Once more the Campbells won three VCs, though this is a statistic that need not suggest that the MacDonalds did any less. Brigadier John or Jock Campbell from Thurso served in the 7th Support Group and was a pioneer of casual desert dressing in North Africa with silk neckerchief and goatskin jacket. More importantly, he also created the concept known as Jock's Columns, or convoys of armoured cars, at the battle of Sidi Rezegh against the German 15th Panzer Division. His decoration was for jumping onto a tank and firing a Verey pistol at the attacking Hessians. His promotion to general had just come through when he was killed in a car crash in 1942.

Flying Officer Kenneth Campbell of 22 Squadron won a posthumous VC for flying in his Beaufort torpedo bomber to attack the German ship *Gneisenau* in 1942. Campbell's torpedo hit the ship's stern below the waterline and it took eight months to repair. Campbell and his crew of four were all killed. The third VC went to Colonel Lorne M. Campbell (d. 1991), from Airds, of the Argyll and Sutherland Highlanders who won it in 1943 at Wadi Akarit in Tunisia where he took some 600 German prisoners after attacking through a minefield. But there were, in addition, thousands of acts of gallantry by many MacDonalds and Campbells. MacDonald seamen were at Narvik and Dunkirk, sank submarines and were sunk in them in the Atlantic, survived the Russian convoys and helped the D-Day landings. Captain Alan Bell MacDonald gave out beer to the troops at Dunkirk as they waited for rescue. A medical colonel, John MacDonald, noted his horror at the stench, filth and gore of the massacre at Les Pardins. Captain Ian Campbell RN in the destroyer *Milne* led a number of Arctic convoys to Russia under horrendous conditions.

Two MacDonald Spitfire pilots from 603 Squadron were shot down during the battle of Britain. Aeneas Ranald MacDonell, Chief of Glengarry, shot down at least two Junkers and shared in a Bf 109 but was himself shot down twice and survived to become an air commodore. Pilot Officer G.L. Campbell also shot down two Junkers over Sicily but was killed in 1942. There were two Canadian Campbell pilots in the battle of Britain, one of whom was killed in his Hurricane in 1940. Lieutenant H.B. Campbell landed a Catalina Flying Boat in the North Sea to take over command of a German U-boat U570 out of Trondheim after it had suffered bomb damage and hoisted the white flag. She was towed to Iceland.

Captain R.F. Campbell took part in one of the early special commando raids, later formalised as the Special Air Service. It was a behind-the-lines effort to kill Rommel, Hitler's chief in North Africa, in his own headquarters. General Levin Campbell was Chief of Ordnance in the US army in 1941, responsible for General Dwight Eisenhower's supply lines. John McDonald of the King's Own Scottish Borderers went on to become a major-general commanding 28th Commonwealth Brigade in the Korean War of 1951, while Alan Campbell, later Baron of Alloway, spent five years in Colditz.

The most exotic Campbell participant in the war was William or Villi, the stepson of John Ross Campbell, the Greenock Communist whose trial had led to the fall of Ramsay MacDonald in 1924 (see p. 147). Finding work hard to get during the Depression, Villi emigrated to Russia in 1931 and after a short spell in a factory found his niche as an entertainer. He became a clown in the Soviet State Circus, then when war started he toured the front with his dancer wife Elena, entertaining the troops, including at a concert in the newly captured Reichstag in 1945. Latterly he was a commentator for Radio Moscow until deciding to return to London in 1977 where his wife became a ballet teacher.

Of the politicians from our two clans at this time the most interesting was probably Malcolm Macdonald (1901–81), son of Ramsay. He was Secretary for the Dominions in 1935 under his father and again under Prime Minister Neville Chamberlain, when he negotiated the handing over of three naval bases in Ireland to the Irish, which led Churchill to call him 'rat poison'. Despite this he soon became Minister of Health during the London blitz in 1940–1 under Churchill himself and was given the job of offering Ulster to Eamon de Valera as a prize for Ireland's helping Britain in the war. Luckily perhaps for Churchill's reputation, de Valera refused and yet again the Irish problem remained unsolved. Macdonald then had a five-year spell as Commissioner in Canada, followed by two years as Governor-General of Malaya and Borneo. After a brief appointment as High Commissioner in Kenya in 1964–5 he had a five-year stint as special representative in east and central Africa. Overall, therefore, he played a key role in the awkward decolonisation period, advising the emergent states, and his abilities as both administrator and negotiator were widely recognised. His versatility was such that he could walk on his hands round Jawaharlal Nehru, went bird-watching with Eamon de Valera and played nursery games with Jomo Kenyatta.

Another MacDonald who made a significant contribution to Africa was Sir Murdoch (1866–1950), a former Liberal MP who subsequently played a major part in the planning and construction of the Aswan Dam in Egypt. Gordon McDonald (1888–1966), later Lord Gwaenysgor, a former coal miner from Wigan became a Labour MP, Postmaster-General and Governor of Newfoundland in 1946.

Meanwhile, the Chief of the Clan Campbell, Ian Douglas Campbell, 11th Duke of Argyll (1903–73) suffered a most macabre humiliation. In 1963 he sued his second wife Margaret Whigham or Sweeney for divorce on grounds of adultery with eighty-eight different men. The case became notorious because of the production as evidence of photographs taken in a mirrored bathroom in Belgravia. The duchess was portrayed clad in nothing but three strings of pearls and entwined with a man whose head was not visible. There were also lists of various accoutrements for a selection of lovers, three specifically but the fourth perhaps the mysterious man with no head. Some suggested that he was the actor Douglas Fairbanks Junior, others mentioned a variety of well-known political figures.

Rather more romantic was Roy Campbell (1901–57), the South African poet. Born in Durban he ran away from school at an early age and after trying various jobs in 1924 produced 'The Flamingo Terrapin', an allegory of regeneration that won him some critical notice. He then edited a magazine called *Voorslaag* with Laurens van der Post before moving to France where he set up home at Martigues in Provence and, among other activities, tried his hand at bullfighting. Surprisingly for a poet he preferred Franco to the Communists in the Spanish Civil War and unfashionably went out of his way to help rescue Catholic priests on the run from the Republicans. When the Second World War began, he put aside any right-wing leanings, volunteered to fight in East Africa and did so as a sergeant. He was eventually killed in his mid-fifties in a car crash in Portugal. Also a fine poet was Alistair

Ariki Campbell (b. 1925), born of a Polynesian mother in the Cook Islands and author of 'The Frigate Bird', while Marcus Campbell was a Dutch writer and Frederico Campbell a Mexican novelist.

Perhaps the two clan members who most neatly typified the end of one era and the beginning of another were Clarence Sutherland Campbell, the Canadian hockey player turned advocate who acted as a prosecutor at the Nuremburg war trials of 1945–6, and Douglas M. Campbell, the Australian judge who did the same job in Yokohama.

23

RED PERILS AND ICE CREAM

In the closing decades of the twentieth century the roles played by members of our two clans and the areas where they played them became ever more diverse. There were, of course, still a few warriors. Admiral L. Wesley McDonald (b. 1924) was commander-in-chief US Atlantic Command in 1983. He had been an ensign in 1946, held the Distinguished Flying Cross plus Gold Star and was successively captain of the USS *Hermitage* and *Coral Sea* in the Atlantic Fleet. In 1983 President Ronald Reagan gave him the job of invading the island of Grenada, which had a Marxist regime and was regarded as a potential threat to the US along the same lines as Fidel Castro's Cuba. It was a very sensitive time in American military history because of the psychological disasters of Vietnam: anything but rapid success would be a serious humiliation. In fact, despite numerous minor problems McDonald did accomplish the conquest of Grenada in two weeks. The CIA had hugely miscalculated the level of the island's defences and communications between sea and land troops were totally chaotic, but by sheer numbers McDonald won through and Ronald Reagan was delighted by this blow to what he thought was Communist expansion in the Caribbean. McDonald became an American hero.

Twenty years earlier a Campbell had come close to rocking the American establishment. Judith Campbell was a Catholic convent-school girl who grew up with blue eyes and raven hair, married and divorced a young actor called Campbell and was introduced to President John F. Kennedy by Frank Sinatra in Las Vegas. It seems she was already Sinatra's mistress, though she had apparently refused to succumb to his overtures until he took her with him on a trip to Hawaii. Peter Lawford, Kennedy's brother-in-law and another show business member of the so-called 'brat pack' that followed Sinatra, also made a pass at Campbell. He and his wife Patricia were present when Judith was introduced to the president. John Kennedy took her out for a long lunch and, according to her, they discussed Catholicism. A month later he sent her an airline ticket to New York and when she arrived she put up no more than token resistance before becoming yet another of his conquests. She was described as a more erotic, voluptuous version of his wife Jackie.

This affair might have been no more consequential than any of Kennedy's others but for the fact that soon afterwards, perhaps by prior arrangement, Judith Campbell also became the mistress of Sam Giancana, a constitutional psychopath and boss of the Chicago syndicate of the Mafia. She thus became potentially, if not actually, a conduit from the Mafia to the Oval Office. Even this might have made no particular difference to events had J. Edgar Hoover, head of the FBI, not acquired information about all these relationships. Hoover was no great admirer of the Kennedy brothers and might have made direct use of the information himself. He certainly offered it to Barry Goldwater, the Republican candidate for the presidency, who honourably refused to use what he called 'that crap'. Judith Campbell, by that time also called Exner, subsequently wrote her version of events in *My Story*. As Frank Sinatra put it, 'Hell hath no fury like a hooker when she becomes an author.'

Even less reputable was the career of Thomas C. Campbell, a Glasgow professional criminal who was gaoled in 1984 for causing the death by fire of five members of the Doyle family in the Ruchazie district of that city. This was the so-called 'Ice Cream War' in which ice-cream vans were a cover for the distribution of drugs: their sales pitches could therefore become a matter of life and death. Campbell professed his innocence of this particular crime and went on a hunger strike to show his confidence, managing to father a child on his mistress while out on bail for his appeal.

He was described as having a remarkable power to intimidate just by lowering his voice. Other members of the Campbell underworld included the brothers Colin and William or Big Bill Campbell, albeit they claimed a political rationale for their acts of violence. They were convicted in Glasgow of being members of the Ulster Volunteer Force

(UVF) and with seven others received long prison sentences for the bombing of two Catholic pubs in the city in 1979. They were also convicted of criminal conspiracy as part of western Scotland's strange obsession with supporting the late King William of Orange and once more 'wading in Fenian blood'. Big Bill was believed to be the overseas commander of the UVF. The family tradition was kept up by Colin's son Jason, an unemployed teenager living in Bridgeton who almost always wore an orange jacket. In October 1995 he stabbed a passing supporter of the Celtic Football Club, which was perceived by Jason and his peers as personifying the world plot machinations of the Pope and his Irish republican allies. The reason for the killing was that the victim and his friends had objected to being spat upon while passing the Windsor Bar. Jason was convicted of murder and followed his father into prison.

If they disapproved of Irish Catholics these Campbells would probably also, sadly, have disapproved of two black footballers who shared their surname. Kevin Campbell moved from Nottingham Forest to Turkey where his own new club hectored him out with racist abuse – 'We bought a cannibal who calls himself a striker.' Kevin moved to Everton Football Club and pronounced 'I am first of all a black man.' Whether he or Sol Campbell, an English international footballer, had actual Campbell blood or were simply descended from slaves on a Campbell plantation is hard to assess. The same may be true of Naomi Campbell, born in London, the first black model to have her picture on the front cover of *Vogue* magazine and Darren Campbell, who aged twenty-four won the European 100 metres title in 10.04 seconds at Budapest in 1998. There have also been a number of outstanding black MacDonalds. Trevor (b. 1938), the television news-reader from Trinidad, is regarded as the best proponent of spoken English of his generation. Gabrielle Kirk McDonald was President of the International Criminal Tribunal of Yugoslavia at the Hague in 1998 and prepared the charges of war crimes against Bosnian Serb leaders both political and military.

Certainly of mixed blood were a number of Native American Campbells and MacDonalds. Arizona-born Peter McDonald, a Navajo, (b. 1937) became an aerospace engineer but was accused of corruption and sent to prison. Ben Nighthorse Campbell (b. 1933), a Republican, was voted into the Senate for Colorado in 1992.

There were a number of reasonably successful politicians from the two families in the final third of the twentieth century. Alexander Campbell, a Liberal, became the youngest premier of a Canadian province when he took charge of Prince Edward Island in 1966 and in 1993 Kim Campbell (b. 1947) was briefly the first woman prime minister of Canada. In 1972 Donald MacDonald (b. 1909) the Canadian miners' leader from Cape Breton became the first non-European to be chosen President of the International Federation of Free Trades Unions. Gordon Campbell (b. 1921), later Lord Campbell of Croy (near Cawdor), was Conservative Secretary of State for Scotland 1970–4. Labour Prime Minister Tony Blair's Scottish Office team included two MacDonalds. Lord Gus Macdonald (b. 1940), a retired television executive, became UK Transport Minister in 1999 and Calum, the Outer Isles MP, was dropped from office after the setting up of the new Scottish parliament, while the extremely influential spin doctor, Alastair Campbell (b. 1957) was in charge of press relations in London. One personal press story which the latter allowed to leak out was about how he and Colonel Alastair Campbell, then defence attaché to the British embassy in Kuwait and son of Campbell of Croy, played the bagpipes together to relax during one of the West's confrontations with Saddam Hussein. Menzies Campbell (b. 1941) was a long-serving and influential Liberal MP and a respected spokesman on foreign affairs. Anne Campbell was the Labour MP for Cambridge and Caroll Ashmore Campbell (b. 1940) became governor of South Carolina. Flora McDonald (b. 1926) was Canadian Tory spokesperson on Indian affairs. In the United Nations at the end of the millennium there was, predictably, one representative from each clan: Sybil Campbell from Jamaica was Chief of Staff at UNESCO, Paris; Alphonse Macdonald from Suriname was a UN expert on fertility, based in Nigeria.

Science, the arts and show business also had a number of talented performers from both clans. Dr William Campbell of Philadelphia was the first to diagnose Legionnaires' Disease in 1976. Jeanette Macdonald (1907–68) was a popular Philadelphia soprano who starred in *Rose Marie* and other films. Sharon Ethel Macdonald (b. 1952) became a highly regarded Pittsfield ballerina, while Elaine MacDonald (b. 1943) was principal dancer at Scottish Ballet. Glen Campbell (b. 1936) was a popular singer of country and western music.

The Campbells produced great folklorists on both sides of the Atlantic: John Francis Campbell (1822–85) and John Lorne Campbell

(1906–96) in Scotland and Josiah Campbell (1904–88), an Irish Catholic, at Columbia who wrote *The Hero with a Thousand Faces*, which was part of the inspiration for the *Star Wars* series of films. The MacDonalds had Donald Archie (1929–99) a great recorder and collector of traditional songs and stories.

Ian Campbell, 12th Duke of Argyll (b. 1937) was meanwhile working hard to prevent the erosion by tax of the family fortune and was still the 367th richest man in Britain. A former captain in the Argyll and Sutherland Highlanders, he remained a member of the queen's bodyguard, Keeper of the Great Seal of Scotland, Keeper (but not owner) of Dunoon, Dunstaffnage, Tarbert and Carrick Castles and hereditary Sheriff of Argyll. Lady Colin Campbell, the ex-wife of the duke's brother, used her friendship with Princess Diana to produce one of many biographies and his half-sister was married for a while to novelist and journalist Norman Mailer. Godfrey, Lord Macdonald of Slate* (b. 1947), ran a luxury hotel on Skye with his wife Claire, herself a successful author of cookery books.

Meanwhile, Dr Jeffrey MacDonald, a former US Marine Corps doctor, still languished in a medium security Massachusetts gaol, serving three life sentences for the murder of his wife and two daughters in 1970. He claimed he was innocent of all three crimes and blamed a drug-crazed hippie.

At sea Captain D.R.F. Campbell, commanding the aircraft carrier *Ark Royal* in 1955, conceived the idea of the angled flight deck which avoided the use of a crash barrier for landing planes. His idea was soon afterwards successfully adopted by the United States Navy. Rather less technological was the building of the boat *Aileach* by the Macdonald family of Moville, County Donegal, in 1991. She was a replica of a Highland birlinn and was sailed with some difficulty to the Faroes in 1992 by Wallace Clark.

With so many talented people from such different backgrounds the idea of any continued antipathy between the two clans must seem ridiculous. To some degree the extended myth of Glencoe was the result of anti-Orange propaganda which had quite a different motivation. Yet still there are apocryphal stories like the one of a Campbell who

---

* An Irish peerage bestowed in 1776 that just happens to be an anagram of Sleat, the title used by the Yorkshire branch of the family.

introduces himself to a stranger on a train. The stranger announces that he is a MacDonald and promptly moves to the next compartment. Or the ones about Campbells not being able to buy a drink at the Clachaig Inn in Glencoe and campers in the glen hearing strange voices in the middle of the night.

The Edinburgh Glencoe Society has commemorated the massacre each year recently at the memorial erected in 1833 to the MacDonalds of Glencoe and for the tercentenary in 1992 the Clan Donald Society spent £30,000 renovating the site. On 13 February that year, since there were no known descendants of the MacIain MacDonalds of Glencoe, a wreath was laid there by Lord Macdonald of Sleat.

But the real memorials to the two clans are scattered over every corner of the globe from Toubacanti and Ticonderoga to Botany Bay and Mangalore. Certainly there were rivalries and some bitterness in the past but both rose above the collapse of their traditional way of life, spread, multiplied and continued to leave their mark everywhere in the world.

A Tour Round the Sites and Monuments of the Great Feud

Scotland and Ireland

What follows is a suggested tour by car or coach and it should not be used without a good road map, up-to-date ferry timetable and accommodation register.

A natural starting point is **Edinburgh** where there are no specific monuments relating to the Campbell–MacDonald story, but a lot of key events occurred here including the humiliation of the 3rd Lord of the Isles at Holyrood Palace and the execution of two Campbell earls in Edinburgh Castle (1661 and 1685). There are a number of portraits of characters from the feud in the Scottish National Portrait Gallery and some fine sculpted stones and other artefacts in the Museum of Scotland. A detour to the east also takes in the battlefield of **Prestonpans**, where Campbell of Loudoun was put to flight with General John Cope in 1745, and **Tantallon Castle**, where the 3rd Lord of the Isles was imprisoned.

Heading north-west out of Edinburgh and over the Forth Road Bridge on the A/M90, bearing left on to the A823 and A91, there are two excellent Campbell monuments managed by Historic Scotland. **Castle Campbell** just off the A91 at Dollar is a fine late medieval castle in a most dramatic setting and gives an excellent idea of the Campbells in their Reformation splendour. Twelve miles further along the A91, the **Argyll Lodging** in Stirling is a delightful Restoration town house with fine room settings and excellent display material on the background of the ill-fated 9th Earl. Stirling Castle houses the excellent museum of the Argyll and Sutherland Highlanders and was for many years the prison that held Donald Dhu MacDonald.

From Stirling head north on the A9 to the site of the battle of **Sheriffmuir**, then turn onto the A85 at Perth, near which are two other battlefields – **Methven**, where Neil Campbell fought alongside Bruce, and **Tippermuir**, where in 1644 the MacDonalds under Montrose scored their first major victory in the Civil War. Take the A85 and A826 via Crieff and Aberfeldy through Campbell country, including **Monzie** which features in the Darien story, then the A827 to Kenmore where the semi-derelict **Taymouth Castle** stands as an extraordinary monument to late Campbell opulence. Built round Black Duncan's tower of Balloch, where he excecuted a McGregor chief, it is now surrounded by a modern golf course. Most of the huge 1801 Gothic building where the Breadalbane Campbells entertained Queen Victoria is not occupied or open to the public but can be viewed from the outside. Near Kenmore is the Isle of Loch Tay, the site of an earlier Campbell fort, and Acharn.

Head west on the A827 along the north side of Loch Tay, turning north at Fearnan and then left into spectacular **Glenlyon**. There are the ruins of a Campbell castle at Carbane where the young MacGregor chief was brainwashed, then go up the lovely glen to **Meggernie Castle**, once the home of the infamous Captain Robert Campbell, perpetrator of the Massacre of Glencoe. The castle is in private hands and has been restored; it looks like a white gem in the green lushness of this glen, which reminds us of how attractive it must have seemed to MacDonalds who came over from Glencoe and Rannoch to lift its cattle.

Return halfway down Glenlyon to Bridge of Balgie and take the Lawers road past the National Trust Visitor Centre. **Lawers** was another famous Campbell family which produced a number of well-known military leaders and took over the barony, later an earldom, of Loudoun. Turn right at the main road A827 and head into Killin. Turn left at the Pier Road and drive to the neglected ruins of **Finlarig Castle**, a very forlorn remnant of one of Black Duncan's most famous castles and the burial place for him and many of his descendants. The ruins are dangerous and should only be approached with care but it is to be hoped that they will soon be properly conserved.

Back on the main road, head south and add a detour if there's time down the A85 to Lochearnhead. This is the home area of Campbell of Fonab, the only hero of Darien, who befriended his near neighbour Rob Roy of Balquhidder. Near by, in front of **Ardvorlich House** are the graves of seven MacDonalds of Glencoe, killed by the owner during a raid in 1620. On Loch Earn also is **Edinample Castle**, number three of Black Duncan's seven castles, a Z-shaped tower in a beautiful setting, modernised and in private hands. Return to the A85 and retrace the route to the junction for Crianlarich. Head west, stopping at **Loch Dochart** where ruins of the fourth of Black Duncan's castles can be seen on their island – there is a lay-by and you can cross the fence onto the former railway line that skirts the south side of the loch. It is obvious why MacColla's troops found it hard to get through Strathfillan when the guns of this castle could fire on them and were themselves protected by the waters of the loch.

Head now for Tyndrum on the A82, passing **Dalry** battlefield where Bruce and Campbell were thrashed by the MacDougalls. Then pass Dalmally and turn left to the car park of **Kilchurn Castle**, the fifth and probably most impressive of the Black Duncan castles. In 1999 it was put on the market by Historic Scotland, but deserves better, is still open to the public and is very well worth a visit. It faces Cruachan, the mountain whose name was the Campbell warcry, and Glenstrae where the MacGregors were ethnically cleansed – their castle has disappeared. A couple of miles further on is St Conan's, the strange church built around 1889 by Walter Campbell as an extravagant Victorian monument to the Campbells, but it does have a certain attraction. Just beyond it is the site of the battle of the **Pass of Brander**, which ended the power of the MacDougalls.

Now return back towards Dalmally and turn right on to the A819, passing further magnificent views of Kilchurn, then bear right again at Cladich on to Loch Awe road, the B840. Opposite this shore are **Inishail Island**, with its monastery of St Findocha, and **Fraoch Eilean Castle** built by the McNaughtons and later owned by the Campbells of Inverawe (of Ticonderoga fame) and the Campbells of Monzie; each of these can be reached by boat although the second is in private ownership. Ten miles further on is the superb island fortress of **Inchconnel**, original home of the Campbells. It also requires a boat for access and is not normally open to the public, though it should be. Eight miles further on out of sight of the road are the twisted ruins of **Fincharn Castle**, a Campbell outpost from 1315, beautiful and dramatically set on the water's edge. Now return to Cladich and head south to **Inveraray** and the present seat of the Dukes of Argyll, more handsome at a distance than close up but inside full of interesting portraits and other artefacts. The new town of Inveraray is also a monument to the power and wealth of the dynasty, which simply destroyed the old town to make room for the castle and gardens, building a new settlement that is now a superb surviving example of eighteenth-century town planning and architecture. A short diversion northwards, 4 miles up the A83, takes in **Dunderave Castle**, which the Campbells won from the MacNaughtons by cheating. It has been restored and is used for holiday accommodation. Across the loch can be seen **Ardkinglas**, seat of the Campbell sheriff at the time of Glencoe.

Head south now to Lochgilphead, passing **Crarae** Gardens, founded by Grace Campbell and the site of the Campbell castle at **Lochgair**, where the leading Jacobite Campbell was arrested in 1745. Bear right on the A816 to **Kilmartin** where the Z-shaped sixteenth-century tower house manse formerly held by Campbells has been restored and the church has a number of fine Campbell tombs, including, according to the records, that of the crusading Black Knight of Rhodes. A few miles further on is an even more elaborate fortified manse, **Carnasserie Castle**, managed by Historic Scotland. Its roof and interiors were destroyed in the 1685 rebellion but is still impressive and there are fine views from the battlements.

Just after Carnasserie turn right up the B840 to Ford, go up the west side of Loch Awe and turn left up to **Loch Avich**, which has its tiny castle ruins on the little island at the far end. Return to Loch Awe road, turn left again by Inverinan onto farmtrack for the **String of Lorne** and walk up to see the cairn marking the spot where Sir Colin Campbell was killed at the start of the long feud. Return to road and visit his reconstructed tomb at St Peter's Church, **Kilchrenan**.

Return to main Oban road, the A85, travel down Loch Etive through Connel to **Dunstaffnage**, the key fortress which changed hands so often in the early part of the feud, a magnificent old castle with a delightful ruined chapel near by, both well cared for and presented by Historic Scotland. In Oban itself is the spectacular keep of **Dunollie Castle**, the ancient MacDougall stronghold which is not particularly well maintained but can be reached by a path from the road and is well worth it, though treat with caution.

Oban is a good centre and there are four useful ferry routes that start from here. The shortest is to **Lismore** with its **Coeffin Castle**, which went to the Campbells in 1470, and tiny cathedral. **Colonsay** is also highly recommended for those who have the time, though more for its wonderful scenery. The architectural relics are limited except for Good John's superb priory on **Oronsay** which can be reached by foot at low tide (check carefully). Note that the steamer to Colonsay passes the remote MacLean island castle of **Dunchonnel** on the Garvellach islands. The third ferry route, to Mull, can be taken at this point or left until the return trip of this tour to avoid retracing old ground. The fourth is to the Clanranald outposts of **Boisdale** on South Uist, birthplace of Flora Macdonald, with its **Caisteal Bheagram**, and Benbecula, with its **Borve Castle** and **Nunton Nunnery**. South Uist has some vestiges of kelp kilns on its shores.

Head south again on the A816 passing the **Knipoch** Hotel, the rebuilt version of the house where John Campbell of Calder was murdered. A short detour up **Glen Euchar** on the left leads to the Barn of Bones, site of a massacre of Campbells by MacDonalds under MacColla. To the west also are the ruined Campbell outposts of Ardfad on Seil and Castael nan-Con on Torsay. Pass **Kilmelford** and Melfort, home of the two Campbell heroes of the Napoleonic Wars, the Campbell Lerags Cross and **Craignish**, associated with the Campbell supporter of Bismarck. **Ardmaddy Castle** was built by Colin Campbell in 1732. After Kilmartin bear right across the Great Moss between ancient Dunad, the early Scots capital, and **Duntrune Castle** at the mouth of the River Ad. This castle, haunted by a MacDonald piper, was also an ancient Campbell stronghold and figured in the MacColla campaign. It is now restored and privately owned, although occasionally open to visitors.

Cross the Crinan Canal at Bellanoch, turn right on the B841 towards Crinan and then bear left down the B8025 and left again to **Castle Sween**, the oldest and one of the most famous castles of the long feud. It changed hands on numerous occasions, finally going to the Campbells of Auchinbreck. Four miles beyond it is **Kilmory Knap** Chapel with its fine collection of carved tombstones. For those with the time there is a matching chapel on the other side of Loch Sween with a further collection of stones and if a boat is available a third, with a tiny monastery on the **Eilean Mhor** which was rebuilt by the 1st Lord of the Isles.

Return to Crinan Canal and turn briefly left to see the MacDonald council mound at **Kilchumaig**, by tradition referred to as **Dundonald**. Then bypass Lochgilphead and keep on Campbeltown road, the A83, past Inverneil, another Campbell family seat, **Tarbert** where the Campbells manned the now ruined royal castle for many years. A detour off the Tarbert road on to the A8024 can take in **Kilberry**, a lesser-known Campbell outpost, but it has a fine collection of tombstones from its former monastery.

Turning west from Tarbert there are no real remains of the former MacDonald stronghold on **Eilean Ghallagan**, an island in West Loch Tarbert which deserves archaeological exploration. Just beyond this is the Kennacraig ferry terminal which can be used now or on the return journey, whichever is more convenient, to visit Islay.

The fertile island of Islay is the heartland of MacDonald territory. The highlight has to be a visit to **Finlaggan**, the Lords of the Isles' palace on an island on a lake itself on an island. Now receiving welcome, if long overdue, attention from archaeologists and run by the Finlaggan Trust, this fascinating site can be visited in the summer with access both to the castle island and the council island near by. Radar images taken from a NASA spacecraft in 1994 showed up a network of previously undiscovered medieval roads leading from Finlaggan to the galley harbour at Fionnport Bhoraic and the lead/silver mines believed now to be one reason why the Lords of the Isles chose this remote location. The second highlight is a visit to the badly ruined but exciting remains of **Dunyveg Castle**, which played such a dramatic part in the fortunes of the MacDonalds over several centuries. En route it is possible to visit **Loch Gorm** where the smaller MacDonald outpost is barely visible but also saw a number of dramatic events and the battlefield of **Loch Gruinart**. There are also a number of fine medieval church ruins with carved tombstones from the feud period. **Bowmore** was a model eighteenth-century new town built by Daniel Campbell. Bowmore Round Church was built for Daniel Campbell in 1717 and the distillery was constructed in 1779.

For those with the time a visit to **Jura** by the little ferry from Port Askaig is well worth it and the island did have both a MacDonald and Campbell stronghold, albeit there is now little of them to see.

Returning by the main ferry to Kennacraig turn south again and bear left on to Carradale road, the B8001. **Skipness Castle**, home to the Lady Glamys (burned as a witch) and several other characters, is another Campbell castle in good condition although the main tower is not open to the public. It also has a partially ruined chapel.

Head south past **Carradale**, where Airds Castle was held by MacDonalds up to 1493, to **Saddell Abbey**, founded by the early MacDonalds, burial place of several senior MacDonalds and Campbells, with **Saddell Castle**, an early MacDonald tower house now restored and used as a holiday venue. Just before Campbeltown is Lower Smerby and the remains of **Island Muller**, a small MacDonald castle on an island by the shore. Then comes **Fort Argyll**, part of the fortification put up at the start of the Civil War and minimal vestiges of **Kilkerran Castle**. South of **Campbeltown** on the B842 is Southend with the dramatic site of **Dunaverty Castle**, scene of some of the greatest acts of violence in the long feud. Although very little is left but the great rock on which it was built, this is still a very evocative sight. Near by is the fourteenth-century St Columba's Chapel, a small graveyard for the MacDonald victims of the 1647 siege and MacDonald's Cave where the baby son of their commander was taken for safety.

Returning to Campbeltown there is the opportunity during summer months of using the ferry to Ballycastle in **Northern Ireland**, which is a convenient way of visiting the main MacDonald sites there. (Alternatively, fly from Glasgow or take ferry from Stranraer.) **Davaar Island**, given by the Lord of the Isles to the church, is passed to starboard, as is Sanda Island another early MacDonald outpost and across the channel is **Rathlin Island**, the scene of several events in the feud and part of the original MacDonald Antrim estate. To the west of Ballycastle is majestic **Dunluce Castle**, not built by the MacDonalds originally but much developed by them and very much the centre for their expansion in Ireland. It is square, still with two round towers set on a rock with a narrow ridge to the mainland. A succession of good marriages with O'Cahans, Bissets and others had extended MacDonald lands far southwards, though the senior branch here remained the MacDonalds of Dunyveg and the Glens. They reached their most ambitious under Sorley Boy and his descendant the Earl of Antrim, most well known for his failure to dislodge the apprentice boys of Londonderry. To the south are the ruins of **Red Bay Castle** near Waterfoot and the **Layde Church**, burial place of the Antrim MacDonalds. **Glenarm Castle** to which they moved, when Dunluce became old-fashioned, is a picturesque medley of architectural styles. To the west, Strabane Castle was occupied by the MacDonalds and the remarkable Agnes Campbell. For those with a special interest there are a number of other sites to visit in both Northern Ireland and the Republic, including the scenes of Alastair MacColla's early and final battles. The last was Knocknanus and he is buried at Clonmeen. Beyond Dublin in County Wicklow, which became known as Clan Donald country, the MacDonells became Constables of the Pale and held the castle of **Tinakilly** which still stands as a ruin with its 'murthering hole'. A more modern version near by has been converted into a hotel.

Returning by ferry to Campbeltown head northwards up the main road A83 passing **Rhunahaorine** where MacColla's men fought their last battle and Largie, another former MacDonald estate. Then on up the A816 to Oban taking in any visits that have been postponed when coming down this road before. If the Mull–Iona trip has not been done now is the time, but before that a short detour northwards over the Connel Bridge is worthwhile, taking a left after Benderloch to visit **Barcaldine Castle**, another of Black Duncan's seven which has recently been repurchased and restored by descendants of the original Campbell family. It is supposedly haunted by the murdered brother of an early Campbell and the Glencoe chief was delayed here in 1692. A short, pretty detour can also take in **Ardchattan Priory** on the north shore of Loch Etive, founded by the MacDougalls but taken over by the Campbells.

Those not going to Mull at this point should keep northwards over the Ballachulish Bridge to the small Corran ferry, near where Alistair Macdonell of Glengarry met his untimely death leaping from a sinking steamer to the shore. Take the ferry and then the A861 en route to **Ardtornish**, near Lochaline, one of the most important and most neglected of all MacDonald sites. It is a virtually unmarked rock with a few poorly repaired stretches of wall and a couple of miles from the end of the road, but very well worth a visit for its evocative setting and its superb view. At night the string of MacDonald castles on the Mull and Argyll coastlines could be linked by a warning chain of bonfires. Drimnin, about 8 miles north of Ardtornish, was an even more remote MacDonald outpost.

The alternative way to reach Ardtornish is to take a single ferry ticket from Oban to Mull, do the sites of Mull and Iona and then take the other ferry route from Fishnish to Lochaline. The Oban–Mull ferry passes **Lismore**, the cathedral island of the MacDonalds, and the infamous **Lady Rock** where a MacLean stranded his Campbell wife and later paid for the attempted murder with his own life. Mull itself offers

Duart Castle, the restored headquarters of the MacLean branch of the MacDonald Lordship, and not far away **Torosay Castle**, a more modern ex-Campbell mansion built in 1858 by Colonel Campbell of Possil with delightful gardens. Now head west on the A849.

Iona is always worth a visit but it is also very rich in memories of the long feud. Two Lords of the Isles and their ancestors are buried here and there is one more or less identifiable carved stone inscribed Angus Og, though the man it refers to is more likely the last lord's bastard than the first lord's father. The nunnery was built originally by Somerled and this, as well as the abbey, certainly received attention from Good John and Donald, the 2nd Lord, who in later life supposedly became a monk here. Ironically this island, sacred for saints, early kings of Scotland and the MacDonald Lords of the Isles, came into Campbell ownership and it was they who passed on the abbey to the Church of Scotland.

North of Iona are the **Treshnish Islands**, which can be visited by boat and have the remarkable twin castles of **Cairnaborg** and **Isleborg**.

Ruined **Aros Castle** is another of the MacLean/MacDonald coastal chain of castles and is now a picturesque ruin off Mull's A848 with a Gaelic Visitor Centre near by. **Tobermory Bay** is where the Spanish galleon that helped the MacLeans attack the MacIains of Ardnamurchan sank and whose treasure was searched for in vain by the 11th Duke of Argyll. And to the west is **Bloody Bay**, scene of the civil warfare which finally split the MacDonald Lordship.

Now take the Fishnish–Lochaline ferry, from which it is just a short drive and walk to Ardtornish (see above). Then take the A884, A861 and B8007 to Kilchoan and nearby **Mingary Castle** on the Ardnamurchan peninsula, another impressive ruin of a Lordship castle founded by the ill-fated MacIain branch of the MacDonalds. Near by is the site of the attack by sailors from the Spanish Armada, Port na Spainneach. Heading northwards on the A861, **Castle Tioram** on an island on the shore of Loch Moidart is one of the most beautiful of all MacDonald castles. It was founded by Amy MacRuari, ex-wife of the 1st Lord, and her son Ranald, founder of the Clanranald. The castle was deliberately burned by its chief in 1715 who was correctly pessimistic about his chances when he went off to fight for the Old Pretender. Recently it has changed hands again and there have been controversial plans for its restoration. From the castle an avenue of stones leads to Loch Shiel and the landing place for Eilean Fhionain with its **St Finan's Chapel**, burial place of Clanranald.

Head north again by **Kinlochmoidart**, a well-known MacDonald seat which has a Plate Rock where the owner buried his family silver in 1745. Join the A860 and passing Loch nan Uamh where Bonnie Prince Charlie landed, detouring if desired up to Glenfinnan and its monument for the '45 and **Glenaladale** where the first white rose was plucked. Then head up to Mallaig and take the ferry to **Skye**. As the ferry heads north note the remote Knoydart peninsula, producer of many well-known MacDonalds, which can only be reached by boat or a long trudge from the Lochgarry road. Also reachable by boat from Mallaig is the island of **Canna** where Donald Gorm kept his wife a prisoner in An Coroghon Castle.

In **Armadale**, Skye, is the **Clan Donald Centre** with interpretation centre, restaurant, shop and delightful gardens surrounding the shell of **Armadale Castle**. This was the former stately home of the Macdonalds of Sleat, built first as a dower house in 1773 where Samuel Johnson stayed, then extended in toy fort style in 1815. The current Lord Macdonald and his wife Claire, the cookery expert, now have a luxury hotel, the **Kinloch Lodge**, about 8 miles up the A851. Meanwhile, there are four older MacDonald castle sites to visit on Skye. **Dunskeath** on its dramatic stack on the west coast of the Sleat peninsula, taken by the MacDonalds from the MacLeods in the fourteenth century, had seven ramparts and a pit full of snakes, and can be reached by turning left at Kilbeg. **Camus** or Knock Castle on the east coast is 3 miles north of Kilbeg, a ruin on 50 feet high cliffs. **Uisdean** Castle belonged to the piratical Hugh Macdonald who died of thirst after being fed on salt beef in the dungeons of Duntulm, which his ghost subsequently haunted. **Duntulm Castle** itself, home of the irascible Donald Gorm, right up at the north of Trotternish by the A855 is another clifftop ruin with galley grooves on the rocks below and earth from seven kingdoms in its garden. They staged a ball here in 1715 to celebrate the Pretender but by 1732 it was deserted in favour of **Monkstadt Castle** closer to Uig. Dunvegan is, of course, the best-known castle on Skye but does not play any real part in our particular narrative. More relevant are the homes of Flora Macdonald at **Kingsburgh** off the A87 and at **Flodigarry**.

On Vatersay are the ruins of Trumpan Church where the MacDonalds of Eigg burned the MacLeods in 1577. On Eigg itself is the cave where the MacLeods burned the MacDonalds in retaliation.

Take the ferry from Uig to **South Uist**, which has the MacDonald stronghold of **Ormiclate Castle**, burned down in 1715, Howmore, burial place of Clanranald, **Calvay Castle** at Boisdale where MacDonalds sheltered Bonnie Prince Charlie and the birthplace of Flora Macdonald at Milton. To the south is the MacDonald island of Eriskay where Prince Charlie first landed in 1745. To the north, **Benbecula** has **Borve Castle** (probably built by John of Islay), the ruins of the MacDonald nunnery at **Nunton** and Nunton House, home of Clanranald, where Prince Charlie was dressed up as Mary Burke. **North Uist** has its Ditch of Blood near Carinish (where the MacDonalds fought the MacLeods) and Sollas, famous for the brutal clearances of MacDonalds by Lord MacDonald of Sleat.

Return now to the mainland by the Skye Bridge A87 or, for a scenic detour in summer, by the Glenelg ferry. **Glenshiel** is the site of the Jacobite battle in 1719 when Spanish troops were employed. **Eilean Donan Castle** off the A87, a MacRae stronghold that also figures in a number of incidents of the feud, was blown up at this time, and Macdonald of Sleat died on the nearby islet after being fatally wounded by an arrow from its ramparts. Turn north now via Plockton and the A890 to Lochcarron; on the far side is the most northerly of the mainland MacDonald fortresses, ruined **Strome Castle**, home of the violent MacDonalds of Lochalsh, worth the extra drive round the loch if you have the time.

Now a change and quite a distance as we have to cross back over to the east coast – A832/835/834. . . . **Dingwall** became the headquarters of the MacDonalds when they at long last won the Earldom of Ross and held it for two generations, but there is little to see of Dingwall Castle. Dingwall does, however, have its monument to Sir Hector MacDonald and **Rogart** to the west has its to Sir John Macdonald, first prime minister of Canada. To the south-west is Urray where the Glengarry MacDonalds burned the MacKenzies in their church in 1603. The **Tain Distillery** is also a MacDonald business. The Chanonry of Ross at **Fortrose Cathedral** where the 3rd Lord was buried is well worth a visit. A long detour to the far north can take in the monument for the Campbell battle of Altimarlach outside Wick.

Cross the Black Isle on the A835 joining the A9 over the Kessock Bridge, then left on to the B9006, pausing inevitably at **Culloden** where for the last time the Campbells and MacDonalds shed each other's blood in a general combat. Then comes the fourth of the great Campbell baronial castles, **Cawdor**, which they acquired by the marital abduction of an underage bride. It is in immaculate condition, full of interesting Campbell portraits and still lived in by the Campbell Earls of Cawdor, despite their earlier emigration to Wales. Near by, **Ardersier** village was built by the Campbells of Cawdor in the eighteenth century and has the alternative name of **Campbeltown**. Beyond it on the B9090 is **Auldearn**, another battlefield from the Civil War period where there is a monument to Alastair MacColla the talented MacDonald general and Sir Mungo Campbell was among the dead. Further on is **Lossiemouth** where the birthplace of Ramsay MacDonald can be seen in Gregory Place.

Return now to Inverness and take the A82 down the Caledonian Canal and the Great Glen to **Castle Urquhart** on Loch Ness. This is one of Scotland's largest and most impressive castle ruins and it was several times taken over by MacDonalds as the key to the Earldom of Ross. Near by are Invermoriston, Lochgarry and Aberchalder, junior MacDonald seats. On Loch Oich the precarious tower of **Invergarry** Castle, burned by Monck and blown up by Cumberland, totters on its cliff above the loch beside the grounds of the Glengarry Castle Hotel, itself built in 1866. A detour can take in the newly rediscovered MacDonald village of **Daingean**, deep now in the forests. Beyond Lochgarry a diversion can be made to Kinloch Hourn to visit on foot the deserted MacDonald clachans of Knoydart cleared in 1852: **Skiary**, **Runival**, **Barrisdale** and **Scotas**.

Now keep on the A87, passing the Seven Heads Well which commemorates the killing of the seven murderers of the MacDonald of Keppoch and was erected in 1812 by Macdonell of Glengarry, to Spean Bridge, but there, if interested, make a small detour eastwards up the A86 to **Keppoch**, where the old castle was destroyed several times. It features significantly in the history of the feud and there were a number of other interesting MacDonald branches up these glens such as **Bohuntine**. This route also gives an idea of the great feat of Montrose and MacColla's MacDonalds in their winter traverse of the mountains to take the Campbells by surprise at Inverlochy.

Return to the A82 and just before Fort William turn right down to **Inverlochy Castle**, a magnificent and newly conserved fortress built by the Comyns. It features in our narrative as the site of two crucial battles – the first between the MacDonalds and the royal army in 1429, the second the heaviest and bloodiest defeat of the Campbells by the MacDonalds in 1645. The homeland of the Keppoch MacDonalds is 5 miles east of Spean Bridge on the A86.

From Fort William head south on the A82 to **Glencoe**, watching out for **Eilean Munde**, the MacDonald burial island lying off its mouth. By now the traveller will have seen enough sites of violence perpetrated by both clans to put Glencoe in perspective, but with its natural grandeur and its memories it is always an impressive place to stop. The rather mundane National Trust Visitor Centre is now happily being replaced by something more sympathetic to the surroundings. If nothing else it is also worth walking up to the Hidden Valley (Coire Gabhail) where the MacDonalds kept their stolen herds out of sight. An alternative is to walk up the **Devil's Staircase**, now incorporated in the West Highland Way, the remains of the road dug by General Wade's soldiers to open up a route to Fort William.

Emerging from Glencoe and passing over Rannoch, on the left there are the ruins of **Achallader Castle**, the last of the seven associated with Black Duncan of the Seven Castles and the site at which he tricked the Fletchers into handing over to him. Heading down to Tyndrum we rejoin the Oban road having completed a huge figure of eight and drop down past Loch Lomond towards Glasgow. At **Tarbet** divert westwards again, if there is time, to take in the Campbell sites on Cowal. **Carrick Castle** on Loch Goil has recently been restored and a bottle dungeon was discovered – used for Campbell prisoners – but there is little else left of the Auchinbreck patrimony as the island fortress of **Eilean Dearg** on the east side of Loch Riddon was blown up in 1685. The Campbell church of **Kilmun** with its fine medieval tombs is worth seeing but of the ducal castles at **Rosneath** – one burned down in 1802, the other an Italian style palazzo demolished in the 1940s – there is nothing left. Near Mamore is a stone marking the place where miracle worker Isabella Campbell 'was wont to pray' beside a small waterfall. Of **Dunoon Castle**, captured by Colin Campbell from the English in 1334, the first step in the Campbell expansion, there are very few remains, but the town does have its statue of **Mary Campbell**, the Highland Mary made famous by Robert Burns.

Reaching **Glasgow** by the A82 we find one of the city's newer hotels, The Art House, is in the shell of a former Campbell mansion in Bath

Street, once owned by the family which produced Campbell-Bannerman, who was born in the mansion by the Kelvin used by the BBC. There are several hotels in the region owned by Macdonald, one of Scotland's largest hotel groups. If it is open, **Paisley Abbey**, 7 miles away, is worth a visit to see the supposed tomb of John, the last Lord of the Isles.

There is one final short trip to the sites associated with the Ayrshire Campbells. **Loudoun Castle**, though its roof and interior were destroyed by fire and it is now surrounded by an amusement park, is still a very impressive mansion, with the ancient tower house of the Campbells dating from 1315 at the core of the stately home built in quasi-Palladian style in 1807. The famous yew tree of the Campbells of Loudoun still stands to the south and the site itself is imposing. **Loudoun Kirk** at nearby Glaston contains the 1622 vault of the Campbells. A few miles further south is **Cessnock Castle**, an ancient Campbell keep with walls 14 feet thick joined to a 1675 mansion built by Sir Hugh Campbell. This castle has been beautifully restored and is not open to the public but can be viewed from the outside. At **Sorn Castle**, Lady Campbell, widow of the 3rd Earl of Loudoun, lived till she was 100 (1672–1772). South of Ayr is **Craigie House**, which was extended by William Campbell in 1783 as a seven-bay Georgian mansion and near by on the sea cliffs stand the dramatic ruins of **Greenan Castle**, which was briefly owned by the Lord of the Isles. En route back to Glasgow is Dundonald Castle where Alexander Og MacDonald probably met his death and nearby Symington, associated with the early Campbells as was Doon Castle in south Ayrshire. Greenock's **Cathcart Square** was the first home of Robert Campbell, the Australian pioneer.

OTHER SITES

No one would suggest that what follows should be treated as a recommendation for a tour of Europe or the rest of the world, but for those who are travelling anyway, it is well worth pausing at some of these monuments to recall the Campbell/MacDonald contribution.

England

LONDON
• Ham House in Petersham, London, is a National Trust property and the birthplace of the 2nd Duke of Argyll. He later built Sudbrooke House, which is now a golf club house in the same area.

- Westminster Abbey has carved tombs of the 2nd Duke of Argyll (by Roubiliac), Lord Clyde and Thomas Campbell, the latter in Poets' Corner.

PORTSMOUTH – HMS *Victory's* first captain was John Campbell.

BRIDLINGTON, YORKSHIRE – Thorpe Hall is the Yorkshire home of the Macdonalds of Sleat.

Wales

PEMBROKE – Stackpole Court and Castlemartin, homes of the Cawdor Campbells who repelled a small French invasion here in 1793, are beside the Pembroke Coast National Park.

Belgium

WATERLOO – Hougoumont Farm, site of the heroic stand by Sir James MacDonell of Glengarry in 1815, is marked as private but visits are allowed and there is a plaque.

JEMAPPES – Near Mons where Marshal Macdonald scored his first success in 1792.

BRUGES – Where the unhappy Campbell of Glenlyon died and was buried in 1696.

France

SEDAN – Birthplace of Marshal Macdonald, Duke of Tarento, in 1765. It still has its château fort, the largest in Europe.

PARIS – Hotel Regina, Place des Pyramides, by the Tuileries, where 'Fighting Mac' MacDonald shot himself in 1903, still retains its Victorian grandeur.

RIVER NIVELLE – In the far south-west corner of France where Highlanders stormed fortifications to invade Napoleonic France in 1813.

Holland

BERGEN OP ZOOM – At the mouth of the River Scheldt, it still has some of the fortifications left from the period when it was defended by Campbell of Loudoun and MacDonell of Leek in 1749.

WALCHEREN – Also at mouth of Scheldt where Colin Campbell and others fought hard and in vain against the French and swamp fever in 1809. It now has Walcheren Miniature, a model of the old town.

NAARDEN – Captured by Marshal Macdonald after he had crossed the frozen River Waal in 1794.

Spain

CORUNNA – In north-west Spain, the fortress on the peninsula still guards the harbour where Highlanders, including MacDonald of Dalchosnie under John Moore, fought a brave rearguard action in 1809.

BADAJOZ – Moorish fortress in Estremadura commanding Guadiana Valley and road to Portugal. Sir John Macdonald was involved in its capture.

TORRE BARROSA – Hill in the far south, heroically stormed by a group including Flora Macdonald's son John in 1811.

ARROYO DOS MOLINOS – A small village 6,000 feet up in Sierra de Montanches where Highland regiments braved foul weather to play pipes and capture the pass in 1811.

CIUDAD RODRIGO – 54 miles south of Salamanca, the battlements stormed by Highland regiments can still be explored for some distance.

SALAMANCA – The city still has many of the walls and buildings of the Peninsular War period.

TALAVERA – Walled town west of Madrid on River Tagus where General Alexander Campbell played a key part in the British victory of 1809.

VITTORIA – The battle site where several men of both clans fought in Basque country, 41 miles south of Bilbao. It has a statue of Wellington.

SAN SEBASTIAN – Where young Colin Campbell led the Forlorn Hope in 1813 and was twice wounded in the failed attempt to storm the town. Much of the walls still stand.

Portugal

VIMEIRO – Portuguese seaside town where Wellington began his invasion of Napoleonic Europe in 1810 with Highlanders in an action that was followed by the capture of nearby ravine of Torre Vedras.

VILA POUCA – A Campbell and Macdonald defeat in the Portuguese civil war of 1832–4.

Germany

REGENSBURG, BAVARIA – Formerly Ratisbon, where the poet Thomas Campbell stayed in the monastery and wrote 'Hohenlinden' in 1801.

LEIPZIG – The scene of a massive defeat in 1813 for Napoleon and Marshal Macdonald, who covered his retreat and had to swim the river after blowing the bridges. It now has a massive German monument on the site and an elegant Russian church in memory of the huge number of Russian casualties.

Italy/Switzerland

SPLÜGEN PASS – North of Lake Como, the high pass over the Alps into Switzerland where Marshal Macdonald amazingly led a whole army through the snow in December 1800.

TREBBIA – In north-west Italy, scene of Marshal Macdonald's extremely hard battle with Russians under Suvurov in 1799.

Ukraine

SEBASTOPOL – This is still a fortess city and naval base so it is hard to visit, but a stretch of the battlements from the Crimean War period survives and there is a 115-metre mural of the 1855 fighting.

BALACLAVA – The British base was 10 miles away from Sebastopol.

INKERMAN – The battle site of the 'Thin Red Line' is now a suburb of Sebastopol.

Russia

ST PETERSBURG – The stonework of the Admiralty building was the responsibility of Alexander Campbell (1760–1802), working for the Scottish architect Cameron. Retired Russian naval captain, John McDonald, lived here in 1797.

Bulgaria

SHIPKA PASS – Where Alastair 'Shipka' Campbell led Turks to a surprise victory against Russians in 1877. It is over 4,000 feet high and is on road to Gabrovo.

United States

CALIFORNIA
CAMPBELL – 5 miles from San Jose. Campbell Highland games are still held on the ranch bought by Ben Campbell in 1881. Richard Campbell first pioneered a direct overland route to California via Colorado in 1827.

GEORGIA
DARIEN – Scottish colony 150 miles south of Savannah set up by Colonel James Oglethorpe as an advance post. It became a major timber exporter. There are also Campbell connections with Fort Jackson, Savannah's oldest surviving brick fort, which hosts Highland games.

SAVANNAH – It was captured by Archibald Campbell in 1776, as was Augusta.

BANKS/ELBERT COUNTY – Settlement of the pioneer Donald McDonald on the Grove River, south of Homer.

IDAHO
SNAKE RIVER – Explored by the red-haired giant, Finan Buffalo McDonald in 1810 with an armed band of Iroquois to set against the Blackfoot. He was wounded by his own Indians after a row. He set up a trading post at Spokane, now in Washington. Snake River is now a wildlife reserve.

KENTUCKY
FORT CAMPBELL – Near Bowling Green on the border with Tennessee, this is a former tobacco marketing centre. Also, Campbell County is south of Cincinnati beside Boone. Fort Boonsborough State Park on the Kentucky River has a reconstructed fort.

MASSACHUSETTS
BOSTON – Hugh Campbell was a merchant here in 1679. John Campbell founded *The Boston Newsletter* here in 1695, the first American newspaper. The city has the Old South Meeting House of 1728 where Tea Party plotters met, including Nicholas Campbell.

MONTANA
MCDONALD PEAK – 10,000 feet high, named after fur trader and explorer Angus MacDonald. It is above Fort Connah in the Mission Valley where he lived with his Indian wife and adopted Selish Indian lifestyle, as did his son Duncan: one timber building of time survives. Waterton Glacier International Peace Park includes McDonald Lake and Valley called after Duncan, near Libby Fort, which was founded by Finan McDonald. McDonald ranch at Niarada is in the Flathead Reserve. McDonald Pass at 6,330 feet is named after Alexander McDonald who built the first road over it in 1870.

NEBRASKA
GRAND ISLAND – Home of pioneer Peter Campbell on the River Platte in about 1860.

NEW JERSEY
SOMERSET COUNTY AND EAST NEW JERSEY, on Raritan River – Site of a Campbell settlement led by Lord Neil Campbell in 1685 and centred at Perth Amboy, opposite Staten Island and south of Woodbridge. Millington hosts Bonnie Brae Highland Games each June. Campbells also settled at Mount Pleasant, Frenau, in 1685 and Burlington on Delaware.

TRENTON – Has Old Barracks, which are now a museum, built in 1758. Both clans had soldiers in this area.

NEW YORK STATE
TICONDEROGA – The famous fort by Lake Champlain where MacDonalds and Campbells died fighting the French in 1758 has been a museum since 1909. Some of the boats used were sunk deliberately and have been recovered.

SCHOHARIE CREEK – Scene of a battle fought by Macdonell of Aberchalder in 1812. There is an old stone fort near by.

OGDENSBURG – It was captured by Red George Macdonnell after a surprise attack over the frozen river in 1812.

WASHINGTON COUNTY – Site of settlement by eighty-three Islay families led by Lachlan Campbell after 1738, north of Albany on Lake George.

SCHENECTADY COUNTY – 400 Macdonell of Glengarry settlers came here in 1773, 30 miles from Albany in the Mohawk Valley.

FORT MONTGOMERY, beside West Point and Highland Falls – Colonel Mungo Campbell was killed in an attack on a Patriot position here in 1777.

NORTH CAROLINA
MOORE'S CREEK BRIDGE, near Wilmington – Site of the defeat of Loyalists under Brigadier Donald McDonald and where Alan Macdonald, husband of Flora, was made prisoner. Their farm was at Barbecue Creek, Upper Cape Fear. Wilmington itself still has buildings from the early nineteenth century and is well wooded with oak and pecan trees.

NEW BERN – Here Farquhar Campbell attended revolutionary meetings and the Tryon Palace of 1794 has been reconstructed.

FAYETTEVILLE – Formerly Campbellton and Cross Creek. Hugh Campbell started farming at Rockfish Creek in Bladen County in 1733. At nearby Red Springs the Flora Macdonald Highland Games are held annually. Cape Fear River was an early Scots settlement near Fayetteville on the lumber route that crossed Orange, Rowan and Cumberland Counties. John Campbell built a mill on Buffalo Creek.

LAURINBURG – Scottish Heritage Centre.

OHIO

MUSKINGUM RIVER – Discovered by Major Angus McDonald who led a party of 400 from Fort Fincastle to fight through the Shawnee Indians in 1774.

DELAWARE – Where George Washington Campbell developed the Campbell Early and Delaware grapes. Campbell Hill in west-central Ohio is the region's highest.

SOUTH CAROLINA

KING'S MOUNTAIN MILITARY PARK – 15 miles north-east of Gaffney by the Watauga River where Colonel William Campbell and his sharpshooters achieved a crucial victory in 1780 during the War of Independence.

PORT ROYAL – Site of an early George Campbell of Cessnock colony from 1685. This settlement was the start of the Ayrshire Campbell presence in South Carolina/Tennessee.

CHARLESTON – Several Campbells settled as planters in the area in 1774 and in 1776 Lord William Campbell was the ill-fated governor who died of wounds received in an offshore battle.

TENNESSEE

HOLSTON – Originally part of South Carolina, this town near Bristol was home of Colonel Arthur Campbell, explorer friend of Daniel Boone. He crossed the Kentucky River in 1776, losing several colleagues to Indian attacks, then laid waste Cherokee country in 1780. Colonel William Campbell, another local Cherokee fighter, the victor of King's Mountain, lived at nearby Aspenville. Close by is the Chattanooga home of old John MacDonald who came to Savannah, then settled by Look Out Mountain, South Chickamauga Creek, in 1766 with a half-Cherokee wife and maintained good relations with the Cherokee, unlike the two Campbell colonels.

FORT LOUDOUN – Near Knoxville, a further Campbell connection, with Campbell County to the north. It was attacked by Cherokee in 1760.

VIRGINIA
PORT NORTH POTOMAC – Where Jacobite MacDonalds and Campbells landed in 1746.

BETHANY COLLEGE – Founded by Thomas Campbell in 1841.

MONTEREY – Has Campbell House, a Civil War hospital built in 1855.

BLADENBURG, OCCAQUAN AND FREDERICKSBURG – All three towns had Campbell tobacco factors.

WASHINGTON
FORT COLVILLE – Located at Colville on the Columbia River, it had MacDonald connections. It was closed by the Hudson's Bay Company in 1871.

WYOMING
FORT LARAMIE NATIONAL HISTORIC SITE – Originally Fort William, then Fort John, it was built by Ulsterman Robert Campbell as a trappers' rendezvous on the Oregon Trail, near the junction of Rivers Laramie and Platte. It has a restored officers' club and was the site of the battle of Pierre's Hole where Campbell fought the Blackfoot.

LITTLE SCOTLAND – By the east fork of the Wind River and associated with John Campbell, first governor of Wyoming in 1868.

Canada

ALBERTA
FORT AUGUSTUS – Founded by John Macdonell for the North West Fur Company in 1794 across the River Saskatchewan from the rival Hudson's Bay Company's Fort Edmonton in Fort Edmonton Park. Finan McDonald was born here in 1807.

BRITISH COLOMBIA
VANCOUVER ISLAND – Has Strathcona Provincial Park wilderness area with its Glencoe connection – oil mogul Lord Strathcona also had Invercoe House in Glencoe.

THE CAMPBELL RIVER – This logging settlement is now mainly famous for salmon.

MOUNT MACDONALD – This dangerous avalanche area has the longest railway tunnel in North America, near Rogers Pass on the Trans-Canada Highway.

MANITOBA

WINNIPEG – The remains of Upper Fort Garry, part of the original Red River settlement founded by Lord Selkirk, are beside the Fort Garry Hotel and Fort Garry Park. Cruises on the Red River start near by. The city also has Dalnavert, a large Victorian house built in 1895 for Sir Hugh Macdonald, son of Sir John, who became premier of Manitoba in 1899. He kept the basement as a lodging for poor vagrants.

LOWER FORT GARRY – Stone fort built by the Hudson's Bay Company to replace Upper Fort Garry in 1830–4. It is 32 miles from Winnipeg in the National Historic Park by Selkirk.

RED RIVER – Is a restored Hudson's Bay Company fort dating from 1870.

SELKIRK – Hosts the Manitoba Highland Gathering, which includes Red River boat races.

FORT DOUGLAS – On the Assinboine River was founded by Miles MacDonell.

YORK FACTORY – Hudson's Bay trading post wooden building from 1832 floats on permafrost, 150 miles south-east of Churchill and is only reachable by canoe or plane from Charlottetown. From here both Archibald (in 1814) and later Angus McDonald (in 1838) started epic journeys.

NEW BRUNSWICK

CAMPBELLTON – on the Quebec border, a harbour town on the Restigouche River at the foot of Pain de Sucre Mountain was originally a French settlement but was renamed after the governor Sir Archibald Campbell in the 1760s. It was the scene of the last naval battle in the Seven Years War.

ROOSEVELT CAMPOBELLO INTERNATIONAL PARK – This is on Campobello Island, a settlement founded by Admiral Owen in 1766 and named after Governor William Campbell. It is linked to Maine, USA, by bridge.

MACDONALD FARM HISTORIC SITE – overlooks the Miramichi River. The farm was owned by Alexander MacDonald in 1820. Its Scottish-type stone farmhouse is still preserved.

NOVA SCOTIA
PICTOU – has Hector Heritage Quay. A replica of the immigrant ship *Hector*, which arrived here in 1773 with a large number of half-starved Highlanders, is under construction.

ANNAPOLIS, ST ANNS – Major Scots centres. Campbell of Glenorchy was one of founding barons of Nova Scotia as were several other members of both clans.

HALIFAX – Has Angus McDonald Suspension Bridge.

LOUISBOURG FORTRESS – Original French fortress on Cape Breton Island guarding the entrance to St Lawrence and the approach to Quebec, which was besiged by John Campbell of Loudoun in 1756. The fortress was destroyed but was then reconstructed in 1961.

MABOU – on the Ceilidh trail, home of Cape Breton bard John McDonald.

ONTARIO
TORONTO – has Campbell House, 160 Queen Street, built about 1824 for Sir William Campbell, Chief Justice of Upper Canada, who moved here from York.

KINGSTON – The home of Sir John Macdonald, Bellevue House, is nicknamed the Pekoe pagoda. At 35 Centre Street, it is a national historic site with fine views over the St Lawrence River.

MACDONALD PARK – Situated on Lake Ontario, this is the site of an 1812 naval battle.

GLENGARRY COUNTY – At the junction of the Ottawa and St Lawrence Rivers, where Macdonnells resettled after migrating from Cornwall and Charlottenburg. The area is now industrialised but Upper Canada Village preserves relics. Maxville, north of Cornwall, hosts Glengarry Highland Games, supposedly the world's largest. Also, Lochgarry and Macdonald Grove placenames recall the clan.

PRINCE EDWARD ISLAND
CAMPBELLTON AND CAMPBELL'S COVE PROVINCIAL PARK – Orwell's Corner Historic Village was settled by Scots in 1766. Scotchport and Tracadie were settled by Macdonnell of Glenaladale.

CHARLOTTETOWN – Province House Historic Site was the scene of Macdonald's launch of the Canadian confederation concept in 1864 and still has a Highland gathering. By Prince Edward Island National Park is Dalway by the Sea, the Victorian summer home of the Standard Oil magnate Alexander MacDonald. It is now a hotel.

QUEBEC

QUEBEC – city has the Parc des Champs de Bataille beside the Citadel of the Old Upper Town and includes the Plains of Abraham where men of both clans fought under General Wolfe in 1759. The ship *Macdonald* brought 520 crofters from Moidart to Quebec in 1786.

YUKON

THE CAMPBELL HIGHWAY – Follows the trail of the explorer and fur trader Robert Campbell and takes in Simpson lake, Fort Selkirk and Fort Pelly Banks (which Campbell founded in 1844), Pelly River and Yukon River (which he explored). At Fort Selkirk (originally called Fort Campbell) Campbell survived ransack by Chillat Indians. He is credited with finding gold in the Yukon but was not interested in it.

Jamaica

The relics of Campbells are hard to find here but for some time they did run major plantations in the west around the Hanover, Westmorland, and St Elizabeth areas. Colin Campbell had the Holland estate. Campbells of Glassary ran Orange Bay. There are some remains of the British Fort Charlotte. Petersville at Fish River was founded by Campbell of Kilmory. Archibald Campbell lived at Minard and there were others in St Ann's Bay, Lucea, Wakehouse, St Andrews, Salt Spring and Morvern, Hanover. John Campbell, the Darien survivor, was at Black River, the centre for the logwood trade and export of valuable blue dye. Lucea was the Jamaican base of Duncan Campbell, where the ship *Bethia*, later *Bounty*, was based, and William Bligh was his resident agent.

St Lucia

Conquered by General Colin Campbell from the French in 1799. He landed at Longueville.

Tobago

Peter Campbell was Lieutenant-Governor in 1772 and James Campbell, President of the Council, died at Argyll, Tobago, in 1805.

Panama

NEW EDINBURGH – 40 miles north-east of La Palma are the remains of New Edinburgh, the colony built mainly by Campbells on Darien. It was excavated in 1979 but since then the jungle has once more covered it and it is extremely difficult both to get to the area and find the site. It was on a promontory near Cap Escoce and a canal was dug across to turn it into an island with the guns of Fort St Andrew to fend off the Spaniards. The area still has virtually no roads, is undeveloped and surrounded by inhospitable jungle where the Choco Indians are still hunter-gatherers. The famous fort of Toubacanti or Yoratuba would be even harder to find.

Australia

NEW SOUTH WALES

CAMPBELLTOWN – South-west of Botany Bay, a MacDonald was among the earliest convicts and a Campbell officer was in charge.

PARRAMATTA – Now a suburb of Sydney, this was a farm settlement in 1788 with a Campbell marine officer in charge.

SYDNEY – Port Jackson was Robert Campbell's first base in Sydney Cove after he arrived at Dawes Point. It is now a park. Campbell's Store House was built in 1838 by his son. It now houses four restaurants. A replica of the former Campbell ship *Bounty* now does excursions from the harbour.

NORTHERN TERRITORY

MACDONNELL RANGES – These are in West Macdonnell National Park and Artlunga Historical Reserve, which includes a gold ghost town, south of Alice Springs. The Ranges are called after Sir Richard MacDonnell (1814–81), governor of South Australia 1855–62, who helped open up the Murray River area.

TASMANIA

CAMPBELL TOWN – A garrison settlement, with early colonial buildings, named after Governor McQuarrie's wife Elizabeth Campbell. One of the first Scots to settle in Tasmania was a convict, Archibald Campbell.

VICTORIA

PORT CAMPBELL NATIONAL PARK – South-west of Melbourne, it stretches from Moonlight Head to Peterborough and includes Glenample homestead. The first settler in Moonlight Creek in 1787 was a Campbell. Campbell Field, a suburb of Melbourne, was named after an early settler.

LA TROBE RIVER – Gippsland, an Old Pioneer Township on Princes Highway. The area was settled by Glengarry MacDonells and Campbells. Port Albert and Greenmount, with Glencoe and Armadale, recall the connection.

PORT FAIRY – An original Campbell whaling base in Portland Bay settled by Alexander Campbell (1805–90).

WESTERN AUSTRALIA
MACDONALD LAKE – is salt water, 20 miles long and usually dry.

New Zealand

AUCKLAND – One Tree Park was donated by John Logan Campbell, the 'Father of Auckland'. Acacia Cottage, built in 1841 by Campbell, is the city's oldest building.

WAITANGI – Campbell built the first European house here; the town, now has Treaty House Museum 1½ miles from Paihia.

KORARARIKA – Admiral MacDonell was wounded here when he arrived with shore party in the Maori Wars in 1845.

CAMPBELL ISLAND – This is the only inhabited island in the New Zealand subantarctic, and is a Campbell sealing settlement. It is now mainly the home of the royal albatross and other seabirds.

CAMPBELL PLATEAU – An undersea feature of the South Pacific.

CAPE CAMPBELL – Named after Captain John Campbell, the patron of James Cook.

India

CALCUTTA – Fort William, the base that housed many Scottish soldiers, still stands. Campbell, Clark & Co. had its office in Theatre Street.

LUCKNOW – The capital of Utra Pradesh under the Muslim Nawabs was the site of the 1857 siege that lasted eighty-seven days and was ended by General Colin Campbell. The pock-marked ruins of the Residency built in 1800 have been conserved as they were in 1857.

MANGALORE – A major fort of Hyder Ali in the Karnaka. The sultan's battery once defended by John Campbell of Stonefield is still visible.

SERINGAPATAM, NOW SRIRINGAPATNA – Palace of Tipu Sultan 10 miles from Mysore, where some Campbells were kept prisoner and Tipu was killed in 1799. There is a large mural painting of the battle.

ANNANPORE, NOW ANANDPUR – Captured by John Campbell.

TRICHINOPLY, NOW TIRUCHIRAPPALI – Rock Fort Temple hewn out of rock by Pallavas, scene of Sir James Campbell's attack in 1803 and his introduction of bagpipes to India.

PONDICHERRY – French Indian city captured with Campbell as senior officer.

AHMEDNAGAR – Imposing fort in North Maharashtra, scene of epic attack by Colin Campbell of Melfort that so impressed Wellington.

Pakistan

CHILIANWALLA – Scene of the other General Colin Campbell, later Lord Clyde's suspect victory over the Sikhs in 1847.

GUJARAT – Site of another Colin Campbell success against the Sikhs.

LAHORE – The Mogul fort occupied by Campbell still stands.

CAMPBELLPUR – Railway junction.

Myanmar/Burma

YANGON/RANGOON – Superb golden Dagon Pagoda where Sir Archibald Campbell led the attack in 1820.

Afghanistan

KABUL – Where 'Fighting Mac' Hector MacDonald won promotion in 1878 and several MacDonalds and Campbells were involved in frontier wars, railway building and exploration.

South Africa

PAARDEBERG – East of Kimberley, this was the scene of Hector MacDonald's successful attack on a Boer laager in 1900.

LAING'S NEK – On the pass into Natal, scene of Hector MacDonald's epic stand in the First Boer War in 1880 – near Majuba Hill where he also fought.

GRIQUALAND WEST – Kimberley area where John Campbell helped run free a black state in early nineteenth century until another Campbell and other diamond prospectors made it impossible (see p. 143).

BIBLIOGRAPHY

Balfour, Paul J., *The Scots Peerage*, Edinburgh, 1904–14
Beattie, W., *Life and Letters of Thomas Campbell*, London, 1849
Belich, J., *Making Peoples*, Auckland, 1996
Billington, R.A., *Westward Expansion*, New York, 1967
Black Book of Taymouth, Edinburgh, 1855
Boylan, H., *Dictionary of Irish Biography*, Dublin, 1978
Buchan, John, *Montrose*, London, 1928
Bumsted, J.M., *The Scots in Canada*, Toronto, 1982
——, *The People's Clearance*, Edinburgh, 1982
——, *A History of the Canadian Peoples*, Toronto, 1998
Campbell, A.A., *Voyage Round the World 1806–12*, London, 1813
Campbell, Alastair, *The Life and Troubled Times of Sir Donald Campbell*, Isle of Coll, 1992
Campbell, D., *The Records of the Clan Campbell in the Honourable East India Company*, Edinburgh, 1925
Campbell, D., *The Clan Campbell*, Edinburgh, 1913–22
Campbell, George, *Afghanistan*, Edinburgh, 1879
Campbell, George Douglas, 8th Duke of Argyll, *Autobiography*, London, 1908
Campbell, Gina, *Bluebirds: Story of the Campbell Dynasty*, London, 1988
Campbell, John L., *Canna*, Oxford, 1984
Campbell, Phyllis, *Book of Fear*, London, 1916
Campbell, Roy, *Selected Poems*, Oxford, 1982
Campbell, Thomas, *Poetic Works*, Edinburgh, 1918
Campbell, Victor, *Antarctic Diary*, Aldburgh, 1988
Campbell, William, *Villi the Clown*, London, 1981
Campbell Exner, Judith, *My Story*, New York, 1975
Clark, Thomas P., *Frontier America*, New York, 1959

Clarke, Wallace, *Lord of the Isles Voyage*, Dublin, 1993

Craig, David, *The Crofters' Trail*, London, 1990

Creighton, Donald, *John A. Macdonald*, Toronto, 1952

Denning, Greg, *Mr Bligh's Bad Language*, Cambridge, 1992

Dickson, Pat, *Red John of the Battles*, London, 1973

Divine, T.M., *Scottish Elites*, Edinburgh, 1994

Dobson, David, *Original Scots Colonists*, Baltimore, MD, 1989

——, *Scottish Emigrants to Colonial America*, Athens, GA, 1994

Donaldson, Gordon, *Scots Overseas*, London, 1966

Douglas, Hugh, *Flora Macdonald*, Stroud, 1993

Dubreton, J. Lucas, *Life of Murat*, London, 1944

Dukes, Paul, *Caledonian Phalanx*, Edinburgh, 1987

Duncan, A.M.M., *Scotland: the Making of the Kingdom*, Edinburgh, 1975

Elton, G.E., *Ramsay MacDonald*, London, 1939

Featherstone, David, *Macdonald of the 42nd*, London, 1971

Fergusson, Bernard, *Argyll in the Forty-Five*, London, 1960

Fitzpatrick, Roy, *God's Frontiersmen*, London, 1989

Foote, Shelby, *Civil War*, New York, 1980

Forbes, A., *Colin Campbell*, London, 1985

Gordon, Seton, *Highways and Byways in the West Highlands*, London, 1935

Graham, I.C.C., *Colonists from Scotland*, New York, 1956

Grant, I.F., *The Lordship of the Isles*, Edinburgh, 1935

Grant, Neil, *The Campbells of Argyll*, Edinburgh, 1959

Gregory, D., *History of the Western Highlands*, London, 1881

Haswell-Smith, Hamish, *Scottish Islands*, Edinburgh, 1996

Helland, Jane, *The Studio of Frances and Margaret Macdonald*, Manchester, 1996

Hewitson, Jim, *Tom Blake & Co. – The Story of the Scots in America*, Edinburgh, 1993

Hill, J.M., *Fire and Sword: Sorley Boy MacDonnell*, London, 1993

Hopkins, Paul, *Glencoe and the End of the Highland War*, Edinburgh, 1986

Hunter, James, *A Dance Called America*, Edinburgh, 1994

——, *Glencoe and the Indians*, Edinburgh, 1996

Johnston, Tom, *Our Noble Families*, Glasgow, 1907

Landsman, Neil, *Scotland and its First American Colony*, Princeton, 1985

Lang, Andrew, *Pickle the Spy*, London, 1897

Linklater, Magnus and C. Hesketh, *Bonnie Dundee*, Edinburgh, 1992

Livingston, Alistair (ed.), *The Muster Roll of Prince Charles Edward Stuart's Army*, Aberdeen, 1984

Lofaro, M.A., *Daniel Boone*, Kentucky, 1986

Macdonald, A. and A., *Clan Donald*, Inverness, 1890

MacDonald, Angus H., *The Troublesome Macdonalds*, Washington DC, 1974

MacDonald, Colin M., *History of Argyll*, Glasgow, 1950

Macdonald, Jacques Etienne, *Recollections*, trans S.L. Simeon, London, 1892

MacDonald, John, *Orain Iain Luim, Songs of John MacDonald*, ed., Annie MacKenzie, Edinburgh, 1964

MacDonald, Norman H., *Clan Ranald of Lochaber*, Edinburgh, 1972

——, *Clan Ranald of Knoydart and Glengarry*, Edinburgh, 1995

Macdonald, R. Andrew, *Kingdom of the Isles*, Edinburgh, 1997

Macgibbon, D., and T. Ross, *Castellated Domestic Architecture of Scotland*, Edinburgh, 1997

MacKaras, George, *Life of Admiral Bligh*, Sydney, 1931

Mackay, Donald, *Scotland Farewell*, Edinburgh, 1980

Mackenzie, Alexander, *Macdonalds of Clanranald*, Inverness, 1831

Mackerral, A., *The Clan Campbell*, Edinburgh, 1979

Macleod, K.I.E., *The Ranker: the Story of Hector Macdonald*, New York, 1976

Marquand, David, *Ramsay MacDonald*, London, 1977

Meyer, Duane, *The Highland Scots of North Carolina*, North Carolina, 1961

Miller, Mary, *Thomas Campbell*, Boston, MA, 1978

Millner, C.A., *Oxford History of the American West*, New York, 1992

Mocker-Ferryman, A., *Up the Niger: Narrative of Major Claude MacDonald's Mission up the Niger*, London, 1892

Moody, T.W., *New History of Ireland*, Oxford, 1976

Morgan, Austin, *J. Ramsay MacDonald*, Manchester, 1987

Morgan, Hiram, *Tyrone's Rebellion*, Woodbridge, 1993

Murray, W.H., *Rob Roy*, Edinburgh, 1982

National Dictionary of Biography, London, from 1917

Newman, C.E.T., *Campbells of Sydney*, Sydney, 1961

Newman, P.C., *Caesars of the Wilderness. Hudson's Bay Company*, Markham, Ontario, 1985

Pike, Douglas (ed.), *Australian Dictionary of Biography*, Melbourne, 1966

Prebble, John, *Highland Clearances*, London, 1963

——, *Culloden*, London, 1967

——, *The Darien Disaster*, London, 1968

——, *Glencoe*, London, 1968

——, *Mutiny: Highland Regiments in Revolt*, London, 1977

Ramsay, F. (ed.), *The Daybook of Daniel Campbell of Shawfield*, Aberdeen, 1997

Rattray, W.J., *The Scot in British North America*, Toronto, 1888

Rice, G.W., *History of New Zealand*, Auckland, 1992

Richards, Eric H., *History of the Highland Clearances*, London, 1982

Rixson, Denis, *West Highland Galley*, Edinburgh, 1998

Roy, J.M., *Old Take Care: the Story of Field Marshal Sir Colin Campbell*, Glasgow, 1985

Royal Commission on the Ancient and Historical Monuments of Scotland, Inventory of Argyll, 1971–92

Sayer, Clyde, *Malcolm Macdonald*, London, 1993

Scott, Sir Walter, *The Poetical Works*, Edinburgh, 1841

Sellar, W.D.H., 'The Earliest Campbells', *Scottish Studies*, 17, 1973

Smout, T.C., *A History of the Scottish People 1560–1830*, London, 1969

Snodgrass, J.J., *Narrative of the Burmese War*, London, 1827

Steer, K.A. and W.M. Bannerman, *Late Medieval Sculptured Stones of the Western Isles*, Edinburgh, 1977

Steven, M., *Merchant Campbell*, Oxford, 1965

Stevenson, David, *Alastair MacColla and the Highland Problem in the Seventeenth Century*, Edinburgh, 1980

Stevenson, Robert Louis, *Ballads*, London, 1887

Stirling, A.M.W., *Macdonald of the Isles*, London, 1913

Swainson, Donald, *John A. Macdonald*, Kingston, 1989

Watson, Don, *Caledonia Australis*, Sydney, 1984

Watson, W.J. (ed.), *The Book of Lismore*, Edinburgh, 1937

Whyte, Ian and Kathleen, *On the Trail of the Jacobites*, London, 1990

Williams, M.W., *The North West Company*, Vancouver, 1983

Williams, Ronald, *The Lordship of the Isles*, London, 1984

——, *The Heather and the Gale*, Colonsay, 1997

——, *The Sons of the Wolf*, Colonsay, 1998

Wilson, John, *Life of Sir Henry Campbell-Bannerman*, London, 1973

WORLD WIDE WEB SITES

Clan Donald – www.highlandconnection.org
Clan Campbell – www.tartans.com

INDEX

Only key individuals have been included